Mathematics Every Elementary Teacher Should Know

DEREK HAYLOCK is senior lecturer in education at the University of East Anglia, Norwich, England, where he is chair of primary initial teacher education and responsible for the mathematics components of the primary programmes. He has worked for 25 years in teacher education, both initial and in-service, but also has considerable practical experience teaching in primary classrooms. His work in mathematics education has taken him to Germany, Lesotho, Kenya, Brunei, and India. He was coauthor (with Anne Cockburn) of *Understanding Early Years Mathematics* (London: Paul Chapman Publishing, 1989) and author of *Teaching Mathematics to Low Attainers, 8–12* (London: Paul Chapman Publishing, 1991). His other publications include four books of Christian drama for young people and a Christmas musical (published by Church House/National Society), as well as frequent contributions to education journals. He is editor of *Mathematics Education Review.*

DOUGLAS McDOUGALL is an assistant professor and coordinator, preservice, (elementary north option) at the Ontario Institute for Studies in Education of the University of Toronto. He teaches preservice elementary school teachers in a one-year graduate program and graduate education students in masters and doctoral programs. He has taught nine years in secondary schools and seven years in elementary schools and spent one year as an elementary school mathematics consultant with the Waterloo County Board of Education in Ontario. He has been president of the Independent Schools of Ontario Mathematics Association and the Educational Computing Organization of Ontario. He is the national chair of the Gauss Mathematics Contest for Grades 7 and 8 students.

SPRINGBOARDS FOR
TEACHING

Mathematics Every Elementary Teacher Should Know

Derek Haylock
Douglas McDougall

Trifolium Books Inc.
Fitzhenry & Whiteside
TORONTO, CANADA

Trifolium Books Inc.
a Fitzhenry & Whiteside Company
195 Allstate Parkway,
Markham, Ontario L3R 4T8

In the United States:
Fitzhenry & Whiteside Limited
121 Harvard Avenue, Suite 2
Allston, Massachusetts 02134

www.fitzhenry.ca
godwit@fitzhenry.ca

Authorized adaptation based on the original edition published by Paul Chapman Publishing Ltd.: Mathematics Explained for Primary Teachers © 1995 Derek Haylock

Canadian Cataloguing in Publication Data

Haylock, Derek
    Mathematics every elementary teacher should know: grades K-8

(Springboards for teaching)
Includes bibliographical references and index.
ISBN 1-55244-012-5

1. Mathematics — Study and teaching (Elementary). I. McDougall, Douglas Emerson, 1956 -
II. Title III. Series

QA135.5.H418 1999   513'.1'024372   C99-931596-X

Project Editor: Rosemary Tanner / Lee D'Anjou
Design, layout, original graphics: Heidy Lawrance Associates
Cover design: FIZZZ Design Inc.

Printed and bound in Canada
10 9 8 7 6 5 4 3 2

Fitzhenry & Whiteside acknowledges with thanks the Canada Council for the Arts, the Government of Canada through its Book Publishing Industry Development Program, and the Ontario Arts Council for their support in our publishing program.

Contents

Acknowledgments

Our appreciation is due to the many student-teachers and elementary school teachers with whom we have been privileged to work over the years on initial training and in-service courses in teaching mathematics. We thank especially those with little background in mathematics for their willingness to come to grips with understanding mathematics, for their patience with us as we have tried to find the best ways of helping them understand mathematical ideas, and for their honesty in sharing their own insecurities and uncertainties about the subject. Dr. McDougall is particularly thankful to Annamaria Iantorno for her assistance in typing and editing the text and for providing advice for the North American edition. He is also grateful to Trudy Rising, Lee d'Anjou, Rosemary Tanner, and Heidy Lawrance Associates for their guidance and assistance.

The publisher and authors would like to thank the many educators and associates who took the time to provide valuable reviews; in particular, Trevor Brown of the Toronto District School Board, Lee McMenemy of the Algoma District School Board, and Ann Louise Revells of the Ottawa-Carleton Catholic District School Board.

Introduction

Mathematics Every Elementary Teacher Should Know is a book that student-teachers and elementary school teachers have asked to have written. We have both had experiences in which we have been explaining mathematical ideas to such audiences and have been asked, is there a book which explains all this?

Many people may be surprised that such a book is needed. But all our work with elementary school teachers and student-teachers convinces us that it is. Even well-qualified graduates feel insecure and uncertain about much of the mathematics they have to teach and appreciate a systematic explanation of even the most elementary mathematical concepts and procedures of the elementary school mathematics curriculum. The book is written to explain mathematics to elementary school teachers, so that they, in turn, will have the confidence to provide a classroom that encourages students to explore mathematics and develop understanding, rather than merely learning by rote.

After the introductory chapter, each of the subsequent chapters follows the same format. An opening that describes the objectives of the chapter is followed by a summary of the ideas explained in it. Each section of the chapter describes a concept and provides some explanation and some examples. Then comes a set of self-assessment questions, to enable readers to reinforce their learning from the chapter. We strongly encourage readers to engage with these. (Answers are provided at the end of the book.) Each chapter then concludes with some teaching suggestions for the mathematics in question in the elementary school classroom.

Derek Haylock
University of East Anglia, Norwich,
School of Education and Professional Development

Douglas McDougall
Ontario Institute for Studies in Education
University of Toronto

Elementary school teachers' insecurity about mathematics

One of the best ways for students to learn the mathematical concepts being taught in the elementary school curriculum is for teachers themselves to have a better understanding of those concepts. Much of the criticism of elementary school teaching of mathematics in recent reports (OFSTED, 1993a; 1993b) suggests too much reliance on approaches to the organization of students' activities which allow insufficient opportunities for teachers to provide this explanation.

Haylock (1991) is particularly critical of the way in which some teachers rely on commercial programs to help them teach mathematics. Many students experience mathematics in elementary school by working on their own, page by page through the textbook, hardly ever getting any substantial explanation or teaching other than at a procedural level when they get stuck on a particular question (Ball, 1988). Of course, studying mathematics can be — and should be — more than having a teacher just explain something and then assign homework. Exploring, using, and applying mathematics must always be at the heart of learning the subject. Students need explanation, and teachers must organize lessons and activities in ways that give children opportunities to explore and investigate mathematical concepts, patterns, procedures, and principles (Franke & Carey, 1997; Richards, 1991).

The lack of exploration and investigations in elementary schools is often a consequence of the insecurity about mathematics experienced by many elementary school teachers. This insecurity has made it likely that teachers rely heavily on textbooks to do their teaching for them. This book is written, therefore, to encourage teachers to redress the balance, and to provide more opportunities to explain mathematical ideas to their students. We set out to provide explanations of key mathematical ideas with the aim of improving elementary teachers' own understanding and increasing their personal confidence in discussing these ideas with their students.

This book originated from our experiences working with student-teachers enrolled in an elementary, one-year teacher-training program, highly motivated honors graduates, whose degree studies ranged across the curriculum. Over a number of years, it became clear that many of them started the course with a high degree of anxiety about having to teach mathematics.

Haylock invited student-teachers who felt particularly worried to join a group that would meet for an hour a week throughout the course to discuss their anxieties and to identify which aspects of the elementary school mathematics curriculum gave them most concern. A surprisingly large number turned up for these sessions. Discussions with these student-teachers revealed a great sense of personal anxiety that had emerged from their own experiences of learning mathematics at school. In addition, many were troubled by their own lack of understanding of the mathematical concepts they were expected to teach.

The students' comments on their feelings about mathematics closely reflected the findings of various studies of the responses to mathematics of adults in general and elementary teachers in particular.

Mathematics anxiety

Anxiety about mathematics and feelings of inadequacy in this subject are widespread among the adult population (Buxton, 1981; Handler, 1990). This phenomenon is clearly demonstrated by surveys of adults' attitudes to mathematics (Sewell, 1981; Cockcroft, 1982; Levine, 1995). Findings indicate that many adults admit to feelings of anxiety, helplessness, fear, dislike, and even guilt in relation to mathematical tasks. Feelings of guilt are particularly widespread among those with high academic qualifications, who think they ought to be more confident in their understanding of the subject. A common feeling is that there are proper ways of doing mathematics and that the subject is characterized by questions to which the answers are either right or wrong. Many adults identify their feelings of failure, frustration, and anxiety as rooted in the unsympathetic attitudes of teachers and the expectations of parents.

Teachers' anxieties

Many elementary teachers still experience feelings of panic and anxiety when faced with unfamiliar mathematical tasks (Briggs, 1993; Briggs and Crook, 1991). They are often muddled in their thinking about many of the basic mathematical concepts that underpin the material they teach to students, and they are all too aware of their personal inadequacies in the subject (Haylock and Cockburn, 1989; Jones, 1995).

Student-teachers' anxieties

The most common experience the student-teachers cited was their own teachers' expectation that they should be able to deal successfully with all the mathematical tasks they were given. They recalled clearly the negative effect on them of teachers' responses to their failure to understand.

When these student-teachers talked freely about their memories of mathematics at school, their comments were sprinkled liberally with such words as *frightened, terror, horrific.* Several recalled having nightmares. These memories were very vivid and still lingered in their attitudes to the subject today, even though they were academically successful adults:

> *I was very good at geometry but really frightened of all the rest.*

> *Math struck terror in my heart: a real fear that has stayed with me from over twenty years ago.*

> *I had nightmares about math as well: I really did, I'm not joking. Numbers and figures would go flashing through my head. Times tables, for example. I especially had nightmares about math tests.*

> *It worried me a great deal. Math lessons were horrific.*

Others recalled feelings of stupidity or frustration when faced with mathematical tasks:

> *I remember that I would always feel stupid. I felt sure that everyone else understood.*

> *Things used to get hazy and frustrating when I was stuck on a question.*

Teaching and learning styles

The student-teachers spoke with considerable vigor about their memories of the way mathematics was taught to them, recognizing now, from their adult perspective, that part of the problem was a significant limitation in the teaching style to which they were subjected:

> *Surely not everyone can be terrible at math. Is it just that it's really badly taught?*

> *I remember one teacher who was good because she actually tried to explain things to me.*

Clearly most of the student-teachers in this group felt that they had been encouraged to learn by rote, to learn rules and recipes without understanding. This rote-learning style was then reinforced by apparent success:

> *I was quite good at math at school but I'm frightened of going back to teach it because I think I've probably forgotten most of what I was taught. I have a feeling that all I learned was just memorized by rote and now it's all gone!*

> *I could rote learn things, but not understand them.*

> *I got through the exams by simply learning the rules. I would just look for clues in the question and find the appropriate process.*

The limitations of this rote-learning syndrome were sometimes apparent to the students:

> *I found you could do simple problems using the recipes, but then they'd throw in a question which was more complex. Then when the recipe I learned did not work, I became angry.*

> *We would be given a real-life situation, but I would find it difficult to separate math concepts out of it.*

But it seems that some teachers positively discouraged a more appropriate learning style:

> *I was made to feel like I was a nuisance for trying to understand.*

> *Lots of questions were going round in my head but I was too scared to ask them.*

> *I always tried to avoid asking questions in math lessons because you were made to feel so stupid if you got it wrong. There must be ways of convincing a child it does not matter if they get a question wrong.*

The following remark from the group highlights how the role of student-teacher focuses the feelings of anxiety and inadequacy arising from the rote-learning strategy adopted in the past:

I have a real fear of teaching young children how to do things in math as I have just learned the rules and recipes myself. I have a great personal fear of having to explain why we perform a specific math function.

Expectations

It seems as though the sources of anxiety for some student-teachers were the expectations of others:

It was made worse because Dad's best subject was math.

My teacher gave me the impression that she thought I was bad at math. So that's how I was labeled in my mind. When I got my … [math] result, she said, "I never thought you'd get an A!" So I thought it must just be a fluke and that I was not competent in math.

But the most common experience cited by these student-teachers was the teacher's expectation that they should be able to deal successfully with all the mathematical tasks they were given. They recalled clearly the negative effect of teachers' responses to their failure to understand:

There were few math teachers who could grasp the idea of people not being mathematical.

The teacher just didn't understand why I had problems.

Teachers expect you to be good at math if you're good at other things. They look at your other subjects and just can't understand why you can't do math. They say to you, "You should be able to do this."

I remember when I was seven and I had to do 100 long divisions. The headmaster came in to check on our progress. He picked me up and banged me up and down on my chair, saying, "Why can't you do it?" After that I wouldn't ask if I couldn't understand something.

Image of Mathematics

Some student-teachers had had an image that mathematics was such a difficult subject that not being any good at it was socially acceptable:

Math has an image of being hard. You pick up this idea from friends, parents and even teachers.

My Mum would tell me not to worry, saying "It's alright, we're all hopeless at math!" It was as if it was socially acceptable to be bad at math.

Among my friends and family it's OK to be bad at math, but it's not acceptable in society or employment.

For some, the problem seems to lie with the feeling that mathematics was different from other school subjects because the tasks given in mathematics are seen as essentially convergent and uncreative.

Math is not to do with the creativity of the individual, so you feel more restricted. All the time you think you've just got to get the right answer. And there is only one right answer.

There's more scope for failure with math. It's very obvious when you've failed, because things are either right or wrong, so you feel a fool, or look a fool in front of the others.

Language

A major problem that all student-teachers confront is that mathematical language seems to be too technical, too specific to the subject, and rarely reinforced through their language use in everyday life:

I find the language used to explain math to be, on the most part, obscure, but the handling of numbers is fine.

Many of the terms used in math are never used in everyday conversations.

Some words seem to have different meanings in math, thereby making it even more difficult to comprehend.

I was always worried about saying the wrong thing in math lessons because math language seems to be so precise. I worry now that I'll say things wrong to children in school and get them confused. You know, like, 'Which is the bigger half?'

When we discussed the actual content of the curriculum guidelines for mathematics, it became clear that the majority of the students' anxieties were related to the language used when discussing math. Even as mathematicians, we agree that little of this kind of technical language comes into everyday conversation, apart from when we are actually doing mathematics.

I can't remember what prime numbers are... Why are they called prime numbers anyway?

Is a product when you multiply two numbers together?

What's the difference between mass and weight?

What is congruence? A mapping? Discrete data? A measure of spread? A quadrant? An inverse? Reflective symmetry? A translation? A transformation?

Oh, is that what they mean? Why don't they say so, then?

Why do they have to dress it up in such complicated language?

Mathematics explained

Given this background of anxiety and confusion among elementary school student-teachers and, indeed, among many elementary school teachers in general, a major task for initial and in-service training is the promotion of positive attitudes toward teaching mathematics. The evidence from conversations with student-teachers suggests that achieving such attitudes requires shifting perceptions away from the notion of teaching recipes toward the development of understanding. Teachers need to give time to thinking about mathematical ideas, to grappling with explanations, and to ironing out confusions over the content and, in particular, the language of the mathematics curriculum.

Thus, this book focuses specifically on explaining the language and content of the mathematics taught to students in elementary schools. We hope it will help other student-teachers and elementary school teachers in general to develop confidence in approaching the core elements of the curriculum for students who are at such an important stage in their educational development.

References

Ball, D.L. (1988) "Unlearning to Teach Mathematics." *For the Learning of Mathematics* 8(1), 40–48.

Briggs, M. (1993) "Bags and Baggage Revisited." *Mathematics Education Review* 2: 16–20.

Briggs, M. and Crook, J. (1991) "Bags and Baggage." In E. Love and D. Pimm, eds., *Teaching and Learning Mathematics*. London: Hodder & Stoughton.

Brown, Martha A. & Gray, Mary W. (1992). *Mathematics Test, Numerical, and Abstraction Anxieties and Their Relation to Elementary Teachers' Views on Preparing Students for the Study of Algebra.* School Science and Mathematics. 92 (2), pp 69–73.

Buxton, L. (1981) *Do You Panic About Maths?* London: Heinemann.

Cockcroft, W.H. (1982) *Mathematics Counts.* Report of the Committee of Inquiry into the Teaching of Mathematics under the chairmanship of Dr. W.H. Cockcroft. London: Her Majesty's Stationery Office.

Franke, M.L. and Carey, D.A. (1997) "Young Children's Perceptions of Mathematics in Problem-Solving Environments." *Journal for Research in Mathematics Education* 28(1), 8–25.

Handler, Janet R. (1990). *Math Anxiety in Adult Learning.* Adult Learning. 1(6), pp 20—23.

Haylock, D. (1991) *Teaching Mathematics to Low Attainers, 8–12.* London: Paul Chapman Publishing.

Haylock, D. and Cockburn, A. (1989) *Understanding Early Years Mathematics.* London: Paul Chapman Publishing.

Jones, D. (1995) "Connecting Research to Teaching: Making the Transition: Tensions in Becoming a (Better) Mathematics Teacher." *Mathematics Teacher* 88(3), 230–234.

Levine, G. (1995) "Closing the Gender Gap: Focus on Mathematics Anxiety." *Contemporary Education* 67(1), 42–45.

OFSTED (Office for Standards in Education). (1993a) The Teaching and Learning of Number in Elementary Schools. London: Her Majesty's Stationery Office.

——— (1993b) *Curriculum Organization and Classroom Practice in Elementary Schools: A Follow-Up Report.* London: Her Majesty's Stationery Office.

Richards, J. (1991) "Mathematical discussions." In E. Von Glaserfeld (Ed), *Radical Construction in Mathematics Education.* Boston, MA: Kluwer Academic Publishers, 13–51.

Sewell, B. (1981) *Use of Mathematics by Adults in Daily Life.* Leicester: Advisory Council for Adult and Continuing Education.

Place Value

Students should learn to read, write, and order whole numbers; to understand the position of a digit that signifies its value; and to extend their understanding of the number system to decimals in the context of money and measurement.

THIS CHAPTER EXPLAINS:

- the way in which our Hindu-Arabic system of numeration uses the principle of place value;
- numeration systems from other cultures;
- powers of ten;
- two ways of demonstrating place value with materials;
- the role of zero as a placeholder;
- the extension of the place-value principle to tenths, hundredths, and so on; and
- the decimal point used as a separator in the context of money and measurement.

What is meant by *place value*?

Various cultures have developed many number systems through the centuries.

The system of numeration we use today is derived from an ancient Hindu system that was picked up in the ninth and tenth centuries and developed by Arab traders, who spread it throughout Europe. Various cultures have developed many number systems through the centuries, each with its particular features. Comparing some of these with the way we write numbers today inspires appreciation of the power and elegance of the Hindu-Arabic legacy. Unfortunately, space here does not permit going into much detail, but the history of different numerical systems is a fascinating topic, with considerable potential for curriculum integration in schools.

The Egyptian hieroglyphic system, used as long ago as 3000 BC, had separate symbols for ten, a hundred, a thousand, ten thousand, a hundred thousand and a million. The Romans, some 3000 years later, used a numeration system still based on the same principle as the Egyptians', but with symbols added for a few extra numbers, including five, fifty and five hundred. Figure 2.1 illustrates how various numerals are written in these systems and, in particular, how the numeral 366 is constructed. Clearly, our Hindu-Arabic system is far more economical in its use of symbols. The reason is that it is based on the highly sophisticated concept of place value.

Egyptian hieroglyphics	Roman numerals	Hindu-Arabic
I	I	1
II III	V	5
∩	X	10
∩∩∩∩∩	L	50
૭	C	100
૭૭ ૭૭ ૭	D	500
૭૭૭∩∩∩∩∩∩ IIIIII	CCCLXVI	366

FIGURE 2.1 *Some numbers written in different numeration systems*

In the Roman system, for example, representing three hundreds requires three Cs, and each of these symbols represents the same quantity: namely, one hundred. Likewise, the Egyptian system needs three "scrolls," each representing one hundred. But the Hindu-Arabic system does not use a symbol representing a hundred to construct three hundreds; it uses only a symbol representing three. Just this one symbol is needed to represent three hundreds.

We know that it represents three hundreds, rather than three tens or three ones because of the place in which it is written. Another example of the use of place value is the two sixes in 366. They do not stand for the same number. Reading from left to right, the first stands for six tens and the second for six ones because of the places in which they are written.

In our Hindu-Arabic place-value system, all numbers can be represented using a finite set of digits: 0, 1, 2, 3, 4, 5, 6, 7, 8, 9. Like most numeration systems (doubtless because humans have ten fingers for counting purposes), the system uses ten as a base. Whole numbers that are larger than nine are constructed using powers of the base: 10, 100, 1000, and so on. Of course, these powers of ten are not limited; they can continue indefinitely with higher powers.

> In our Hindu-Arabic place-value system, all numbers can be represented using a finite set of digits: 0, 1, 2, 3, 4, 5, 6, 7, 8, 9.

Here is how some of these powers are named, written as numerals, constructed from tens, and expressed as powers of ten in symbols and in words:

A million	1 000 000 =	10 x 10 x 10 x 10 x 10 x 10	= 10^6 (ten to the power six)
A hundred thousand	100 000 =	10 x 10 x 10 x 10 x 10	= 10^5 (ten to the power five)
Ten thousand	10 000 =	10 x 10 x 10 x 10	= 10^4 (ten to the power four)
A thousand	1 000 =	10 x 10 x 10	= 10^3 (ten to the power three)
A hundred	100 =	10 x 10	= 10^2 (ten to the power two)
Ten	10 =	10	= 10^1 (ten to the power one)

The place in which a digit is written represents that number of one of these powers of ten. So, in the numeral 2345 for example, working from right to left, the 5 represents five ones, the 4 represents four tens, the 3 represents three hundreds and the 2 represents two thousands.

We work from right to left in determining the place values, with the powers of ten increasing as we move in this direction. Since we read from left to right, the numeral is read with the largest place value first: 2 thousands, 3 hundreds, 4 tens, and 5 ones. Then we use the conventions of language to state this amount in a more customary form: 2 thousand, 3 hundred, 45.

In brief, the numeral 2345 is essentially a clever piece of shorthand, condensing a complicated mathematical expression into four symbols, as follows:

$$(2 \times 10^3) + (3 \times 10^2) + (4 \times 10^1) + 5 = 2345$$

Notice that each of the powers of ten is equal to 10 times the previous one: one hundred equals 10 tens, one thousand equals 10 hundreds, and so on. Thus, whenever ten accumulates in one place, this amount can be exchanged for one in the next place to the left.

This principle of being able to *exchange one of these for ten of those* as we move left to right along the powers of ten (or to *exchange ten of these for one of those* as we move right to left) is a significant feature of the place-value system. It is essential for understanding the way in which we count. For example, the next number after "56, 57, 58, 59 ..." is 60, because we fill up the units position with ten ones and exchange them for an extra ten in the next column.

This principle of exchanging is also fundamental to our calculations with numbers. When we do additions, we use the principle of exchanging one (see Chapter 5). When we do subtraction, we can, when necessary, exchange one in any place for ten in the next lower place (see Chapter 7).

What are the best ways of explaining place value in concrete terms?

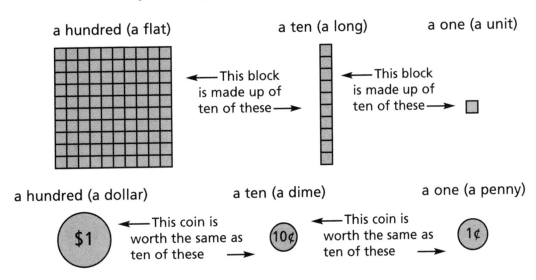

FIGURE 2.2 *Materials for explaining place value*

Two sets of materials can provide particularly effective concrete embodiments of the place-value principle and therefore help teachers to explain the way our number system works. They are base-ten blocks and sets of coins (1¢, 10¢, and $1).

Figure 2.2 shows how the basic place-value principle of exchanging one for ten is built into these materials, for ones, tens, and hundreds. With the blocks, of course, ten of one kind of block actually make one of the next kind. With the coins, it is simply that ten 1¢ coins are worth the same as one 10¢ coin, and ten 10¢ coins are worth one $1 coin.

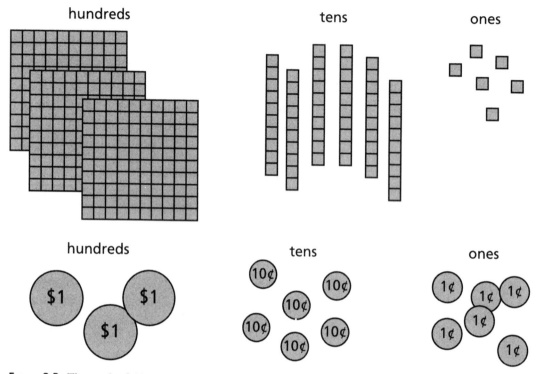

FIGURE 2.3 *The number 366 in base-ten blocks and in coins*

Figure 2.3 shows the number 366 represented with these materials. Notice that with both the blocks and the coins we have 3 hundreds, 6 tens, and 6 ones. The blocks are equivalent to 366 units, and the coins amount to 366 cents. Representing numbers with these materials enables us to build up images that help students to make sense of the way we do calculations such as addition and subtraction (as will be seen in Chapters 5 and 7).

What is meant by saying that zero is a placeholder?

The Hindu-Arabic system is not the only one to use a place-value concept. The Babylonians developed a system that incorporated this principle, although it used sixty as a base as well as ten. A problem with that system was that the user could not easily distinguish between, say, three and three sixties.

The difficulty was that the Babylonians did not have a symbol for zero. Scholars generally think that the Mayan civilization of South America was the first to develop a numerical system that included both the concept of place value and the consistent use of a symbol for zero. Clearly, rich potential exists for including a

> The Babylonians developed a system that used a place-value concept, using sixty as a base as well as ten.

mathematical dimension for students studying, for example, the ancient Egyptian and Mayan civilizations.

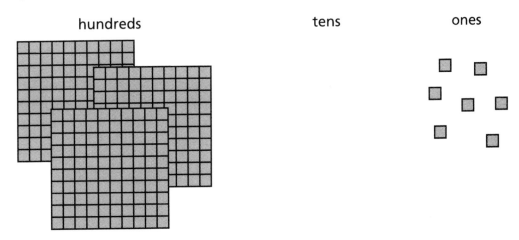

hundreds   **tens**   **ones**

FIGURE 2.4 *Three hundred seven in base-ten blocks*

Figure 2.4 shows the number 307 represented in base-ten blocks. When the amount is translated into symbols without the use of a zero, it could easily be confused with 37. The zero is used to indicate that the number 307 includes no units of of ten to the power of one.

Therefore, when we see a numeral such as 300, we should not think to ourselves that the 00 means hundred. The position of the 3 indicates that it stands for 3 hundreds; the function of the zeros is to make this position clear while indicating that there are no tens and no ones. Confusion about this point leads some children to write, "30045" for "three hundred forty-five."

What's the difference between a *numeral* and a *number*?

A *numeral* is the symbol, or collection of symbols, used to represent a number. The *number* is the concept represented by the numeral. As demonstrated in Figure 2.1, the same number (for example, the one we call "three hundred sixty-six") can be represented by different numerals, such as 366 and CCCLXVI. Because the Hindu-Arabic system of numeration is now more or less universal, the distinction between the numeral and the number is easily lost.

> A numeral is the symbol, or collection of symbols, used to represent a number.

How does the place-value system work for quantities of less than one?

Once we establish the principle of being able to exchange one of these for ten of those, we can continue with it to the right of the units position for tenths, hundredths, thousandths, and so on. These positions, which are usually referred to as *decimal places*, are separated from the units by the decimal point. Since a tenth and a hundredth are what we get when we divide a unit into 10 and 100 equal parts respectively, it follows that 1 unit can be exchanged for 10 tenths, and 1 tenth can be exchanged for 10 hundredths. In this way, the principle of one of these being exchanged for ten of those continues indefinitely to the right of the decimal point, with the values represented by the places getting progressively smaller by a factor of ten each time.

A useful way to picture decimals is to explore what happens if we decide that the flat piece in the base-ten blocks represents one whole unit. In this case, the long piece represents tenths of this unit and the small cubes represent hundredths. The collection of blocks shown in Figure 2.3 is made up of 3 units, 6 tenths, and 6 hundredths. This quantity is represented by the decimal number 3.66. Similarly, the blocks in Figure 2.4 represent the decimal number 3.07 — that is, 3 units, no tenths and 7 hundredths.

Do teachers have to explain tenths, hundredths, and decimal places when they introduce decimal notation in the contexts of money and measurement?

If a dollar coin is the unit, then the collection of coins in Figure 2.3 represents the number 3.66, since the dimes are tenths of a dollar and the pennies are hundredths of a dollar. And this amount of money written in dollars, rather than in cents, is recorded conventionally as $3.66.

In terms of decimal numbers in general, the function of the decimal point is to indicate the transition from units to tenths. Therefore, a decimal number such as 3.66 is read as "three point six six," with the first figure after the point indicating the number of tenths and the next the number of hundredths. Reading it as "three point sixty-six," would be confusing since the phrase might be taken to mean 3 units and 66 tenths. A different convention rules, however, when using the decimal point in recording money: the amount $3.66 is read as "three dollars sixty-six." In this case there is no confusion about what the "sixty-six" refers to; the context makes clear that it is 66 cents.

> *In terms of decimal numbers in general, the function of the decimal point is to indicate the transition from units to tenths.*

In practice, children first encounter the decimal point in money notation. In this form the decimal point is simply something that separates the dollars from the cents, so that $3.66 represents 3 whole dollars and 66 cents. No reader or listener needs any more specification that the first 6 represents 6 tenths of a dollar and the next 6 represents 6 hundredths.

Because the decimal point is no more than a separator of the dollars from the cents, we have the convention of always writing two figures after the point when recording amounts of money in dollars. For example, we write $3.20, rather than $3.2, and read it as "three twenty (that is, twenty cents)." By contrast, if we were working with pure decimal numbers, then we would simply write "3.2," meaning "3 units and 2 tenths."

Since 100 centimeters (cm) makes 1 meter (m), just as 100 cents make 1 dollar, the measurement of length in centimeters and meters offers a close parallel to recording money. For example, a length of 366 cm can also be written as 3.66 m. Once again the decimal point is something that separates the 3 whole meters from the 66 centimeters.

Teachers find it helpful to press the parallel quite strongly, following the same convention of writing two figures after the point when expressing lengths in meters — for example, writing 3.20 m rather than 3.2 m. We can then interpret this as 3 meters and 20 centimeters. (A convention that is very useful when dealing with additions and subtractions involving decimals is explained in Chapter 17.)

This principle extends to the measurement of mass, where, because 1000 grams (g) make 1 kilogram (kg), it is best to write a mass measured in kilograms with three figures after the point. For example, 3450 g is 3.450 kg. The decimal point can then be easily seen as something that separates the 3 whole kilograms from the 450 grams. Similarly, in recording liquid volume and capacity, where 1000 milliliters (mL) make 1 liter, a volume of 2500 mL can be written as 2.500 liters, with the decimal point separating the 2 whole liters from the 500 milliliters.

When working with elementary-school children, teachers should explain about tenths and hundredths by using the decimal point in the context of money, length, and other measurements. Money and measurement activities provide fertile contexts for explaining the ideas of tenths, hundredths and thousandths. Later teachers can use the decimal point as a separator and build up the student's confidence in handling the decimal notation in these familiar and meaningful contexts. For example, a decimal number such as 1.35 can be explained as a length by setting in a line a 1-meter stick, 3 decimeter rods (tenths of a meter), and 5 centimeter cubes (hundredths of a meter), as shown in Figure 2.5.

> Money and measurement activities provide fertile contexts for explaining the ideas of tenths, hundredths, and thousandths.

1 meter | 3 decimeters

5 centimeters

FIGURE 2.5 *The decimal number 1.35 shown as a length*

Check yourself

2.1 Arrange the following amounts from the smallest to the largest without converting them to Hindu-Arabic numerals:

(a) DXI
(b) CCLXVII
(c) CLXXXVIII
(d) DCC
(e) CCC

Now convert them to Hindu-Arabic numerals, repeat the exercise, and note any significant differences in the process.

2.2 Add one to four thousand ninety-nine.

2.3 Write the following numbers in Hindu-Arabic numerals, and then write them out in full using powers of ten:

(a) five hundred sixteen
(b) three thousand sixty
(c) two million, three hundred, five thousand, four

2.4 I have 34 pennies, 29 dimes, and 3 dollar coins. Apply the principle of exchanging ten of these for one of those to reduce this collection of coins to the smallest possible number of 1¢, 10¢, and $1 coins.

2.5 Interpret the following decimal numbers as collections of base-ten blocks (using a flat to represent a unit), and then arrange them in order from the smallest to the largest:

(a) 3.2   (b) 3.05   (c) 3.15   (d) 3.10

2.6 A thousand millimeters (mm) make a meter. Write lengths of 3405 mm and 2500 mm in meters.

2.7 Write the following:

(a) 25¢ in dollars   (b) 25 cm in meters
(c) 7¢ in dollars   (d) 45 g in kilograms
(e) 50 mL in liters   (f) 5 mm in meters

➤Teaching suggestions

1. Incorporate some study of numeration systems into history-focused topics, such as Egyptian and Mayan civilizations, highlighting the advantages and significance of the place-value system we use today.

2. Explore with the students various cultures that have contributed so much to the development of numeration.

3. Use coins (1¢, 10¢, and $1) and base-ten blocks to develop students' understanding of the place-value system.

4. Use the same materials to reinforce the principle of exchanging one of these for ten of those while moving left to right along the powers of ten, and exchanging ten of these for one of those while moving right to left.

5. Give particular attention to the function and meaning of zero when writing and explaining numbers to students.

6. Articulate the words tenths and hundredths very carefully when explaining decimal numbers. Students may think you are saying tens and hundreds.

7. Explain decimal numbers by using the flat pieces in the base-ten materials to represent units, the long ones to represent tenths, and the small cubes to represent hundredths.

8. Remember that most students first encounter the decimal point as a separator in the context of money (dollars and cents) and then length (meters and centimeters), with two figures after the point. They can use the notation in these contexts initially without having any real awareness of figures representing tenths and hundredths.

9. Extend the experience with coins to further use of decimal notation in the context of mass (kilograms and grams) and of liquid volume and capacity (liters and milliliters) with three figures after the point.

10. Reinforce the explanation of the idea that the figures after the point represent tenths, hundredths, and thousandths.

3

Mathematical Modeling

Students should learn to select and use appropriate mathematical models; to recognize situations to which the operations of addition, subtraction, multiplication, and division apply; to understand and use the features of a basic calculator; to interpret the calculator display in the context of the problem; and to develop their use of the four mathematical operations to solve problems, including those involving money and measures, using a calculator where appropriate.

THIS CHAPTER EXPLAINS:

- three approaches to calculations: the use of algorithms, informal methods, and calculators;
- the fundamental process of mathematical modeling;
- the contribution of electronic calculators to the modeling process;
- three different kinds of answers that may be obtained from a calculation done on a calculator; and
- truncation.

What is the best way to do calculations?

We can do a calculation, such as the cost of 16 items at 25¢ each, in a number of ways. The solution clearly demands working out 16 x 25. But what is next?

One approach to the problem above is to use an *algorithm*. The word (derived from the name of the ninth-century Arabian mathematician, Al-Khowarizmi) means a step-by-step process for obtaining the solution to a mathematical calculation or, in this case, the result of a calculation. In other words, algorithms are the formal, paper-and-pencil methods that we might use for doing calculations. If the procedures are followed correctly, they always lead to the required result.

Algorithms include, for example, subtraction by decomposition and long division. Answering the question above using an algorithm might involve performing the calculation for 16 x 25 as shown in Figure 3.1, using the method known as long multiplication.

$$
\begin{array}{r}
16 \\
\times\ 25 \\
\hline
320 \\
80 \\
\hline
400 \\
\hline
\end{array}
$$

FIGURE 3.1 *Using an algorithm for 16 x 25*

What are informal methods of calculation?

Second, people do calculations using a vast array of informal methods, most of which are not written down in textbooks or explained by teachers to students, but which are the actual methods most numerate adults employ for the calculations they encounter in everyday life.

> People do calculations using a vast array of informal methods, most of which are not written down in textbooks or explained by teachers to students.

For example, to solve the problem above, we might make use of the fact that four groups of 25¢ make $1, so 16 of them must be $4. Or we might work out that the problem involves ten 25s (250), four 25s (100), and two 25s (50) and then add up these amounts, to get 400. Or we could reason: two 25s is 50, so four 25s is 100, so eight 25s is 200, so sixteen 25s is 400.

These kinds of approaches, which make use of the particular numbers and relationships in the problem in question, may be called *informal methods*. These informal approaches to calculations are equally as valid as the formal, algorithmic approaches and have the advantage of being based on individuals' personal level of confidence with numbers and number operations. (Chapters 5, 7, 9, and 11 discuss various algorithms and informal methods for each of the four operations.)

How can calculators be used in mathematical modeling?

A third approach to doing calculations is to use a calculator. Many people have misconceptions about calculators. They think they are a form of "cheating" — or at least avoiding mathematics. In fact, using a calculator to solve a practical problem involves a fundamental mathematical process called *mathematical modeling*. This means using and applying mathematics in the real world.

> Using a calculator to solve a practical problem involves a fundamental mathematical process called mathematical modeling.

Example 3A

How many boxes are needed to hold 150 games if each box can hold 18?

Thinking it through

Using a calculator, we divide 150 by 18. The result is 8.3333333, which is just a bit more than 8 boxes. If only 8 boxes are available, some games will be left over (although the calculator answer doesn't actually tell us how many). Therefore, 9 boxes are needed for the 150 games.

The process involved in the reasoning here is an example of mathematical modeling, which is summarized in Figure 3.2. A problem in the real world is translated into a problem expressed in mathematical symbols. In this example, the real-world problem about buying boxes to hold games is modeled by the mathematical expression 150 ÷ 18.

The result of the calculation must then be interpreted back into the real world: for example, by saying that the calculator result means the approximate answer is 8 boxes and a bit of a box.

The final step is to compare the result with the reality of the original situation. In this case, recognizing that 8 boxes would leave some games not in a box, the appropriate conclusion is that we actually need 9 boxes.

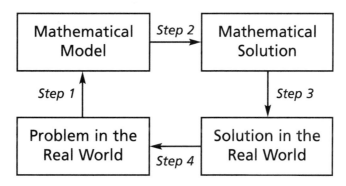

FIGURE 3.2 *The process of mathematical modeling*

This process, basically has four steps:
1. set up the mathematical model;
2. obtain the mathematical solution;
3. interpret the mathematical solution back into the real world; and
4. compare the solution with the reality of the original situation.

A potential fifth step exists. If the solution does not make sense when compared with the reality of the original problem, then we may have to review the mathematical model and check each stage of the process to determine what has gone wrong.

Notice that the calculator helps in only one of the steps in the process. The problem solver must do the others.

In a technological age in which most machines do calculations, surely no one can dispute that knowing which calculation to do is more important than being able to do the calculation. As will be seen in Chapters 4, 6, 8, and 10, recognizing which operations correspond to various real-world situations is not always straightforward. These chapters indicate the range of categories of problems that students should learn to model with addition, subtraction, multiplication, and division.

How is the result of a calculator calculation interpreted?

The interpretation of the calculator result is a significant aspect of the process. For example, in the problem above, the interpretation of the result 8.3333333 requires a decision about what to do with all the figures after the decimal point.

When we carry out a calculation on a calculator in order to solve a practical problem, particularly one modeled by division, we can get four kinds of answers:

- an exact, appropriate answer;
- an incorrect answer;
- an exact but inappropriate answer; or
- an answer that has been truncated.

In the last two cases, we normally have to round the answer in some way to make it appropriate to the real-world situation (rounding is considered in more detail in Chapter 12). For example, consider these three problems, all with the identical mathematical structure:

> We normally have to round the answer in some way to make it appropriate to the real-world situation.

1. If apples are 15¢ each, how many can I buy with 90¢?
2. If apples are 24¢ each, how many can I buy with 90¢?
3. If apples are 21¢ each, how many can I buy with 90¢?

For problem 1, we could enter $90 \div 15$ on a calculator and obtain the result 6. There is no difficulty interpreting this result back into the real world. The answer to the problem is indeed exactly 6 apples. The calculator result is both exact and appropriate.

For problem 2, we could enter $90 \div 24$ and obtain the result 3.75. This result is the exact answer to the calculation entered on the calculator — the solution to the mathematical problem we used to model the real-world problem — and the correct interpretation is 3.75 apples. But since grocers sell only whole apples, the answer is clearly inappropriate. Thus, in the final step of the modeling process, comparing the solution with reality, the 3.75 apples must be rounded to a whole number of apples. In this case, we conclude that we can actually afford only 3 apples.

For problem 3, we could enter $90 \div 21$ on the calculator and find that we get the result 4.2857142. This answer is not exact. Dividing 90 by 21 actually produces a recurring decimal: namely, 4.285714285714…, with the 285714 repeating. Since a simple calculator can display only eight digits, it truncates the result by throwing away all the extra digits. Of course, in this case, the bits that are thrown away are relatively tiny, so the error involved in the truncation process is fairly insignificant. We can interpret the result displayed on the calculator as about 4.2857142 apples. But again, when we compare this result with the real-world situation, we must recognize the constraints of purchasing fruit and round the answer to give a whole number of apples. The conclusion is that we can afford only 4 apples.

Another problem arises when the calculator result in a money problem gives only one figure after the decimal point.

Example 3B
If marker pens are $1.15 each, how much do 24 of them cost?

Thinking it through
We can model this problem with the mathematical expression 24 x 1.15. The calculator gives the result 27.6. Elementary school students have to be taught how to interpret this result (in step 3) as $27.60, in order to draw the conclusion (in step 4) that this amount is the total cost of the 24 marker pens.

Check yourself

3.1 How much must you pay altogether for three books that cost $4.95, $5.90, and $9.95? Use a calculator to answer this question. Then identify the steps in the process of mathematical modeling in what you have done.

3.2 A restaurant bill is for $27.90. If three people share it, what does each pay? Use a calculator to answer this question. Is the calculator result:

(a) an exact, appropriate answer?
(b) an exact but inappropriate answer?
(c) an answer that has been truncated?

Identify the steps in the process of mathematical modeling in what you have done.

3.3 Repeat question 3.2 with a bill for $39.70.

3.4 Luc has been given $50 for his birthday and thinks he may spend it all on his favorite chocolate bars, which cost 89¢ each. He wonders how many he might get. What is the mathematical model of this problem? Obtain the mathematical solution, using a calculator. Interpret the mathematical solution back to the question. Is the calculator result:

(a) an exact, appropriate answer?
(b) an exact but inappropriate answer?
(c) an answer that has been truncated?

3.5 How many months will it take Maria to save $500 if she saves $35 a month? Use a calculator to answer this question. Is the calculator result:

(a) an exact, appropriate answer?
(b) an exact but inappropriate answer?
(c) an answer that has been truncated?

Identify the steps in the process of mathematical modeling in what you have done.

> ## ➤ Teaching suggestions

1. Recognize the validity of the three ways of doing calculations: algorithms, informal methods, and calculators.
2. Provide students with plenty of opportunities to work through the process of mathematical modeling, emphasizing the four steps in the process.
3. Recognize that all the steps of mathematical modeling are important, and that step 2 (doing the calculation) is not actually as important as the other three steps.
4. Allow students to use a calculator when they encounter difficulty with the calculations associated with a real-life problem. Then they can still engage in the modeling process and learn to choose the right operation, to interpret the result, and to compare it with reality.

5. Discuss with students real-life problems, particularly in the context of money, that produce calculator answers that require different kinds of interpretation, including those with (a) an exact, appropriate answer; (b) an exact but inappropriate answer; and (c) an answer that has been truncated.

6. Explain truncation to elementary school students, but use informal language. Here is an example: "When the calculator answer has a decimal point and fills up all the available spaces, then there are probably lots more figures to come after the ones we can see. Because the calculator does not have room for these, it throws them away. This does not usually matter because they represent very small quantities."

4

Addition Structures

Students should learn to understand the operation of addition, and to recognize situations where it applies.

THIS CHAPTER EXPLAINS:

- two structures of real-life problems modeled by addition; and
- situations in which students will meet these structures.

What are the kinds of situations in which elementary students may encounter the operation of addition?

Two basic categories of real-life problems are modeled by the mathematical operation we call addition. The problems in each of these categories vary in terms of their content and context, but they all have the same basic structure. These structures are organized into:

- the aggregation structure; and
- the augmentation structure.

Aggregation refers to a situation in which two or more quantities are combined into a single quantity and the operation of addition is used to determine the total.

For example, 15 marbles are in one circle and 17 in another. How many marbles are there altogether? The idea of *how many (or how much) altogether* is the central notion in the aggregation structure (see Figure 4.1).

Aggregation is when two or more quantities are combined into a single quantity, and addition is used to determine the total.

Augmentation refers to a situation in which a quantity is increased by some amount, and the operation of addition is required in order to find the augmented or increased value.

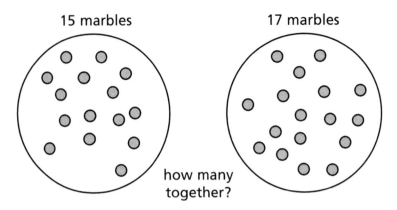

15 marbles   17 marbles

how many together?

FIGURE 4.1 *Example of aggregation structure*

Augmentation refers to a situation in which a quantity is increased by some amount, and the operation of addition is required in order to find the augmented or increased value.

For example, the price of a bicycle that cost $149 is increased by $25. What is the new price? The important language in augmentation includes phrases like *increased by* or *goes up by*. Of course, if the number added is negative, then the addition will results in a *decrease*, not an increase. This extension of the augmentation structure to negative numbers is discussed in Chapter 15, which deals with positive and negative integers. The augmentation structure is the addition structure that lies behind the idea of counting along a number line. Teachers can use a number line with young children who are experiencing simple additions. We say, for example, "for 7 + 5, start at 7 and count up by 5" (see Figure 4.2).

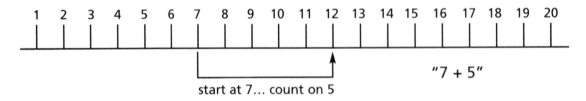

1 2 3 4 5 6 7 8 9 10 11 12 13 14 15 16 17 18 19 20

start at 7... count on 5

"7 + 5"

FIGURE 4.2 *Number line showing 7 + 5*

Distinguishing between the aggregation and the augmentation structures is not always easy, nor is it necessarily helpful to try to do so. Students need not learn the words for them. But teachers find it useful to keep the two structures in mind to ensure that students have opportunities to experience a full range of situations.

What are some of the contexts in which students meet addition in the aggregation structure?

First and most simply, students encounter the aggregation structure whenever they are trying to find a total number by putting two sets of objects into a single set. Examples include combining two discrete sets of students (for instance, 25 boys and 29 girls; how many altogether?) and combining two separate piles of counters (for instance, 46 red counters and 28 blue counters; how many altogether?).

Second, students encounter the aggregation structure in the context of using money. They may want to find the total cost of two or more purchases or the total bill for a number of services. The question is, how much altogether?

Students also have to recognize situations of aggregation in the context of measurements, such as length and distance, mass, capacity and liquid volume, and time. For example, addition is the operation required to find the total distance of a journey made up of two stages of 48 kilometers and 63 kilometers. It is also required to find the total time for the journey if the first stage takes 65 minutes and the second stage takes 85 minutes.

What are some contexts in which students meet addition in the augmentation structure?

The most important and relevant context for the augmentation structure is money, particularly the calculations of increases in price or cost, wage, or salary. The key idea that signals the operation of addition is that of increasing. This idea is occasionally encountered in other measurement contexts, such as length (stretching a piece of elastic by a certain amount), mass (increasing an object by a certain number of kilograms), and time (lengthening the lunch break by a certain number of minutes).

Check yourself

4.1 Using the aggregation structure in the context of shopping, pose a problem that corresponds to the addition 5.95 + 6.99.

4.2 Using the augmentation structure in the context of salaries, pose a problem that corresponds to the addition 19750 + 450.

4.3 Using the aggregation structure and liquid volume in the context of cooking, pose a problem that corresponds to the addition 250 + 125.

4.4 Using the aggregation structure in the context of time, pose a problem that corresponds to the addition 15 + 25 + 55 + 20 + 65.

> **Teaching suggestions**

1. Teach students to connect the operation of addition with a range of problems, including aggregation and augmentation situations.
2. Recognize that the key language to be developed in the aggregation structure includes *how many altogether, how much altogether,* and *the total.*
3. Recognize that the key language to be developed in the augmentation structure includes *count by, increased by,* and *goes up by.*
4. Ensure that students experience these addition structures in a range of relevant contexts including and especially money (shopping, bills, wages, and salaries), and various aspects of measurement.

5
Addition Calculations

Students should learn to apply their understanding of place value to develop methods of computation; to develop a variety of mental methods of computation; and to extend those mental methods to develop a range of computations that involve the addition of whole numbers without using a calculator.

THIS CHAPTER EXPLAINS:
- the idea of carrying in the addition algorithm; and
- various informal methods of doing additions.

Understanding

The key to understanding the process of adding two or more numbers is an understanding of the principle of place value. Recall that when we have ten in one column, they can be exchanged for one in the next column to the left. *Ten of these can be exchanged for one of those* is a key phrase for teachers explaining the process to students.

> The key to understanding the process of adding two or more numbers is an understanding of the principle of place value.

Understanding the things we do with numbers often involves connecting the manipulation of the symbols with appropriate language and concrete materials. To explain addition, the teacher can use $1, 10¢, and 1¢ coins, referring to them as *hundreds, tens,* and *ones.* Some teachers prefer to call the ones *units.* Clearly, the principle that ten of these can be exchanged for one of those applies to the ones and the tens, as well as to the tens and the hundreds. The process can (and with children, should) be equally well experienced with base-ten blocks.

> Some teachers prefer to call the ones units.

Example 5A

Find the sum of 356 + 267.

Thinking it through

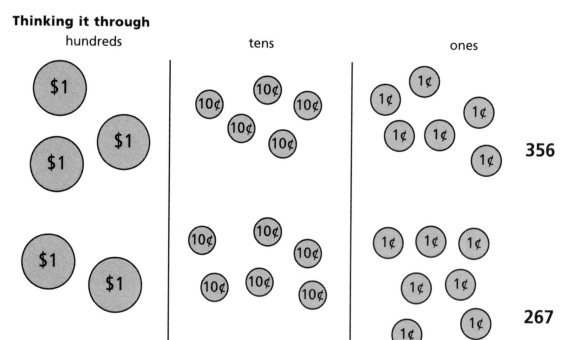

FIGURE 5.1 *356 + 267 using coins*

The individual amounts are shown in Figure 5.1, with 356 interpreted as 3 hundreds, 5 tens, and 6 ones and 267 interpreted as 2 hundreds, 6 tens and 7 ones. The two numbers now have to be combined to find the total. The standard algorithm involves working from right to left, that is, starting with the ones. This order may seem a little unnatural since the obvious thing would be to start with the biggest-value coins on the left. In fact, most people who can cope with this level of addition mentally do just that. They reason something like this: "300 and 200 make 500; 60 plus 50 is 110, so that's 610 so far; 6 and 7 give another 13, making 623 in all."

When we use the standard addition algorithm, however, we work from right to left so that we can use the principle of place value. Remember and apply the principle correctly: ten of these can be exchanged for one of those.

In Figure 5.1, we first put together all the ones, making 13 in all. Ten of these ones can then be exchanged for one ten. Since this ten is literally carried and placed in the tens column, the language of *carrying one* is very appropriate (provided it is clear that we are carrying "one of these" and not "a one"). The coins at this stage are arranged as shown in Figure 5.2.

The figure also shows the recording so far, indicating the relationship between what is done with the symbols and what is done with coins. The 3 written in the ones column corresponds to the three remaining pennies. The 1 written above the line in the tens column corresponds to the one ten that has been exchanged for ten ones.

Next, all the tens are combined: the 1 ten that has been carried, plus the 5 tens in the original top row, plus the 6 tens in the next row. This gives a total of 12 tens. Ten of these are then exchanged for one hundred. So again we carry one, but this time, of course, it is one hundred. Figure 5.3 shows the situation at this stage and, once again, the direct correspondence between the recording in symbols and the manipulation of the coins.

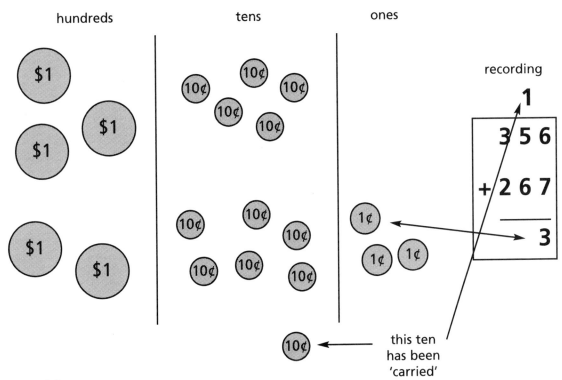

FIGURE 5.2 *Carrying a ten*

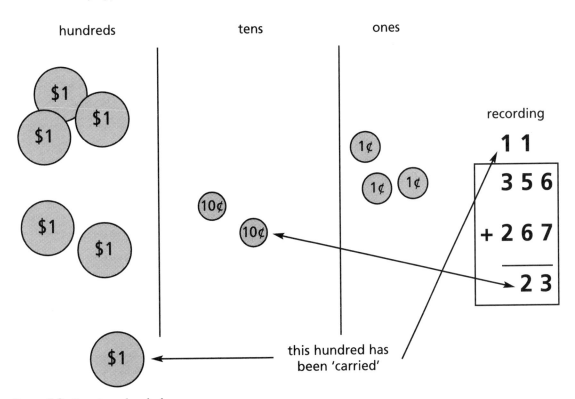

FIGURE 5.3 *Carrying a hundred*

The final stage in this calculation is to combine the hundreds: the 1 hundred that has been carried, plus the 3 hundreds in the original top row, plus the 2 hundreds in the next row, giving a total of 6 hundreds. Figure 5.4 shows the final arrangement of the coins, with the 6 hundreds, 2 tens, and 3 ones corresponding to the answer of 623.

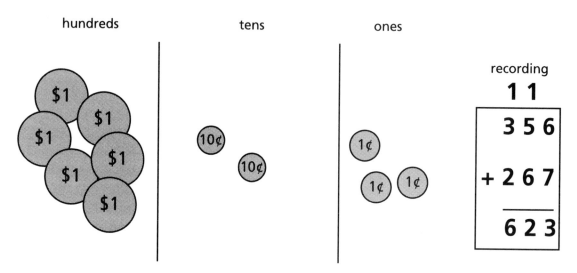

hundreds   tens   ones

recording

11

356

+267

623

FIGURE 5.4 *The result of adding 356 and 267, using coins*

What informal methods of doing addition should be discussed with students in elementary school?

As noted earlier, working from left to right is perfectly acceptable if the problem solver is able to keep track of where he or she is. Many people use this front-end approach when doing arithmetic mentally or even informally on paper. The point about addition is that every three digit number, for example, is made up of so many hundreds, tens, and ones, and problem solvers can combine these in any order they like. Therefore, given 457 + 359, someone may be attracted first to the 2 fifties, because they combine nicely to make a hundred. Adding these to the other hundreds gives 800. Then the 7 and the 9 can be added on to get the answer 816.

In other cases, the question can be converted into an easier one by temporarily adding or subtracting an appropriate small number. For example, many people evaluate 673 + 99 by adding 1 temporarily to the 99, so the question becomes 673 + 100. This gives 773. Now take off the extra 1 to get the answer 772.

A third method is the simple process of breaking up one of the numbers into appropriate parts that can be added to the other number one part at a time. For example, to work out 307 + 424, we might think of the 307 as being 300 + 6 + 1. Then add to 424: first the 6 (making 430), then the 300 (giving 730), and finally the 1 (to get 731).

It is important for students to talk about how they add and to explore informal methods. Sharing of these informal methods, whether mental or written (or a combination of the two), can undoubtedly lead to greater confidence with numbers.

Check yourself

5.1 Using the example of coins such as the one given above, add 208, 156, and 97.

5.2 Find the answer to 538 + 294 by the front-end approach of starting with the hundreds and working from left to right.

5.3 Suggest some informal methods of evaluating:

(a) 423 + 98   (b) 297 + 314   (c) 309 + 492

➤ Teaching suggestions

1. Recognize that important language used in the addition algorithm includes *thousands, hundreds, tens, ones (or units); ten of these can be exchanged for one of those,* and *carrying.*

2. Realize that coins ($1, 10¢, and 1¢) and base-ten blocks are the two most effective models for explaining the addition algorithm to students and letting them experience it.

3. Develop students' understanding of the addition algorithm by giving them opportunities to connect the manipulation of materials (both coins and blocks) with the manipulation of the symbols and the corresponding language.

4. Discuss with students and encourage informal methods of doing addition calculations, both mental and written (or a combination of the two), including the front-end approach.

6 Subtraction Structures

Students should learn to understand the operation of subtraction as taking away and comparison; to see the relationship between addition and subtraction; and to recognize situations in which subtraction applies.

THIS CHAPTER EXPLAINS:

- four structures of real-life problems modeled by subtraction; and
- the situations in which students meet these structures.

What are the kinds of situations in which elementary students may encounter the operation of subtraction?

Subtraction is the appropriate operation in an entire range of situations. They can be categorized as follows:

- the partitioning structure;
- the reduction structure;
- the comparison structure; and
- the inverse-of-addition structure.

One way to connect these mathematical structures with the operation of subtraction is by asking ourselves, what calculation would we use on a calculator in order to solve this problem? In each case, the answer involves using the subtraction key. Indeed, one of the most interesting aspects of mathematics is that the same symbol can have so many different meanings.

Subtraction as partitioning

The *partitioning structure* refers to a situation in which a quantity is partitioned off in some way or other, and subtraction is required to calculate how many or how much remains.

Example 6A

Suppose a box holds 17 marbles, and then 5 are removed. How many marbles are left?

Thinking it through

The calculation that must be entered on a calculator to correspond with this situation is 17 – 5. This structure is the one that teachers most frequently connect with subtraction. It is strongly associated with the phrases *take away* and *how many* (or *how much*) is left.

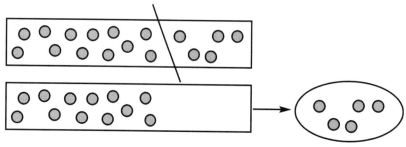

FIGURE 6.1 *Subtraction as partitioning*

What are some contexts in which students meet the partitioning subtraction structure?

This structure is encountered whenever we start with a given number of things in a set and a subset is taken away (removed, destroyed, eaten, killed, blown up, lost, or whatever). In each case, the question being asked is, how many are left? A variation is situations in which a subset is identified as possessing some particular attribute and the question asked is, how many are not? or how many do not? For instance, 58 children from a group of 92 are going on a field trip. The question is how many are not going?, and it has to be associated with the subtraction 92 – 58.

This structure occurs frequently in the context of money and shopping. For example, if Rana spends $72 from her savings of $240, she might want to work out how much is left (carry out the subtraction 240 – 72). Or Jose might spend $6.75 in a shop and need to calculate the amount of change from a $10 bill (carry out the subtraction 10 – 6.75).

Finally, we encounter the partitioning subtraction structure in a number of practical situations in the context of measurement. For example, Anya has a given length of some material, cuts off part of it, and wishes to calculate how much is left. Or Hasim has cooking ingredients that are measured by mass or volume, uses a certain amount in a recipe, and wishes to calculate how much is left.

Subtraction as reduction

The reduction structure is simply the reverse process of the augmentation structure of addition (see Chapter 4). It refers to a situation in which a quantity is reduced by some amount and the operation of subtraction is required to find the reduced value.

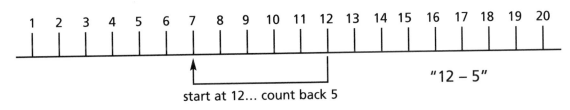

The reduction structure is simply the reverse process of the augmentation structure of addition.

Example 6B

Yesterday a bicycle cost $149. Today it is reduced by $25. What is the new price?

Thinking it through

The calculation that must be entered on a calculator to solve this problem is 149 – 25. The important language in this structure includes phrases such as *reduced by* and *goes down by*. This subtraction structure is the one that lies behind the idea of counting back along a number line, as shown in Figure 6.2.

"12 – 5"

start at 12... count back 5

Figure 6.2 *Subtraction as reduction*

What are some contexts in which students meet subtraction in the reduction structure?

Realistic examples of the reduction structure mainly occur in the context of money. The key idea that signals the operation of subtraction is that of reducing (reducing prices, cutting wages and salaries, and so on). For example, if the price tag on a bike says $325 but it is then cut by $59, the new price is determined by the subtraction 325 – 59. The structure is occasionally also encountered in other measurement contexts, such as a reduction in mass or a fall in temperature.

Subtraction as comparison

The comparison structure refers to a completely different set of situations: those that require subtraction to compare two quantities.

Example 6C

In Figure 6.3, how many more blue cubes are there than red cubes?

Thinking it through

The calculation that must be entered on a calculator to correspond to this situation is 12 – 7. Subtraction of the smaller number from the larger lets us determine the difference — in other words, find out how much greater or how much smaller one quantity is than the other. Because making comparisons is such a fundamental process, with so many practical and social applications, the ability to recognize this subtraction structure and the confidence to handle the associated language patterns are particularly important.

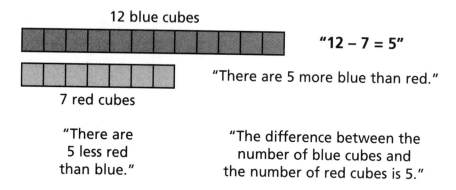

"12 − 7 = 5"

"There are 5 more blue than red."

"There are 5 less red than blue."

"The difference between the number of blue cubes and the number of red cubes is 5."

FIGURE 6.3 *Subtraction as comparison*

What are some contexts in which students meet subtraction in the comparison structure?

Wherever two numbers occur, we often find ourselves wanting to compare them — to determine the difference, or to find out how much greater or smaller one is than the other. We might wish to compare the numbers of items in two sets (for example, the numbers of cards in two packs, the numbers of children in two classes, the numbers of counters in two piles, the numbers of pages in two books). To do this, we have to connect the situation and the associated language of *difference, how many more,* and *how many less* (or *fewer*) with the operation of subtraction.

In the context of money, we encounter this subtraction structure whenever we compare the prices of articles or the costs of services. If holiday package A costs $1109 and package B costs $969, then we ask questions such as, how much more expensive is A?, how much cheaper is B?, how much more does A cost than B?, or how much less does B cost than A? In each case, the question is answered by the subtraction 1109 − 969. Similarly, we use subtraction to compare salaries and wages. For example, how much more does a doctor earn than a teacher? How does this answer change if taxes and expenses are included?

Finally, the process of comparison is a central idea in all measurement. If we measure the heights of two students, we need a subtraction to compare them — to determine how much taller or shorter one student is than the other. If we measure the masses of two articles, we compare them by asking, how much heavier or how much lighter? Again subtraction is involved.

The language of comparison in the context of measurement is extensive. We use words such as *how much longer, taller, higher, further, wider, shorter, nearer,* or *narrower* in the context of length; *how much heavier* or *lighter* in the context of mass or weight; *holds how much more* or *how much less* in the context of capacity; *how much longer* or *shorter* in time taken or *how much sooner, earlier, later, younger* or *older* in the context of time; *how much hotter* or *colder,* in the context of temperature; and *how much faster* or *slower* in the context of speed. The development of this range of language is crucial to children's understanding of the measurement concepts. It is also important in building up their confidence about recognizing situations that are connected with subtraction.

> The language of comparison in the context of measurement is extensive.

Subtraction as the inverse-of-addition

The inverse-of-addition structure refers to situations in which we have to determine what must be added to a given quantity in order to reach some target. The phrase *inverse-of-addition* underlines the idea that subtraction and addition are reverse processes. This means, for example, that since 28 + 52 comes to 80, then 80 – 52 must be 28. The subtraction of 52 undoes the effect of adding 52. Hence, to solve a problem of the form what must be added to *X* to give *Y*?, we subtract *X* from *Y*.

> The inverse-of-addition structure refers to situations in which we have to determine what must be added to a given quantity in order to reach some target.

Example 6D

The chocolate bar is 80¢, but Yanna has only 52¢. How much more does she need?

Thinking it through

The calculation that must be entered on a calculator to solve this problem is the subtraction 80 – 52. Figure 6.4 shows how this subtraction structure is interpreted as an action on the number line: starting at 52, we have to determine what must be added to get to 80.

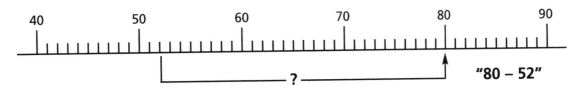

FIGURE 6.4 *Subtraction as inverse-of-addition*

What are some contexts in which students meet subtraction in the inverse-of-addition structure?

This subtraction structure is often the most difficult for elementary students to recognize because the language associated with it, such as how much more is needed? and what must be added?, seems to signal the idea of addition rather than subtraction.

We encounter this structure in many commonplace situations. The category includes any situation in which we have a number of objects or individuals and require more in order to reach a target. For many people, the most convincing examples come from sports. For example, if Lu has scored 180 in bowling, how many more does he need to reach a perfect score of 300? This problem corresponds to the subtraction 300 – 180. If Lili's basketball opponents have a score of 104 and her team has scored only 86, how many more points does her team need to catch up? The calculation to be entered on a calculator to answer this question is 104 – 86.

> Perhaps the most relevant instances of the inverse-of-addition subtraction structure occur in the context of money.

Perhaps the most relevant instances of the inverse-of-addition subtraction structure occur in the context of money. For example, if Shelley has saved $85 toward a bike that costs $325, we use the subtraction 325 – 85 in order to calculate how much more she needs to save.

If anyone is uncertain about the assertion that this situation is an example of subtraction, it will help to ask, what is the calculation you would enter on a calculator to work this out?

Other examples of the inverse-of-addition structure occur in the context of measurement, for example, how much further does Sohrab have to drive to complete a journey of 345 kilometers if he has already driven 196 kilometers.

Check yourself

6.1 An important event is planned for 1 January 2050. On 1 January 1999, how many years are there to wait? What is the calculation to be entered on a calculator to answer this question? Of what subtraction structure is this an example?

6.2 My book has 256 pages, and so far I have read 178 of them. How many more pages do I have to read to finish the book? What is the calculation to be entered on a calculator to answer this question? Of what subtraction structure is this an example?

6.3 A teacher is 52 and has a daughter 25 years old. How many years younger is the daughter than the teacher? What is the calculation to be entered on a calculator to answer this question? Of what subtraction structure is this an example?

6.4 I have collected 565 points from my local service station, but I need 750 points to get a case of glasses from the free-gift catalogue. How many more points do I need? What is the calculation to be entered on a calculator to answer this question? Of what subtraction structure is this an example?

6.5 Pose a problem that corresponds to the subtraction $3.95 - 2.99$ using the comparison structure in the context of shopping.

6.6 Pose a problem that corresponds to the subtraction $25 - 6$ using the comparison subtraction structure in the context of temperatures.

6.7 Pose a problem that corresponds to the subtraction $250 - 159$ using the partitioning structure and the phrase "how many do not...?".

6.8 Pose a problem that corresponds to $1489 - 1350$, using the inverse-of-addition structure.

►Teaching suggestions

1. Ensure that students learn to connect the operation of subtraction with a wide range of problems, including situations that involve the ideas of partition, reduction, comparison, and inverse-of-addition.
2. Let students experience these subtraction structures in a range of practical and relevant contexts, including especially money (shopping, bills, and wages and salaries) and various aspects of measurement.
3. Recognize that the key language to be developed in the partitioning structure includes *take away, how many are left?; how many are not?; how many do not?*

4. Realize that subtraction is not just "take away." Partitioning is only one subtraction structure. Teachers should not overemphasize the language of "take away, how many are left" at the expense of all the other important language that has to be associated with subtraction.

5. Recognize that the key language to be developed in the reduction structure includes *reduced by*, *cut by*, and *count back*.

6. Recognize that the key language to be developed in the comparison structure includes *difference; how many more? how many less (or fewer)? how much greater, smaller, longer, taller, higher, further, wider, shorter, nearer, narrower, heavier, lighter, longer or shorter* (in time taken), *sooner, earlier, later, younger, older, hotter, colder, faster, slower?* holds *how much more, or how much less?*

7. Recognize that the key language to be developed in the inverse-of-addition structure includes *what must be added? how many (much) more are needed?*

8. Be aware that the language of problems with the inverse-of-addition structure often seems to signal addition rather than subtraction, so many students will automatically add the two numbers in the question. They need specific help to recognize the need for a subtraction operation.

9. Remember that asking, "what is the calculation to be entered on a calculator to solve this problem?" helps to focus the student's thinking on the underlying mathematical structure of the situation.

10. Be aware that students should not use the terminology of *partitioning, reduction, comparison*, and *inverse-of-addition*. These words refer to structures that can help teachers explore, with their students, the various ways subtraction is used to solve problems.

7

Subtraction Calculations

> Students should learn to use their understanding of place value to develop methods of computation; to work out a variety of mental methods of computation; and to extend mental methods to develop a range of methods of computation that involve the subtraction of whole numbers without using a calculator.
>
> **THIS CHAPTER EXPLAINS:**
>
> - the decomposition method for doing subtraction calculations;
> - the problem with zeros in the first number in a subtraction calculation; and
> - an informal approach to subtraction based on the principles of equal additions and equal subtractions.

How can the subtraction operation be taught at school?

Subtraction calculations are straightforward when each digit in the first number is greater than the corresponding digit in the second. For example, in 576 – 324, we take the 3 hundreds away from the 5 hundreds, the 2 tens away from the 7 tens, and the 4 ones away from the 6 ones to get the answer 252.

Subtraction calculations are quite different when one of the digits in the first number is smaller than the corresponding digit in the second number. Take, for example, 443 – 267. When we look at the units column, we may find ourselves saying something like, "Three take away seven, you can't do that."

To cope with apparent difficulties of this kind, we use a subtraction method called *decomposition.*

How does subtraction by decomposition work?

As with addition calculations, the key to explaining the decomposition method is a sound grasp of place value and the use of some manipulatives, such as coins or base-ten blocks.

Consider the example 443 – 267, using base-ten blocks. First the 443 is set out with base-ten blocks, as shown in Figure 7.1: 4 hundreds, 4 tens, and 3 ones. The task is to take 267 away from this collection of blocks: that is, to remove 2 hundreds, 6 tens and 7 ones.

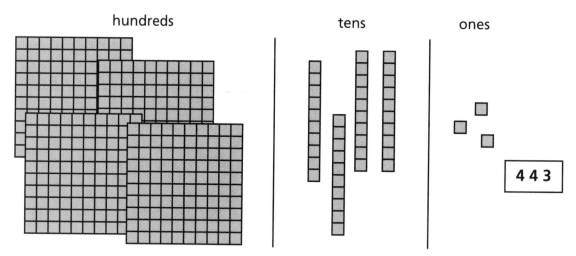

FIGURE 7.1 *The number 443 using base-ten blocks*

As with addition, the natural place to start may be to take away the biggest blocks first — that is, to work from left to right — and this is how many people deal with a calculation of this kind if they are doing it mentally. They think something like this: '443 take away 200, leaves 243; 243 take away 60, leaves 183; 183 take away 7, leaves 176.'

But the standard written algorithm actually works from right to left. We start by trying to remove 7 units from the collection of blocks in Figure 7.1. Since there are only 3 units there, we cannot do this yet. So we take one of the tens in the box of blocks to the left and exchange it for ten ones. Figure 7.2 shows the situation at this stage and the corresponding recording.

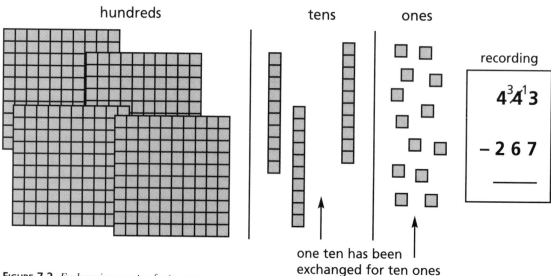

FIGURE 7.2 *Exchanging one ten for ten ones*

Notice how the recording in symbols corresponds precisely to the manipulation of the materials. We cross out the 4 tens in the top number and replace it by 3 because one of these tens has been exchanged for units. We now have 3 tens in our collection. The small

1 placed beside the 3 ones in the top number indicates that we now have 13 ones. We are now in a position to take away the 7 ones as required, leaving 6 ones. This is recorded as in Figure 7.3.

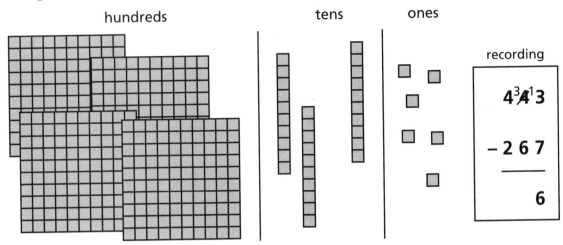

FIGURE 7.3 *After 7 ones have been taken away*

The next step is to deal with the problem of removing 6 tens when we have only 3 of them. So we take one of the hundreds and exchange it for 10 tens, producing the situation shown in Figure 7.4.

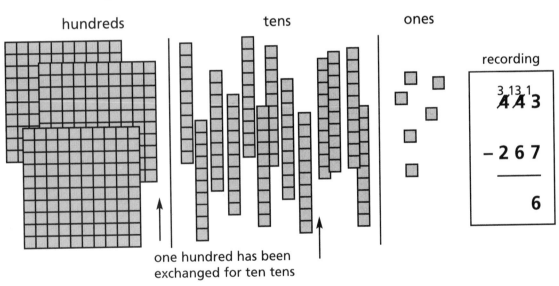

one hundred has been exchanged for ten tens

FIGURE 7.4 *Exchanging 1 hundred for 10 tens*

The recording indicates that after the exchange process we have 3 hundreds and 13 tens. We can now complete the subtraction, taking away the 6 tens and then the 2 hundreds. Figure 7.5 shows the final arrangement of the blocks, with the remaining 1 hundred, 7 tens, and 6 units corresponding to the result of the subtraction, namely 176.

Note three important points about this method. First, the idea of exchanging a block in one column

> The idea of exchanging a block in one column for ten in the next column to the right when necessary is quite natural.

for ten in the next column to the right when necessary is quite natural. Second, a strong connection exists between the manipulation of the materials and the recording in symbols, supported by appropriate language. Thirdly, all the action in the recording takes place in the top line — in the number being worked on, not the number being taken away.

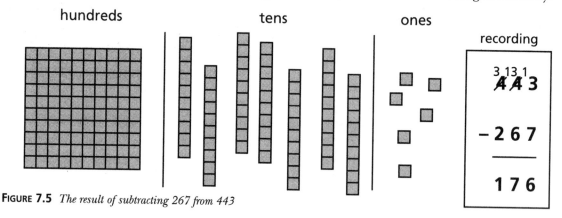

FIGURE 7.5 *The result of subtracting 267 from 443*

How do we approach a subtraction problem with a zero in the first number?

In many problems, a zero is part of the first number used in a subtraction calculation. The method of decomposition uses an exchange from the next largest group of tens. Figure 7.6 shows the steps involved in tackling 802 – 247 by decomposition.

$$
\begin{array}{cc}
8\ 0\ 2 \\
-\ 2\ 4\ 7 \\
\\
\text{(a)}
\end{array}
\qquad
\begin{array}{cc}
{}^{7}\!\!\!\not{8}\ ^{1}0\ 2 \\
-\ 2\ 4\ 7 \\
\\
\text{(b)}
\end{array}
\qquad
\begin{array}{cc}
{}^{7}\!\!\!\not{8}\ ^{9}\!\!\!\not{0}\ ^{1}2 \\
-\ 2\ 4\ 7 \\
\\
\text{(c)}
\end{array}
\qquad
\begin{array}{cc}
{}^{7}\!\!\!\not{8}\ ^{9}\!\!\!\not{0}\ ^{1}2 \\
-\ 2\ 4\ 7 \\
\hline
5\ 5\ 5 \\
\text{(d)}
\end{array}
$$

FIGURE 7.6 *The problem of a zero in the first number*

In Figure 7.6a, the person doing the calculation is faced with the problem of 2 subtract 7. The decomposition method requires a ten to be exchanged for ten units, but the zero in the 802 indicates that there are no tens. It is not difficult to see that the thing to do is to go across to the hundreds column and exchange this for 10 tens, as shown in Figure 7.6b, and then to take one of these and exchange it for ten units, as shown in Figure 7.6c. The subtraction can then be completed, as in Figure 7.6d. Of course, all this can be carried out and understood easily in terms of base-ten blocks or coins, representing hundreds, tens, and ones (units).

Do informal methods have a place in subtraction?

Informal techniques exist for subtraction. We need to allow students to invent their own methods. They might use an addition technique to select "easier" numbers with which to work. For example, to work out 87 – 48, Marco could simply add 2 to both numbers, changing the problem to 89 – 50, a much easier calculation. This method can almost be developed into an "algorithm" that some students may find more to their liking than the formal method of decomposition.

Another example might be useful. Find 443 – 267. We could add 3 to both numbers, to give 446 – 270. Then add 30 to both numbers, to give 476 – 300. So the answer is 176.

This approach can be combined where appropriate with subtracting the same thing from both numbers. For example, to calculate 918 – 436, subtract 6 from both numbers getting 912 – 430. Now add 70 to both numbers: 982 – 500. The answer is 482. With a bit of practice, this method of converting the second number into a round number of tens or hundreds by adding the same thing to both numbers (or subtracting the same thing from both numbers) can become extremely efficient and just as quick as any other.

Check yourself

7.1 Practice the explanation of the process of subtraction by decomposition using coins (1¢, 10¢, and $1 to represent ones, tens, and hundreds respectively) and appropriate examples, such as 623 – 471.

7.2 Practice the explanation of the process of subtraction by decomposition using base-ten blocks to represent units, tens, hundreds, and thousands. Using examples with zero in the first number, such as 2006 – 438.

7.3 Find the answer to 721 – 458 by converting it to an easier subtraction by adding the same thing to both numbers.

7.4 Suggest some informal methods of working out the following subtractions:

(a) 1000 – 458   (b) 819 – 523   (c) 605 – 206

►Teaching suggestions

1. Teach the method of decomposition to all students.
2. Explain the decomposition method in a way that encourages understanding of the process, not just as a recipe without meaning.
3. Provide students with plenty of opportunity to connect the manipulation of coins (1¢, 10¢, and $1) and base-ten blocks with the manipulation of the symbols in the process of subtraction by decomposition, supported by the appropriate language.
4. When explaining subtraction by decomposition, emphasize the idea of *exchange*. Avoid the word *borrow*.
5. Encourage students to set out written subtraction calculations generously, to give themselves plenty of room for crossing-out, writing small 1s, and so on.
6. Discuss with students how the method of adding the same thing to both numbers (or subtracting the same thing from both) can convert a subtraction question into an easier calculation. Ask students to demonstrate, using models such as base-ten blocks, why adding or subtracting the same number to both sides yields the same answer as the original question.
7. Encourage students to share different ideas for working out subtraction calculations by informal methods.

8

Multiplication........
Structures

Students should learn to understand and use the concept of multiplication as repeated addition; use the associated language; and recognize situations to which multiplication applies.

THIS CHAPTER EXPLAINS:

- two structures of real-life problems modeled by multiplication;
- the situations in which students will meet these structures;
- the commutative property of multiplication; and
- the idea of a rectangular array associated with multiplication.

What are the kinds of situations in which elementary students encounter the operation of multiplication?

Structures that correspond to the mathematical operation represented by the symbol for multiplication fall into two categories. They are:

- the repeated aggregation structure; and
- the scaling structure.

These two structures are considered extensions of the two structures of addition that are discussed in Chapter 4.

Repeated aggregation

Repeated aggregation is an elementary concept of describing multiplication as so many sets of. For example, if we have 10 sets of 3 counters, then multiplication as repeated aggregation is considered as 3 x 10. If 10 sets of 3 counters is 3 x 10, how many counters are there altogether (note Figure 8.1)?

This multiplication formula is simply an extension of the aggregation structure of addition, in which 3 x 10 can be displayed as the repeated addition of 3 + 3 + 3 + 3 + 3 + 3 + 3 + 3 + 3 + 3.

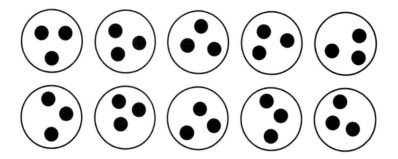

FIGURE 8.1 *Multiplication as repeated aggregation, 3 x 10*

Scaling

The *scaling structure* is an extension of the augmentation structure of addition. Recall that the augmentation structure refers to addition as meaning that we are increasing a quantity by a certain amount. With multiplication, we also increase a quantity, but we are increasing it by a scale factor. Therefore, multiplication by 10 is interpreted in this structure as scaling a quantity by a factor of 10, as illustrated in Figure 8.2.

> The scaling structure is an extension of the augmentation structure of addition.

Multiplication by a number less than 1 corresponds to a scaling that reduces the size of the quantity. For example, scaling 3 by a factor of 0.5 reduces it to 1.5, corresponding to the multiplication $3 \times 0.5 = 1.5$.

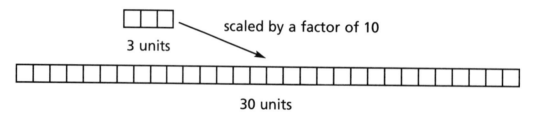

FIGURE 8.2 *Multiplication as scaling, 3 x 10*

Does 3 x 5 mean 3 sets of 5 or 5 sets of 3?

Which of the pictures in Figure 8.3 would we connect with 3 x 5? Some say that 3 x 5 means 5 sets of 3 as illustrated in Figure 8.3a. Many mathematicians, however, are happy to let 3 x 5 refer to either panel a or panel b. The same goes for 5 x 3.

One symbol's having more than one meaning is a feature that makes mathematical symbols so powerful in their application.

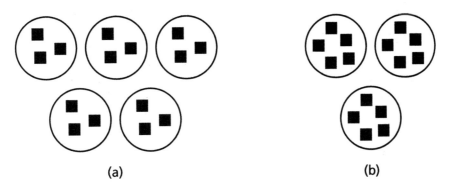

FIGURE 8.3 *a) 5 sets of 3; b) 3 sets of 5*

The commutative property of multiplication

The underlying mathematical principle here is what is called the *commutative property of multiplication*. The basic notion of this theory is that any two numbers can be multiplied together, regardless of the order in which they are written and always result in the same answer. Addition also displays this quality. We can recognize this commutative property formally by the following two generalizations:

$a + b = b + a,$

and

$b \times a = a \times b.$

It is important to note that subtraction and division do not have this commutative property. For example, $10 - 5$ is not equal to $5 - 10$, and $10 \div 5$ is not equal to $5 \div 10$.

In multiplication, the use of the commutative property enables us to simplify some calculations. For example, many of us would evaluate 5 sets of 14 by changing the problem to its equivalent, 14 sets of 5, because we have more experience multiplying by 5 than by 14. The use of the commutative property dramatically reduces the number of different multiplication rules we have to memorize. For example, if we know 7 sets of 5, we also know 5 sets of 7.

Teachers should realize that the commutative property of multiplication is by no means obvious. Aside from counting the squares in each picture, we would not immediately recognize that panel a and panel b of Figure 8.3 have the same number of counters.

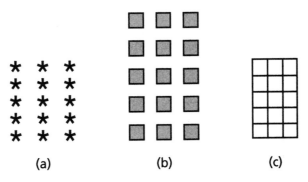

FIGURE 8.4 *Examples of rectangular arrays for 3 x 5*

One significant picture of multiplication does make this commutative property obvious: the image of a rectangular array. Figure 8.4 shows some examples of rectangular arrays that correspond to 3 x 5 (or 5 x 3). This is the image of multiplication that we should carry around in our heads, particularly when we want to talk to students about multiplication and to illustrate our discussions with diagrams. We can see that 3 sets of 5 and 5 sets of 3 come to the same thing because the array can be thought of as 3 rows of 5, if we use the vertical rows or as 5 rows of 3 if we use the horizontal rows.

There are many other valid reasons for strongly associating this image of a rectangular array with multiplication. For example, this idea leads naturally to the use of multiplication for determining the area of a rectangle. In panel c of Figure 8.4, 3 x 5 gives the number of square units in the rectangle and thus determines its area. We can also extend this idea to develop an effective method for multiplying together larger numbers (see Chapter 9).

Multiplication situations

Any situation in which we aggregate a certain number of portions of a given quantity, such as mass, liquid volume, length, or time, provides an application of this multiplication structure. For example, we use it to find: the total distance of 42 trips of 38 km each (42 x 38); the total volume of liquid required to fill 32 glasses if each holds 225 mL (32 x 225); and the total time required for 12 events each lasting 25 minutes (12 x 25).

Not surprisingly, an important context for this structure is shopping, particularly where we have to find the cost of a number of items when given the unit cost. The key words to highlight in working with ratios and money are *each* and *per*. For example, we might want to find the cost of 25 cans of pop at 89 cents each (25 x 89). Or we might purchase 25 tickets at $3.50 per ticket (25 x $3.50). In both cases, we have to associate the language and the structure of the example with the operation of multiplication.

On other occasions we encounter repeated aggregation in the context of cost per unit of measurement. For example, if we purchase 28 liters of gas at $0.56 per liter, we can recognize that a multiplication (25 x $0.56) is required to determine the total cost. In practice, however, the gasoline pump does the calculation for us. Likewise, we can connect multiplication with situations such as finding the cost of a certain number of meters of material given the cost per meter, or someone's earnings for a certain number of hours of work given the rate of pay per hour.

What are some contexts in which students meet multiplication in the scaling structure?

Most obviously, this structure is associated with scale models and scale drawings. For example, if a scale model is built using a scale factor of 1 to 10, then each linear measurement in the actual object is 10 times the corresponding measurement in the model. Similarly, if we have a plan of the classroom made using a scale factor 1 to 100 and the width of the chalkboard in the drawing is 2 cm, then the width of the actual chalkboard is 200 cm (2 x 100 cm).

The same multiplication structure lies behind the idea of a prorated increase. For example, if we each get a 3% increase in salary, then our salaries are multiplied by the same scale factor: namely, 1.03 (see Chapter 18 for an explanation of percentage increases). A similar example of this structure is found during a discussion about doubling or tripling a given quantity, which means increasing the given quantity by applying the scale factors 2 or 3 respectively.

We also use this multiplication structure in order to express a comparison between two numbers or amounts; examples are statements using phrases such as *so many times as much* (or *as many*) or *so many times bigger* (*longer, heavier,* etc.). For example: Nasir earns $125 a week, but his brother earns three times as much; how much does his brother earn? The phrase *three times as much* should prompt the association with multiplication by 3. And the calculation is 125 x 3.

Check yourself

8.1 Pose two problems associated with the multiplication 29 x 12, one using the idea of 29 sets of 12 and the other using 12 sets of 29.

8.2 Using the repeated aggregation structure and the word *per* in the context of shopping, pose a problem corresponding to the multiplication 12 x 25.

8.3 A box of yogurt cups consists of 4 rows of 6 cups arranged in a rectangular array. How can you use this as an example to illustrate the commutative property of multiplication?

8.4 A model of an airplane is built on a scale of 1 to 25. Using the scaling structure, pose a question about the model and the actual airplane.

8.5 A senior teacher earning $4827 a month gets a 2% pay raise. Model this situation with a multiplication by a scale factor, and use a calculator to find her new monthly salary.

►Teaching suggestions

1. Be aware that elementary school students' main experience of multiplication is through the structure of repeated aggregation, although they may also meet some examples of multiplication used for scaling.

2. Do not focus on whether *a* x *b* means *a* sets of *b* or *b* sets of *a*. At this stage, the commutative property and multiplication rules are more important.

3. Recognize that the key language to be developed in the repeated aggregation structure includes *so many groups* (or *sets*) *of so many, how many* (*how much*) *altogether, per,* and *each*.

4. Give special attention to helping students to use the word *per* with confidence and to associate practical problems about unit cost and cost per unit of measurement with the corresponding multiplication statements.

5. Recognize that the key language to be developed in the scaling structure includes *scaling, scale factor, so many times bigger* (*longer, heavier,* etc....), and *so many times as much* (or *as many*).

6. Work with your students to establish the commutative principle in multiplication, and encourage them to use it in recalling results from the multiplication tables.

7. Use rectangular arrays frequently to illustrate and to support explanations of multiplication and particularly to reinforce the commutative principle.

9 Multiplication Calculations

Students should learn to multiply by powers of ten; develop a variety of mental methods of computation; and extend mental methods to develop a range of noncalculator methods of computation for multiplication of up to three-digit by two-digit whole numbers.

THIS CHAPTER EXPLAINS:

- the long multiplication algorithm;
- the distributive law and its relationship to long multiplication;
- a simpler method for multiplication using areas of rectangles; and
- a number of informal multiplication calculations.

Multiplication

Teachers should show students how to use base-ten materials to show multiplication. When the students have a good understanding of the principles of multiplication, they can move to multiplication algorithms.

The standard algorithm for multiplying together two numbers with two or more digits is usually called *long multiplication*. Figure 9.1 shows how the method can be set out for calculating 26 x 34.

```
      2 6
  x   3 4
      7 8 0  ←——— this is 26 x 30
      1 0 4  ←——— this is 26 x 4
      8 8 4  ←——— this is 26 x 34
```

FIGURE 9.1 *Long multiplication, 26 x 34*

Distributive law

The method is based on what is called *the distributive law*. Formally, written out as an algebraic statement, this law of arithmetic looks like this:

$$A \times (B + C) = (A \times B) + (A \times C).$$

What this means is that if we have to multiply the sum of two numbers, *B* and *C*, by another number, *A*, we can multiply *B* and *C* separately by *A* and then add together the results. For example, using some actual numbers:

$$3 \times (6 + 4) = (3 \times 6) + (3 \times 4).$$

The left-hand side is 3 multiplied by 10, which comes to 30. The right-hand side is 18 plus 12, which also comes to 30. Applying this principle to 26 × 34, we can think of the problem as 26 × (30 + 4) and get the answer by multiplying the 26 first by the 30 and then by the 4, and finally adding the results. This is precisely what goes on in long multiplication, as shown in Figure 9.1.

The problem with the method is that multiplications such as 26 × 30 and 26 × 4 are themselves quite difficult calculations; consequently, there is some potential for errors and confusion.

An informal method for multiplying

An informal method for multiplication is based on the idea of splitting up both the numbers being multiplied into their tens and units. So 26 becomes 20 + 6, and 34 becomes 30 + 4. Then we have to multiply 20 by 30, 20 by 4, 6 by 30, and 6 by 4. To make sense of this, we can visualize the multiplication as a problem of finding the number of counters in a rectangular array of 26 by 34 (as described in Chapter 8), as shown in Figure 9.2. Thinking of the 26 and the 34 as 20 + 6 and 30 + 4 respectively suggests that we can split the array into four separate arrays, representing 20 × 30, 20 × 4, 6 × 30, and 6 × 4.

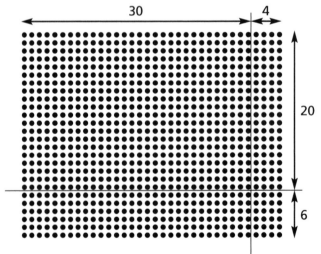

FIGURE 9.2 *A simpler approach for 26 × 34*

Drawing pictures with hundreds of counters in them, like Figure 9.2, helps to explain the method, but it's very tedious. A more efficient picture, therefore, uses the idea, suggested in Chapter 8, that we can extend the notion of a rectangular array into that of the area of a rectangle. We can then explain 26 × 34 very simply by using the diagrams shown in Figure 9.3.

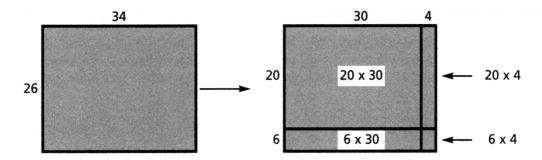

FIGURE 9.3 *Using area to interpret 26 x 34*

The answer to the multiplication calculation is obtained by working out the areas of the four separate rectangles and adding them up. The actual calculation can be written out as follows:

$$
\begin{array}{rcl}
20 \times 30 &=& 600 \\
6 \times 30 &=& 180 \\
20 \times 4 &=& 80 \\
6 \times 4 &=& 24 \\
\hline
26 \times 34 &=& 884
\end{array}
$$

This method extends quite easily to multiplication calculations involving three-digit numbers. Figure 9.4 shows a rough sketch that might be used to visualize 348 x 25. (The rectangles in the diagram are not drawn to scale.) Clearly, this example produces six rectangles to deal with separately, and then add up. As a result, the calculation can be set out as follows:

$$
\begin{array}{rcl}
300 \times 20 &=& 6000 \\
40 \times 20 &=& 800 \\
8 \times 20 &=& 160 \\
300 \times 5 &=& 1500 \\
40 \times 5 &=& 200 \\
8 \times 5 &=& 40 \\
\hline
348 \times 25 &=& 8700
\end{array}
$$

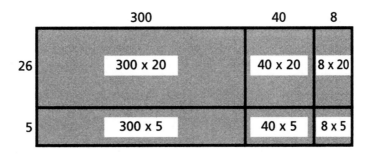

FIGURE 9.4 *The area approach applied to 348 x 25*

Multiplication calculations of this level of difficulty are about as far as most elementary-school students need to go. They still have to be very confident about multiplying 20 x 30 in order to use this method.

Another informal method

As with all calculations, problem solvers can always use those number facts and relationships with which they are confident to find individual approaches that make sense to them. Again, there is great value in encouraging students to build on their growing confidence with numbers in order to develop their own approaches and to share different approaches to the same calculation.

For instance, here are two other ways of evaluating 26 x 34. First, some problem solvers break up the 26 into 10 + 10 + 2 + 2 + 2 on the basis that they are confident about multiplying by 10 and by 2:

$$
\begin{array}{rcl}
10 \times 34 &=& 340 \\
10 \times 34 &=& 340 \\
2 \times 34 &=& 68 \\
2 \times 34 &=& 68 \\
2 \times 34 &=& 68 \\
\hline
26 \times 34 &=& 884
\end{array}
$$

And the numbers on the right do add up to show that 26 x 34 = 884

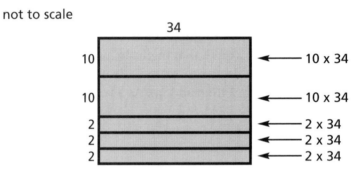

FIGURE 9.5 *Another approach to 26 x 34*

Visually, this method is represented by the diagram in Figure 9.5. Selecting the more common numbers, such as 1, 2, 5, and 10, makes this calculation easier. A second approach to this calculation notices that 26 is quite close to 25, so we can make use of the handy piece of knowledge that:

$$
\begin{array}{lrcl}
& 25 \times & 4 &= 100, \\
\text{so} & 25 \times & 8 &= 200, \\
\text{so} & 25 \times & 16 &= 400, \\
\text{and} & 25 \times & 32 &= 800.
\end{array}
$$

This is 32 twenty-fives, but we need 34. Adding another two 25s (50) gives 25 x 34 = 850. But we're after 26 x 34 so we need another 34 to get 26 x 34 = 884.

Check yourself

9.1 Use the method of Figure 9.3 to find 42 x 37.

9.2 Deduce eight other multiplication results, involving 4, 40, 400, 9, 90, and 900, from the result 4 x 9 = 36.

9.3 Use the method of Figure 9.4 to find 345 x 17.

9.4 Use informal methods, based on your own level of confidence with numbers, to find

(a) 248 x 25   (b) 72 x 16

➤Teaching suggestions

1. Make sure that students know the multiplication tables up to 10 x 10 before they embark on multiplying larger numbers.

2. Teach students how to multiply simple multiples of 10, such as 20 x 3, 2 x 30, and 20 x 30, before going on to multiplication with two-digit numbers.

3. Teach students how to multiply with simple multiples of 10 and 100, such as 2 x 300 and 20 x 300, before going on to multiplication with three-digit numbers.

4. Explore with the students the multiplication method based on areas of four rectangles, splitting each of the two numbers into tens and units (as shown in Figure 9.3).

5. Consider that some students in elementary school may be able to go on to extend this approach to multiply a three-digit number and a two-digit number (as shown in Figure 9.4).

6. Value and encourage informal methods of tackling multiplication statements that build on students' personal confidence with number and number relationships.

7. Show students how, by breaking down one of the numbers in the multiplication into smaller numbers, they can always manage to multiply with only the more common numbers, such as 1, 2, 5, and 10.

10

Division Structures

Students should learn to understand and use the concept of division as sharing and repeated subtraction; to use associated language and recognize situations where division applies; and to understand and use the relationships between the four operations, including inverses.

THIS CHAPTER EXPLAINS

- three structures of real-life problems modeled by division, and
- the situations in which students will meet these structures.

What are the kinds of situations in which elementary students encounter the use of the operation of division?

We can use the operation of division in a wide range of situations. They can be categorized as follows:

- the equal-sharing structure;
- the inverse-of-multiplication structure; and
- the ratio structure.

As we saw earlier, particularly with subtraction in Chapter 6, one of the difficulties in understanding the symbols we use in mathematics is that one symbol, such as the division symbol, can have a number of strikingly different meanings.

Equal-sharing structure

In the *equal-sharing structure*, a quantity is partitioned equally into a given number of portions, and we are asked to determine how many or how much is in each portion. For example, if 4 students share 20 marbles equally in a game, how

> In the equal-sharing structure, a quantity is partitioned equally into a given number of portions.

many does each have? The calculation to be entered on a calculator to correspond to this situation is 20 ÷ 4. This structure, which is illustrated in Figure 10.1, is the one with which teachers most naturally connect division and is strongly associated with the language of *sharing* and *how many* (or *how much*) *each.*

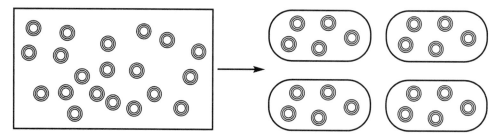

FIGURE 10.1 *Division as equal sharing, 20 ÷ 4*

Inverse-of-multiplication structure

The inverse-of-multiplication structure interprets 20 ÷ 4 in a completely different way. As shown in Figure 10.2 the question being asked is; how many groups of 4 marbles are there in the set of 20 marbles?

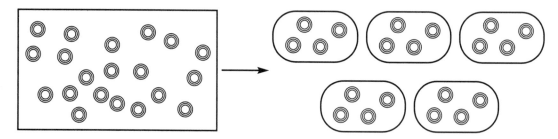

FIGURE 10.2 *Division as inverse-of-multiplication, 20 ÷ 4*

Both Figures 10.1 and 10.2 are equally valid interpretations of the division, 20 ÷ 4, even though they are answering two different questions:
  • share 20 equally into 4 groups; how many are in each group? (Figure 10.1)
  • share 20 into groups of 4; how many groups are there? (Figure 10.2)

The phrase *inverse-of-multiplication* underlines the idea that division and multiplication are *inverse* processes. This means, for example, that since 6 x 9 is 54, then 54 ÷ 9 must be 6. The division by 9 undoes the effect of multiplying by 9. Hence, to solve a problem of the form what must X be multiplied by to give Y?, we divide Y by X. For example, how many tickets costing $1.50 each does the committee need to sell to raise $90? The calculation that must be entered on a calculator to solve this problem is the division 90 ÷ 1.50, and it yields 60 tickets.

Practical problems with this inverse-of-multiplication structure can often be further subdivided. Many problems incorporate the notion of repeated subtraction from a given quantity.

Example 10A

How many sets of 4 can we get from a set of 20?

Thinking it through

The use of base-ten materials is helpful in explaining the process of division. In this example, the process of sharing out the 20 marbles can be thought of as repeatedly subtracting 4 marbles from the set of 20 until none are left, and counting the number of groups as they are removed.

But the problem might also be based on the idea of repeated addition to reach a target.

Example 10B

How many groups of 4 marbles are there in a set of 20 marbles?

Thinking it through

In practical terms, the problem solvers can repeatedly add sets of 4 marbles until the target of 20 is achieved, counting the number of sets as they are added.

Chapter 12 demonstrates that this distinction between the repeated subtraction idea and the repeated addition idea in the inverse-of-multiplication structure is particularly significant when the answer to the division is not a whole number.

Ratio division structure

The *ratio division structure* refers to situations in which we use division to compare two quantities. When a comparison has to be made between two numbers, sums of money, or measurements of some kind, we can make the comparison by subtraction, focusing on the difference between the quantities (see Chapter 6 for further clarification). For example, if A earns $300 a week and B earns $900 a week, one way of comparing them is to state that B earns $600 more than A, or A earns $600 less than B ($900 − $300). But we can also compare A's and B's earnings by looking at the ratio of the two, stating that B earns 3 times more than A. The 3 is obtained by the division: 900 ÷ 300.

> The ratio division structure refers to situations where we use division to compare two quantities.

This process is simply the inverse of the scaling structure of multiplication described in Chapter 8. What we are doing here is finding the scale factor by which one quantity must be increased in order to match the other. This problem could be stated as, by what factor must 300 be multiplied to give 900?

(All the examples of division used in this chapter so far have whole-number answers and no remainders. The problems of remainders and rounding are discussed in Chapter 12.)

What are some contexts in which students meet division in the equal-sharing structure?

Most teachers believe that sharing is a familiar experience for students: sharing candy, sharing pencils, sharing books, sharing toys, and so on. But the concept of sharing a set into subsets corresponds to division only under certain conditions. First, the set must be shared into equal subsets, which is certainly not always the case in most students' experience.

Secondly, the language used in division is "sharing *among*," rather than "sharing *with*." Students' normal experience is to share sets of things *with* a number of friends. Division requires sharing them *among* a number of people by someone not benefitting from the sharing. The division 12 ÷ 3 does not correspond to the statement, "I have 12 marbles, and I share them with my 3 friends." The problem is usually phrased, "Share 12 marbles equally among 3 people."

In the context of measurement, it is not difficult to come up with situations in which we might share a given quantity into a number of equal portions. For example, cutting up a 750-cm length of wood into 6 equal lengths, pouring out 750 mL of wine equally into 6 glasses, and sharing out 750 g of chocolate equally among 6 children, all correspond to the division 750 ÷ 6. However, these problems tend to feel like situations contrived for a mathematics lesson rather than genuine problems.

The context of money does, however, provide some natural, real-life examples for this structure of the operation. For example, a group of people might share a prize in a lottery or a bill in a restaurant. In both cases, it is likely that all the people in the group would share equally.

Another important class of everyday situations occurs when items are sold in multi-packs. People often want to know the price per item. For example, if a shop is selling a pack of 9 audiocassettes for $62.95, the cost per cassette, in cents, is found by the division 6295 ÷ 9. We can think to ourselves that the 6295 cents are being shared equally among the 9 cassettes.

This kind of situation extends naturally to the idea of price per unit of measurement. For example, to find the cost per liter of a 4 L bag of milk that cost $4.96, we recognize that the calculation to be entered on a calculator is the division 496 ÷ 4. It is as though the $4.96 is being shared equally among the 4 liters, giving $1.24 for each liter. Once again the word *per*, meaning *for each*, plays an important part in our understanding of this kind of situation.

This idea of *per* turns up in many other situations in everyday life. For example, we encounter it in calculating how many or how much we get per dollar or per gram, in finding kilometers per liter, in determining how much someone earns per hour, in calculating an average speed in kilometers per hour, in discovering the number of words typed per minute, and so on. All these situations correspond to the operation of division using the equal-sharing structure.

What are some contexts in which students meet division in the inverse-of-multiplication structure?

In many real-life situations, a set has to be sorted into subsets of a given size to answer the question, how many subsets are there?

Example 10C

The principal of a school with 240 students may wish to organize them into classes of 30 students. How many classes does she need?

Thinking it through

This problem is modeled by 240 ÷ 30: that is, how many 30s make 240? Similarly, if a teacher with one of those classes of 30 students wishes to organize them into groups of 5, he calculates how many groups are needed. This problem is modeled by 30 ÷ 5: how many 5s in 30?

The same structure extends quite naturally into the context of money. A familiar question is, how many of these can I afford? This question incorporates the idea of repeated subtraction from a given quantity. For example, items costing $6 each; how many can I buy with $150? The question is basically, how many 6s can I get out of 150? We can imagine repeatedly spending (subtracting) $6 until all the $150 is used up.

Similar situations occur in the context of measurement. For example, how many 150-mL servings of wine are in a 750-mL bottle? In the context of liquid volume and capacity, the calculation is 750 ÷ 150, or how many 150s make 750? Again, the notion of repeated subtraction from a given quantity is evident. We can imagine repeatedly pouring out (subtracting) 150-mL servings until the 750 mL is used up.

Other problems in the context of money and measurement can be stated as, How many do we need? This question incorporates the idea of repeated addition to reach a target. For example, how many items priced at $6 each must the committee sell to raise $150? We can imagine repeatedly adding $6 to our take until we reach the target of $150. In spite of the language used, the problem is modeled by the division 150 ÷ 6.

> **The word *per* is used in division.**

The word *per* turns up again in this division structure. For example, if we know the price per kilogram of potatoes is $1.20, then we might find ourselves asking, how many kilograms can I get for $10? Similarly, if I save $45 per week, I might ask, how long will it take to save $495? If the price of gasoline is $0.58 per liter, how many liters can I get for $22?

The same mathematical structure occurs in finding the duration of a trip given the average speed. For example, how long will it take me to drive 1000 kilometers, if I average 50 kilometers per hour? The question is equivalent to asking, how many 50s make 1000? Using the inverse-of-multiplication structure, I calculate 1000 ÷ 50.

In which situations do students use the ratio division structure?

Many elementary school students can learn to recognize the need to use division in order to compare two quantities by ratio. They encounter many situations in which comparisons can be made between numbers in sets, between amounts of money, or between measurements of various kinds.

The problem is that unless the questions are contrived carefully, the answers tend to be quite difficult to interpret. It's easy enough to deal with, say, comparing two students' journeys to school of 10 minutes and 30 minutes, and by using division (30 ÷ 10), make the statement that one student's journey is three times longer than the other. But it's a huge step from interpreting a whole-number statement like that to making sense of, say, comparing the heights of two students, 125 cm and 145 cm, using a calculator to do the division (145 ÷ 125 = 1.16) and concluding that one pupil is 1.16 times taller than the other.

Check yourself

10.1 A dinosaur is thought to have been 300 cm long and a model of it is 15 cm long. How many times longer is the "real" dinosaur? (that is, what is the scale factor?) What is the calculation to be entered on a calculator to answer this question? Of what division structure is this problem an example?

10.2 A basket of apples weighing 14 kg costs $7.00. What is the price per kilogram of apples? What is the calculation to be entered on a calculator to answer this question? Of what structure of division is this problem an example?

10.3 A new series of CDs cost $12.50 each. How many can I buy with $100? What is the calculation to be entered on a calculator to answer this question? Of what division structure is this problem an example?

10.4 If I save $12 a month, how many months do I need to bank $300? What is the calculation to be entered on a calculator to answer this question? Of what division structure is this problem an example?

10.5 Pose a problem that corresponds to $2.40 ÷ 4 in the context of shopping.

10.6 Pose a problem using the ratio structure in the context of salaries. Use a calculator to answer your own problem.

➤Teaching suggestions

1. Ensure that students learn to connect the operation of division with a wide range of problems, including structures of equal sharing, the inverse of multiplication (including both repeated subtraction from a given quantity and repeated addition to reach a target), and ratio.

2. Explore with students these division structures in a range of practical and relevant contexts including shopping, rates of pay, and the many kinds of problems associated with the word *per*, such as *price per unit*.

3. Recognize that the key idea in the equal-sharing structure is *sharing equally among*.

4. Recognize that division is not only *sharing*. Do not overemphasize the language and imagery of sharing at the expense of the other important language and imagery that should be associated with division, particularly in the inverse-of-multiplication structure.

5. Keep in mind that two key ideas in the inverse-of-multiplication structure are: (a) how many *B*s make *A*? (repeated addition to reach a target), and (b) how many times can *B* be taken away from *A* until there's nothing left? (repeated subtraction from a given quantity). Both these ideas have to be connected with the division $A \div B$.

6. Emphasize division problems built on questions, such as *how many can I afford?*, that incorporate the idea of repeated subtraction from a given quantity, and *how many do I need?*, that incorporate the idea of repeated addition to reach a target.

7. Introduce elementary school students to the concept of using division to find the ratio between two quantities in order to compare them. But remember that the results are difficult to interpret if they are not whole numbers.

8. Keep asking, what is the calculation to be entered on a calculator to solve this problem? It helps to focus students' thinking on the underlying mathematical structure of the situation and hence to make the connection with division.

Division Calculations

Students should learn to divide by powers of ten; to develop a variety of mental methods of computation; and to extend mental methods to develop a range that do not use a calculator, progressing to division of up to three-digit by two-digit whole numbers.

THIS CHAPTER EXPLAINS:

- dividend and divisor;
- the informal repeated-subtraction method of doing division calculations;
- the algorithm known as short division;
- a number of informal approaches to division calculations; and
- the use of the distributive law in division calculations.

Long division is so tedious. Is there a simpler alternative?

Since the use of calculators has become widespread, no one needs to be able to do complicated division by paper-and-pencil methods. Teachers can and should encourage the use of a more informal method described below. It works very well with problems up to the level of difficulty with which most people can cope: dividing a three-digit number by a two-digit number. The approach builds on the individual's personal confidence with multiplication, and the process is easily understood. This contrasts with the conventional algorithm, known as long division, which can involve some tricky multiplications and is, to say the least, not easy to make sense of. So this book does not explain long division.

Take as an example the division 648 ÷ 24. The first number in a division (648 in this case) is technically called the *dividend*, and the second number (24) is called the *divisor*. The informal method uses the inverse-of-multiplication structure and the idea of repeated subtraction, as outlined in Chapter 10. Hence the question is, how many 24s make 648? We approach this problem step by step, using whatever multiplications we are confident with and repeatedly subtracting from the dividend various amounts of the divisor in an informal manner.

	(a)		(b)		(c)		(d)

```
        (a)                    (b)                    (c)                    (d)

     | 648 ÷ 24              | 648 ÷ 24              | 648 ÷ 24              | 648 ÷ 24
  10 | 2 4 0             10  | 2 4 0             10  | 2 4 0             10  | 2 4 0
     | 4 0 8                 | 4 0 8                 | 4 0 8                 | 4 0 8
                        10  | 2 4 0             10  | 2 4 0             10  | 2 4 0
                            | 1 6 8                 | 1 6 8                 | 1 6 8
                                               2   |   4 8             2   |   4 8
                                                   | 1 2 0                 | 1 2 0
                                                                      2   |   4 8
                                                                          |   7 2
                                                                      2   |   4 8
                                                                          |   2 4
                                                                      1   |   2 4
                                                                     27   |     0
```

FIGURE 11.1 *Informal repeated subtraction approach to 648 ÷ 24*

For example, we know easily that ten 24s make 240. We subtract this 240 from the 648. That leaves us with 408 to find. At this stage, our work may be as shown in Figure 11.1a. Try another ten 24s. That's a further 240, leaving us with 168, as shown in Figure 11.1b. We do not have enough for another ten 24s, so we try two 24s (or one 24, if we prefer, or whatever we are confident enough to do mentally). This gives us the situation shown in Figure 11.1c. And so we proceed until we've used up all the 648, as shown in Figure 11.1d.

Adding up the numbers of 24s we've used down the left-hand side gives us the answer to the calculation: $10 + 10 + 2 + 2 + 2 + 1 = 27$.

Someone with greater confidence with multiplication might get to the result more quickly, as shown in Figure 11.2. Here the problem solver went straight in with twenty 24s ($20 \times 24 = 480$), followed up with five 24s ($5 \times 24 = 120$), and finished off with two 24s ($2 \times 24 = 48$).

Note that no one can get far with this method for division by a two-digit number without being fluent in subtraction.

```
       | 648 ÷ 24
   20  | 4 8 0
       | 1 6 8
    5  | 1 2 0
       |   4 8
    2  |   4 8
   27  |     0
```

FIGURE 11.2 *648 ÷ 24 with fewer steps*

Does this method work when there's a remainder?

Yes. Take as an example $437 \div 18$ (Figure 11.3). This time we started with twenty 18s, which is an easy mental calculation ($20 \times 18 = 360$), and followed it up with two more 18s and then another two 18s. At this stage we are left with 5. Since this amount is less than the divisor, 18, we can go no further. The answer to the question is, therefore, 24 remainder 5.

```
        | 4 3 7 ÷ 1 8
   20   | 3 6 0
        |   7 7
    2   |   3 6
        |   4 1
    2   |   3 6
   24   |  rem 5
```

FIGURE 11.3 *An example with a remainder, $437 \div 18$*

The meaning of this answer will, of course, depend on the actual practical situation that gave rise to the calculation. (Remainders in various division situations are discussed in Chapter 12.)

```
      | 4 7 5 ÷ 2 5          | 6 6 9 ÷ 1 2          | 8 0 6 ÷ 3 1
  10  | 2 5 0            50  | 6 0 0            20  | 6 2 0
      | 2 2 5                |   6 9                | 1 8 6
   1  |   2 5             5  |   6 0             2  |   6 2
      | 2 0 0            55  |  rem 9               | 1 2 4
   4  | 1 0 0                                    2  |   6 2
      | 1 0 0                                       |   6 2
   4  | 1 0 0                                    2  |   6 2
  19  |     0                                    26 |     0
```

FIGURE 11.4 *Further examples of an informal repeated-subtraction method of division*

How does short division work? Should teachers use it with students?

Short division is the standard algorithm often used for dividing by a single-digit number. It can be demonstrated clearly using the equal-sharing structure for division and either coins (1¢, 10¢, and $1) or base-ten blocks to represent the numbers. For example, Figure 11.5 shows the division $75 \div 5$ interpreted with 10¢ and 1¢ coins. The 7 tens and 5 ones in the dividend are to be shared equally between five recipients.

> Short division is the standard algorithm often used for dividing by a single-digit number.

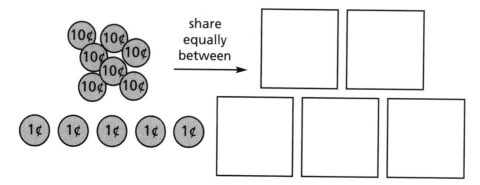

FIGURE 11.5 *Interpreting 75 ÷ 5*

In Figure 11.6, 1 ten has been given to each of the five recipients, and the remaining 2 tens have been exchanged for 20 ones. Therefore a total of 25 ones still has to be shared out. When this is done, each recipient gets 1 ten and 5 ones. The answer to the problem is clearly 15.

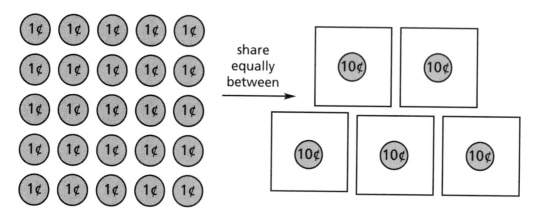

FIGURE 11.6 *Dealing with the tens for 75 ÷ 5*

Figure 11.7 shows one of the standard ways of recording this process. The small 2 written in front of the 5, represents the 2 tens that are exchanged for 20 ones, it indicates that 25 ones are to be shared out at that stage. The 15 written above the line represents the 1 ten and 5 ones that each of the five recipients gets when 75 is shared among them.

$$\begin{array}{r} 1\ 5 \\ \hline 5\overline{)7\,^2 5} \end{array}$$

FIGURE 11.7 *Short division, 75 ÷ 5*

The problem with this explanation is that, in practice, problem solvers using the short division algorithm, particularly with bigger numbers, probably do not use the equal-sharing structure consistently. Rather, they switch between it and the inverse-of-multiplication structure. Figure 11.8a demonstrates, tackling 438 ÷ 6. The first question we ask might be, can we share the 4 hundreds between 6? Since the answer is no, we exchange these 4 hundreds for 40 tens, giving a total of 43 tens.

Now we are looking at 43 tens to be shared among 6. We might say, how many 6s in 43? We have switched from sharing to the inverse-of-multiplication. The answer is 7 with 1 ten remaining. That ten is exchanged for 10 ones, giving a total of 18 ones still to be shared out. Again, we probably switch to inverse-of-multiplication and think, how many 6s in 18? The calculation is completed as shown in Figure 11.8. But the explanation gets unwieldy and wordy.

$$
6\overline{)4\ 3\ 8} \qquad \overset{7\ 3}{6\overline{)4\ 3^1 8}}
$$

(a)   (b)

FIGURE **11.8** *Short division, 438 ÷ 6*

On balance, teachers probably find it easier to introduce division by single-digit numbers using the informal repeated-subtraction approach outlined above, rather than the standard short division algorithm. Figure 11.9 shows this repeated-subtraction method applied to the two examples just considered: 75 ÷ 5 and 438 ÷ 6. Clearly, the more fluent the problem solver is with mental multiplication the easier the method is to use. It therefore encourages practice in handling calculations such as 50 x 6 and 20 x 6 mentally.

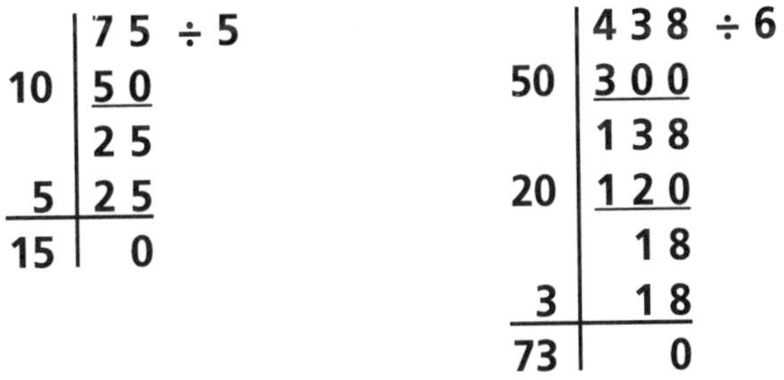

```
        | 75 ÷ 5              | 438 ÷ 6
   10   | 50            50    | 300
        | 25                  | 138
    5   | 25            20    | 120
   15   | 0                   |  18
                         3    |  18
                        73    |   0
```

FIGURE **11.9** *The informal repeated-subtraction alternative to short division*

Do other informal approaches to division calculations exist?

As with all calculations, problem solvers can use whatever number knowledge and relationships they are confident with to devise their own informal approaches to various division questions. In the classroom, teachers find a great deal of value in getting students to share their different ways of arriving at the results. Here are some examples.

The first uses an important principle: the answer to a division calculation does not change if both the dividend and the divisor are multiplied by the same number. Doing so is the equivalent of applying the equal-additions principle in subtraction (see Chapter 7). To understand this point, think of the division in terms of the ratio structure: if both quantities are scaled by the same factor, then their ratio does not change (just as when the same quantity is added to each of two numbers, their difference does not change). For instance, all the following divisions give the same result as 6 ÷ 2:

    60 ÷ 20   (multiply both numbers by 10)
    12 ÷ 4   (multiply both numbers by 2)
    30 ÷ 10   (multiply both numbers by 5)
    6000 ÷ 2000 (multiply both numbers by 1000)

Another good illustration of the application of scaling is one of the calculations done above by short division: $75 \div 5$. If we multiply both numbers by 2, the question becomes $150 \div 10$. So the answer is clearly 15.

We can also use the reverse principle: the answer to a division calculation does not change if dividend and division are both divided by the same numbers. We can use this principle to deal with the first question in this chapter, $648 \div 24$, as follows:

$648 \div 24$ is the same as $324 \div 12$ (divide both numbers by 2)
$324 \div 12$ is the same as $108 \div 4$ (divide both numbers by 3)
$108 \div 4$ is the same as $54 \div 2$ (divide both numbers by 2), which is 27

These scaling-by-multiplication and scaling-by-division principles can be combined. Consider for example, $225 \div 15$. Multiply both dividend and divisor by 2: $450 \div 30$. The question is now easier. And by dividing both numbers by 10, we can change $450 \div 30$ to $45 \div 3$, which gives the answer 15.

Chapter 9 explained how the distributive law applied to multiplication. It also applies to division. Written formally as an algebraic generalization, it looks like this:

$$(A + B) \div C = (A \div C) + (B \div C).$$

This equation means that if we can think of the dividend as the sum of two numbers (A and B), we can divide each of A and B separately by the divisor (C) and add the results.

This principle can often simplify division questions. For example, since $45 = 30 + 15$, we can think of $45 \div 3$ as $(30 + 15) \div 3$, which, using the distributive law, can be split up into $30 \div 3$ and $15 \div 3$. Notice how similar this manipulation is to what happens when we evaluate $45 \div 3$ using the short division algorithm. There, by exchanging one of the 4 tens for 10 ones, we effectively changed 45 into $30 + 15$. Here we transform the 45 into $30 + 15$ *before* we do any division because we are aware that with a divisor of 3, numbers such as 30 and 15 are highly desirable.

The trick in using the distributive law in an informal approach is to look for numbers that are easy to handle with the particular divisor. So, tackling $145 \div 11$, we might make use of the fact that 99 is a good number to have around with 11, and think of 145 as $99 + 46$ as follows:

$145 \div 11 = (99 + 46) \div 11 = (99 \div 11) + (46 \div 11)$
$= 9 + 4$, with remainder 2...
$= 13$ remainder 2

Of course, there's no need to set out the work as formally as done here. Most people work mainly mentally, jotting down a few numbers to keep track of where they are.

One last suggestion. Division can sometimes be made much easier by adding a bit to the dividend to make it into a convenient number. For example, given $638 \div 32$, a problem solver may spot that the question would much easier if it was $640 \div 32$ (answer 20). The 638 is just 2 short of being twenty 32s. So, the answer is 19 with remainder 30.

Check yourself

11.1 A carton holds 6 bottles of pop. I have 288 bottles to put in cartons. How many cartons will I need? In the division calculation corresponding to this problem, which number is the dividend and which the divisor?

11.2 Write down the values of 7 x 3, 7 x 5, and 7 x 10. Now find 126 ÷ 7, using the informal repeated-subtraction method.

11.3 Write down the values of 23 x 2, 23 x 5, 23 x 10, and 23 x 20. Now find 851 ÷ 23, using the informal repeated-subtraction method.

11.4 Write down the values of 8 x 5, 8 x 10, and 8 x 50. Now find 529 ÷ 8, using the informal repeated-subtraction method.

11.5 Use the distributive law and the fact that 154 = 88 + 66 to find the answer to 154 ÷ 22.

11.6 Find informal ways of evaluating

   (a) 385 ÷ 55   (b) 419 ÷ 21

➤Teaching suggestions

1. Teach students the informal repeated-subtraction method for dividing first by using single-digit numbers. Then go to two-digit numbers.

2. Teach short division as a method for dividing by a single-digit number, explaining it with coins or base-ten blocks. Avoid the conventional long division algorithm as a method for dividing by a two-digit number.

3. Provide students with plenty of practice in mental multiplication by 1, 2, 5, 10, 20, and 50. This is all the multiplication required for efficiency in doing divisions by the informal repeated-subtraction method.

4. Remember that fluency in subtraction is another prerequisite for success with this approach. Provide the students with plenty of practice.

5. Share and encourage informal approaches to various division questions.

6. Make explicit the principle that the ratio does not change if two numbers are multiplied or divided by the same amount. Use this principle in various examples.

12

Remainders and Rounding

> Students should learn to understand and use the features of a basic calculator; to interpret the display in the context of the problem; to handle remainders; and to round numbers to the nearest 10 or 100.
>
> **THIS CHAPTER EXPLAINS:**
> - the interpretations required for the results of division calculations done on a calculator and those done by methods that produce a remainder;
> - the relationship between the answer with a remainder and the answer from a calculator;
> - the way in which the context of the problem determines whether to round a result up or down;
> - the idea of rounding to the nearest unit; and
> - how to give answers in decimal places or significant figures.

How do the digits after the decimal point in a calculator answer relate to a division calculation and any remainder?

Consider the problem of seating 250 students in buses that each hold 60 students. Using the process of mathematical modeling (see Chapter 3), we would write the mathematical statement 250 ÷ 60 to find the answer.

Mental calculation

The kind of reasoning involved in interpreting the answer to this division calculation differs depending on whether we do it with or without a calculator. If we divide 250 by 60, using whatever mental or written procedure we are confident with, we get to the result 4 remainder 10. To interpret this result, we note that *remainder 10* does not stand for 10 buses; it represents the 10 students who would be left out if only four buses show up.

Calculator calculation

When we do the calculation on a calculator, we get the result 4.1666666. The digits after the decimal point — 1666666 — represent a portion of a bus, whereas the remainder in the previous calculation represents a number of students. The two are certainly not the same thing. This observation is very significant, and it requires careful explanation to students through discussion of a variety of examples.

How does the interpretation of the results differ in different kinds of mathematical examples?

The way we interpret the previous problems in the real world results in one of two mathematical statements: an answer with a remainder or an answer with digits after the decimal point. The mathematical solution to a calculation involving a division depends on: (a) whether the manipulation of the symbols has led to an answer with a remainder or an answer with digits after the decimal point; and (b) whether the problem giving rise to the division is an *equal-sharing* structure or an *inverse-of-multiplication* structure (see Chapter 10).

Example 12A: Equal-sharing structures

Suppose that the problem arises from an equal-sharing structure. For example, if Katya shares 150 pencils equally among 18 people, how many do they each get?

Thinking it through

The answer is 8 remainder 6 if the problem is worked out mentally or by hand and 8.3333333 if it is done on a calculator. The interpretation of these two results differs. In the first case, the remainder represents the six pencils left over after you have given eight pencils to each person. But the digits after the decimal point in the calculator answer (the .3333333 part of 8.3333333) represents the portion of a pencil that each person would get if Katya were able to share the remainder equally by cutting the pencils into small pieces. So both the remainder and the digits after the decimal point in this example refer to pencils, but the first refers to pencils left over and the second to portions of pencils received if the leftovers are shared equally.

Whether or not a particular remainder can actually be shared in the real world depends, of course, on what the problem deals with. People and pencils, for example, are not usually cut up into smaller pieces. But lengths, areas, weights, and volumes can be further subdivided into smaller units, so the calculator answer may make more sense in measurement contexts.

Example 12B: Inverse-of-multiplication structures

A pencil case holds 18 pencils. How many boxes does Katya need to store 150 pencils?

Thinking it through

Again the answer is 8 remainder 6, if the problem is worked out mentally or by hand and 8.3333333 if it is done on a calculator. But this time, the remainder 6 represents the surplus of pencils after Katya fills 8 cases of 18, while the digits after the decimal point in the calculator answer represent what fraction this surplus is of a full set of 18. That is, the .3333333 means the fraction of a case that is taken up by the 6 remaining pencils.

The remainder in this division problem represents surplus pencils, but the digits after the decimal point represent a portion of a case. In other words, we could say either, Katya needs eight pencil cases and there will be six pencils left over, referring to the answer with the remainder, or Katya needs eight cases and a portion of a case, referring to the answer with digits after the decimal point.

How can we get from the calculator answer to the remainder?

Compare the calculator answer for a division question with the answer with a remainder obtained by some written or mental method. How do we get from one to the other?

Example 12C

Seven people are paying a bill of $100. The calculator method yields $100 ÷ 7 = 14.285714, and the written or mental method gives 14 remainder 2. Note that the calculator answer here is truncated (see Chapter 3). It would actually continue 14.2857142857142857... if the calculator were able to display more than eight digits.

Thinking it through

The question is, how does the .285714 in the first answer relate to the remainder 2 in the second? The easiest way to see what happens is to imagine that the division is modeling a problem with an equal-sharing structure in a measuring context.

We can understand the equivalence of the remainder and of the decimals in the calculator answer in two different ways. First, consider that in the answer from the mental calculation, the 14 represents $14 for each person, and the remainder 2 represents the $2 that still must be paid. If this $2 is also shared between the 7 people, then each pays an extra amount equal to the division $2 ÷ 7. Doing this on the calculator gives the result .28571428. So the digits after the decimal point are the result of dividing the remainder by the divisor.

The implication is that, since multiplication and division are inverse processes, the remainder should be the result of multiplying the digits after the decimal point by the divisor. Checking this with the example above, we multiply .285714 by 7 and expect to get 2. What we actually get is 1.999998, which is nearly equal to 2, but not quite. The discrepancy is due, of course, to the small portion of the answer to 100 ÷ 7 that the calculator discarded when it truncated the result.

Another way of getting from the calculator answer (14.285714) to the remainder (2) is simply to multiply the whole number part of the calculator answer (14) by the divisor (7) and subtract the result (98) from the dividend (100). The reasoning here is that the 14 represents the $14 each person pays. Since there are 7 people, this amounts to $98 (since $14 x 7 = $98). Subtracting $98 from the $100 leaves the remainder of $2.

In summary, allowing for small errors resulting from truncation:
- the digits after the decimal point are the result of dividing the remainder by the divisor;
- the remainder is the result of multiplying the digits after the decimal point by the divisor; and
- the remainder is also obtained by multiplying the whole number part of the calculator answer by the divisor and subtracting the result from the dividend.

Rounding

Numbers obtained from measurements or as the result of calculations in practical examples often have to be rounded in some way in order to make sense and to be of any use to us.

Sometimes we round up and sometimes we round down.

The primary consideration must always be the context of the problem. For example, when buying wallpaper, most people want to be on the safe side in their calculation of how many rolls to purchase so they round up. On the other hand, anyone planning to catch the 7:48 bus should round down to "about a quarter to eight." Rounding the time up to "about ten to eight" would result in missing the bus.

> Numbers obtained from measurements or as the result of calculations in practical examples often have to be rounded in some way in order to make sense and to be of any use to us.

Example 12D

Six children can fit on a particular type of bench. How many of this type of bench are needed to seat 44 children? Use a calculator to obtain the solution.

Thinking it through

To find the number of benches, enter $44 \div 6$ on the calculator and the result 7.3333333 is displayed. The answer is a repeating decimal that has been truncated by the calculator to show just eight digits and is interpreted as about 7.3333333 benches.

Clearly, we cannot have 7.3333333 benches, so we need a rounding operation. Since 7 benches would not be enough for everyone to get a seat, we conclude that 8 benches are needed. In this case, the context determines that we round the 7.3333333 up to 8.

Example 12E

A pencil costs 6 cents. How many pencils can Chee buy with 44 cents?

Thinking it through

Chee can purchase only whole pencils, so the answer about 7.3333333 pencils must be rounded. In this case, the context determines rounding down. Chee can afford only 7 pencils.

In explaining what is going on to students, talk about the .3333333 in Example 12D as representing "a part of a bench." We need 7 benches and a part of a bench so we must get 8 benches; otherwise some people will be left standing. Similarly, the .3333333 in Example 12E represents "a part of a pencil." Chee can afford 7 pencils and a part of a pencil, but he will be able to buy only 7 pencils.

These two examples illustrate the point, noted in Chapter 10, that a division problem with the inverse-of-multiplication structure often takes one of two forms. The first incorporates the idea of repeated addition to reach a target, such as problems that use the question, how many do we need? Problems of this kind, such as Example 12D above, require rounding *up* a calculator answer that has superfluous digits. The second form incorporates the idea of repeated subtraction from a given quantity, such as problems that use the question, how many can we afford? Problems of this kind, such as Example 12E above, require rounding *down* a calculator answer with superfluous digits.

This framework is useful for teachers generating division problems. They should ensure that students get examples of both kinds and experience a range of problems, some in which the context requires rounding up and some in which the context requires rounding down.

What about the rule of rounding up when the next figure is 5 or more?

The context of the problem most often determines whether we should round up or round down. In some situations, however, there is a convention that we round the answer to the nearest unit.

Rounding with measurements

Recording measurements is a situation in which rounding to the nearest something is often employed. Think of examples from everyday life in which measurements are recorded in some form. It is very possible that the measurement is actually recorded to the nearest unit.

Consider the following situations (1) When the gas pump display says that I have put 35.8 liters in my tank, the amount of gas I have taken has been rounded to the nearest tenth of a liter. It could actually be slightly more or slightly less than 35.8 L. (2) When a bathroom scale records a weight of 77 kg, it is actually reporting the weight to the nearest kilogram. (3) When a reporter says that someone has run 100 meters in 9.84 seconds, the time is presumably rounded to the nearest one-hundredth of a second.

In all these examples, the measurement is recorded to the nearest something. The reason is sometimes the limitations of the measuring device and sometimes simply that a more accurate measurement would serve no practical purpose.

Rounding statistical data

The convention of rounding to the nearest something is employed most frequently in the handling of statistical data. For example, people who are calculating averages (means) usually round their answers.

Example 12F

A student's marks are 25, 24, 22, 25, 23, and 23. Calculate the average mark.

Thinking it through

To calculate the average mark, add up the marks and divide by the number of numbers. In this example, the sum is 142 and the average is 23.666666. Normally, no teacher needs to record all these digits. So she rounds the average mark to the nearest whole number, which is 24, or possibly to the nearest tenth, which is 23.7.

How does the process of rounding to the nearest something work?

The concept of *nearest* is essentially spatial, so it helps to imagine the number's position on a number line, as shown in Figure 12.1. In rounding to the nearest something, the decision to round down or up is determined by whether the number is less or more than halfway along the line between two marks on the scale. The crucial questions in this process are always: (1) what number would be halfway? and (2) is the number being rounded less or more than that halfway point? So, to express 23.666666 to the nearest whole number, we have to decide between 23 and 24. The number halfway between 23 and 24 is 23.5 and our number is more than 23.5, so we round up to 24. But to express 23.666666 to the nearest tenth, we have to decide between 23.6 and 23.7. The number halfway between 23.6 and 23.7 is 23.65, and our number is more than 23.65 so we round up to 23.7.

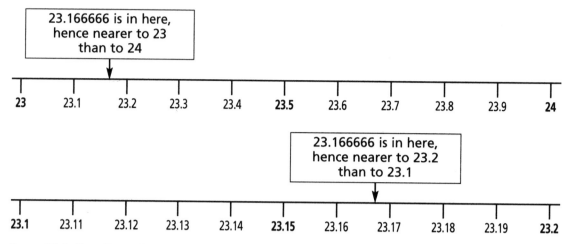

FIGURE 12.1 *Rounding to the nearest something*

What should happen if the number being rounded is exactly halfway on the number line?

Some mathematicians suggest not doing anything if the number to be rounded is at the halfway point. They say that there really isn't much point in rounding a figure such as $8500 to the nearest thousand; just leave it as $8500. Others, however, follow the 0.5 rule and round up.

In elementary school mathematics, teachers should suggest to students that they always round up when the number appears halfway between two numbers on a scale.

What about rounding to a certain number of decimal places?

When a teacher is speaking of rounding a number, such as 23.666666, to talk about rounding it to the nearest tenth, hundredth, thousandth, or ten thousandth is unnecessarily complex. Students may find the terms confusing in themselves, and most of us find it difficult to articulate a word such as *thousandth* in a way that distinguishes it from *thousand*. It is often easier to speak of rounding to a certain number of decimal places. For example, 23.666666, is

24 when rounded to the nearest whole number,
23.7 when rounded to one decimal place,
23.67 when rounded to two decimal places,
23.667 when rounded to three decimal places, and
23.6667 when rounded to four decimal places.

Rounding to significant digits

Rounding to a certain number of significant digits is often appropriate. A full consideration of *significant digits* is beyond the scope of this book, but a few words may give an understanding of the main idea. In many practical situations, we are really only interested in the approximate size of an answer to a calculation, so just the first two or three digits are normally enough.

For example, someone applying for a new job is not terribly concerned about whether the salary offered is $36 237 or $36 231. In either case, the salary is about $36 200. The choice between an additional $37 or $31 is not likely to be particularly significant. On the other hand, to someone buying a pair of pants, the difference between $37 and $31 is likely to be quite significant. This kind of reasoning forms the basis for the practice of rounding to a certain number of significant digits.

Stating the salaries in the previous paragraph as "about $36 200" is the result of rounding them to three significant digits. The first significant figure — indeed the most significant figure — is the 3, which represents the largest part of the salary, ($30 000). Then the 6 and the 2 are the second and third significant digits respectively. This may be all the job applicant wants to know. With a salary of more than $36 200, the digits in the tens and units columns seem relatively insignificant.

Consider two more examples. First, on a weekly trip to the grocery store, Kerry spends $127.96. When he gets home, his wife asks him how big the bill was. He may reply:

- With an exact statement: "the bill came to $127.96."
- Using just one significant figure: "the bill came to about $100" (this is to the nearest hundred dollars).
- Using two significant digits: "the bill came to about $130" (this is to the nearest ten dollars).
- Using three significant digits: "the bill came to about $128" (this is to the nearest dollar).

A second example. A man leaves $270 550 to be shared equally between four children. The mathematical model is $270 550 ÷ 4 = $67 637.50. We can state the answer:

- As the exact solution: "they each inherit $67 637.50."
- To two significant digits: "they each inherit about $68 000" (which is giving the figure to the nearest thousand dollars).
- To three significant digits: "they each inherit about $67 600" (which is giving the figure to the nearest hundred dollars).
- To four significant digits: "they each inherit about $67 640" (which is giving the figure to the nearest ten dollars).

In most practical situations, it is rarely useful to give approximate answers to more than three significant digits.

Check yourself

12.1 A teacher wants to order 124 copies of a mathematics book that costs $5.95. She must report the total cost of the order to a meeting. What is the mathematical model of this problem? Using a calculator, obtain the mathematical solution. Interpret the result as an exact statement back in the real world. What would the teacher say if she reports the total cost to the nearest ten dollars? to three significant digits?

12.2 Jackie knows there are 365 days in a year and 7 days in a week. She wants to work out how many weeks in a year. What is the mathematical model for Jackie's problem? Without using a calculator solve the mathematical problem, giving the answer with a remainder. What is the answer to Jackie's question? What is the meaning of the remainder? Now obtain the mathematical solution using a calculator. Is this calculator answer:

(a) an exact, appropriate answer?
(b) an exact but inappropriate answer?
(c) an answer that has been truncated (see Chapter 3)?

What do the digits after the decimal point in the calculator answer represent?

12.3 Should calculator answers be rounded up or down in the following situations?

(a) 327 children are going on a school trip; each bus can hold 40. How many buses are needed?

(b) Doughnuts cost 65 cents each. How many can you buy with $5?

12.4 Calculate the average (mean) height, to the nearest centimeter, of 9 students with heights 114 cm, 121 cm, 122 cm, 130 cm, 131 cm, 136 cm, 139 cm, 146 cm, and 148 cm.

12.5 A soccer league's teams scored a total of 1459 goals in 462 games one season. How many goals did they score per game on average? Do this problem using a calculator, and give the answer:

(a) rounded to the nearest whole number

(b) rounded to one decimal place

(c) rounded to two decimal places.

12.6 A shipment of 3500 books is to be shared equally among 17 branches of a bookstore chain. A calculator yields $3500 \div 17 = 205.88235$. How many books are there for each store? What is the remainder? What does it represent?

➤Teaching suggestions

1. Explicitly discuss with students the difference in meaning between the remainder in a division problem done mentally or by hand and the digits after the decimal point in the calculator answer.

2. Use the phrase *a part of a...* to explain informally the digits after the decimal point.

3. Provide students with a range of real-life division problems, including some with the equal-sharing structure and some with the inverse-of-multiplication structure. Have the students do them both by a method producing a remainder and on a calculator. Discuss what the remainder means and what the digits after the decimal point represent.

4. Explain, with examples of equal sharing in measurement contexts, the relationship between the calculator answer to a division problem and the answer with the remainder.

5. Discuss rounding up and down to the nearest unit.

6. Use problems that incorporate both the concept of repeated addition, such as those that ask, how many do we need? and the concept of repeated subtraction, such as those that ask, how many can we afford?

7. Emphasize the idea of recording measurements to the nearest unit when doing practical measuring tasks.

8. Use a number-line explanation of rounding to the nearest unit, making use of the crucial questions in this process: what number would be halfway? and is my number less or more than this? Emphasize that we do not always use this process, and that it is most important to first consider the context of the calculation in deciding whether to round up, round down, or round to the nearest unit.

13

Multiples, Factors, and Primes

Students should learn some properties of numbers, including multiples, factors, divisibility rules, square roots, composite numbers, and primes.

THIS CHAPTER EXPLAINS:

- natural numbers;
- whole numbers;
- multiples;
- techniques for finding multiples;
- divisibility rules for 1, 2, 3, 4, 5, 6, 8, 9, and 10
- lowest common multiples;
- factors;
- greatest common factors;
- the transitive property of multiples and factors; and
- prime numbers and composite (rectangular) numbers.

Natural and whole numbers

The natural numbers are 1, 2, 3, 4, 5, 6, and so on. Although many number systems exist, the word *number* in this chapter refers only to the natural number system. Zero, negative numbers, and anything other than the positive whole numbers are excluded.

What are multiples?

The multiples of any given number are obtained by multiplying the number by each of the natural numbers, 1, 2, 3, 4, 5, 6, and so on.

Example 13A

Find the first 10 multiples of 3, 7, and 37.

Thinking it through

A few calculations reveal that:
- the first 10 multiples of 3 are 3, 6, 9, 12, 15, 18, 21, 24, 27, and 30;
- the first 10 multiples of 7 are 7, 14, 21, 28, 35, 42, 49, 56, 63, and 70; and
- the first 10 multiples of 37 are 37, 74, 111, 148, 185, 222, 259, 296, 333, and 370.

The multiples of a given number are easy to generate with a calculator that has a constant facility. Enter a number — for example, 37 — press the plus sign, and then repeatedly press the equals button. The calculator responds by repeatedly adding 37 to the previous total, producing the multiples of 37 on the display.

The transitive property of multiples

The transitive property of multiples is that if *A* is a multiple of *B* and *B* is a multiple of *C*, it follows that *A* is a multiple of *C*.

This property is illustrated in general terms in Figure 13.1a.

> The transitive property of multiples is that if A is a multiple of B and B is a multiple of C, it follows that A is a multiple of C.

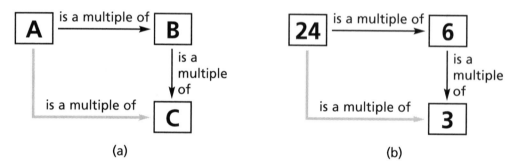

(a)   (b)

FIGURE 13.1 *The transitive property of multiples*

Figure 13.1b illustrates an example of the transitive property. A number, such as 24, that is a multiple of 6 must also be a multiple of 3 because 6 itself is a multiple of 3. Applying this principle, we can deduce that all multiples of 6 are also multiples of 3. However, not all multiples of 3 are multiples of 6 (a good example is 9).

Similarly, all multiples of 28 must be multiples of 7 because 28 is itself a multiple of 7.

Investigating patterns with multiples

Being able to recognize multiples and having an awareness of some of the patterns and relationships within them helps to develop a high level of confidence and pleasure in working with numbers.

Example 13B

Consider the pattern of the multiples of 37:

$$3 \times 37 = 111$$
$$6 \times 37 = 222$$
$$9 \times 37 = 333$$
$$12 \times 37 = 444$$

Find the next three terms of this pattern.

Thinking it through

In each term, we are using the multiples of 3 with 37 and generating a three-digit number with the same digit (note that the digit is the multiple of 3 being used in the product). The next three terms are

$$15 \times 37 = 555$$
$$18 \times 37 = 666$$
$$21 \times 37 = 777$$

Example 13C

$$1 \times 9 = 9$$
$$2 \times 9 = 18$$
$$3 \times 9 = 27$$
$$4 \times 9 = 36$$
$$5 \times 9 = 45$$

Find the next four terms.

Thinking it through

The pattern in the multiples of 9 is that the tens digit increases by 1 and the units digit decreases by 1 each time, this pattern is a useful aid for learning the nine-times table.

Consider the pattern in the multiples of nine: 9, 18, 27, 36, 45, 54, 63, 72, 81, and so on.

Multiples that are easy to find

A number of patterns make spotting certain multiples easy. For example, most adults can tell at a glance that all these numbers are multiples of ten: 20, 450, 980, 7620. The common pattern is clear: all multiples of 10 end with the digit zero. Similarly, most adults know that all multiples of 2 (even numbers) end in 0, 2, 4, 6, or 8, and that all multiples of 5 end in 0 or 5.

Multiples of four

There is also a simple way to spot whether a number greater than 100 is a multiple of 4. Since 100 is a multiple of 4, then any multiple of 100 is also a multiple of 4. A number is divisible by four if the number formed by the last two digits is divisible by four. (The word *divisible* means that a number divides evenly into another number.)

To illustrate, think of 4528 as 4500 + 28. We know that the 4500 is a multiple of 4, because it is a multiple of 100. We need only to determine if 28 is a multiple of 4, which it is. Therefore, if a number has three or more digits, we need only to look at the last two digits to determine whether or not we are dealing with a multiple of 4.

Multiples of nine

Many people can spot immediately that 18, 72, 315, 567, and 4986 are multiples of 9. An interesting technique used to determine if a number is divisible by 9 is to find its digital sum. The *digital sum* of a number is the total from adding up all of its digits. If the digital sum is divisible by nine, then so is the original number. If we cannot quickly determine if the digital sum is divisible by 9, we can continue to add the digits in the digital sum and keep repeating this process of adding the digits until we obtain a single-digit answer. This single-digit answer is called the *digital root*.

For example, the number 4986 has a digital sum of 27 (4 + 9 + 8 + 6 = 27). The digital sum is itself a multiple of 9. If we add the digits of this digital sum (2 + 7), we get the single-digit number, 9, which is the digital root. Interestingly, the digital root of a multiple of 9 is always 9.

Divisibility rules

Here is a summary of some of the divisibility rules for multiples:
- **One:** every natural number is a multiple of 1.
- **Two:** multiples of 2 are even numbers and end in 0, 2, 4, 6, or 8.
- **Three:** the digital sum of a multiple of 3 is always a multiple of 3, and the digital root is always 3, 6, or 9.
- **Four:** the last two digits of a multiple of 4 are themselves a multiple of 4.
- **Five:** multiples of 5 always end in 0 or 5.
- **Six:** multiples of 6 are multiples of 2 and of 3, so they must end in 0, 2, 4, 6, or 8 and have a digital root of 3, 6, or 9. In other words, a multiple of 6 must also be a multiple of 2 and 3.
- **Eight:** the last three digits of a multiple of 8 must be a multiple of 8.
- **Nine:** the digital sum of a multiple of 9 is always a multiple of 9, and the digital root is always 9.
- **Ten:** multiples of 10 always end in zero.

What is a *lowest common multiple*?

If we list all the multiples of each of two numbers, then inevitably some multiples are common to the two sets. For example, using 6 and 10, we obtain the following sets of multiples:
- The multiples of 6 are 6, 12, 18, 24, 30, 36, 42, 48, 54, 60, 66, …, and so on.
- The multiples of 10 are 10, 20, 30, 40, 50, 60, 70, …, and so on.

The numbers common to both sets are 30, 60, 90, 120, and so on. The smallest number of this common set is known as the *lowest common multiple*. Therefore, the lowest common multiple of 6 and 10 is the smallest number that can be split up into groups of 6 and into groups of 10. This concept occurs in many practical situations.

Example 13D

Consider the following problems:
1. What is the smallest class size necessary if the students are to be organized into groups of 7 for mathematics and teams of 5 for games.
2. If Pedro must feed one plant every five days and another plant every eight days, what is the first day on which he must feed both plants at the same time?
3. If Hannah can buy hot dogs only in packages of 12 and she wants to share the hot dogs equally among 8 friends, how many hot dogs must she buy so that each friend gets the same number of hot dogs?

Thinking it through
1. The lowest common multiple of 5 and 7 is 35, so the class size is 35. (Check by listing the multiples of 5 and 7.)
2. The lowest common multiple of 5 and 8 is 40, so both plants must be fed together every 40 days.

3. The multiples of 12 are 12, 24, 36, 48, … and the multiples of 8 are 8, 16, 24, …, so Hannah must buy 24 hot dogs.

Note that in the first two examples, we multiplied the two numbers together. But sometimes, as in the third example, the lowest common multiple is less than the product of the two numbers.

What is a factor?

Factors are all the numbers by which a given number can be divided exactly. Thus, a factor is the reverse of a multiple. That is, if *A* is a multiple of *B*, then *B* is a factor of *A*.

> A factor is the reverse of a multiple.

For example, 24 is a multiple of 6, so 6 is a factor of 24. The factors of 24 are all those natural numbers by which 24 can be divided exactly: 1, 2, 3, 4, 6, 8, 12, and 24. Notice that 1 and 24 are included as factors of 24. One is a factor of all numbers, and every number is a factor of itself.

Recognizing quickly all the factors of a given number is very useful. For example, a set of 24 objects, can be put into groups of 1, 2, 3, 4, 6, 8, 12, or 24. This property makes a number such as 24, which has many factors, more useful for many practical purposes than a number such as 23, which has no factors other than 1 and itself.

```
x x x x x x x x x x x x x x x x x x x x x x x x
                    1 by 24                          x x x x x
                                    x x x x x x x x   x x x x x
    x x x x x x x x x x x x         x x x x x x x x   x x x x x
    x x x x x x x x x x x x         x x x x x x x x   x x x x x
              2 by 12                     3 by 8         4 by 6
```

FIGURE **13.2** *Factors of 24 shown in rectangular arrays*

Rectangular arrays, introduced in Chapter 8, provide good illustrations of the concept of a factor. Figure 13.2 shows all the different rectangular arrays possible with a set of 24. The dimensions of these arrays are all the factors of 24: 1 and 24, 2 and 12, 3 and 8, and 4 and 6.

To determine if a number is a factor of another number, divide the larger number by the smaller factor. If the answer is a whole number, then the smaller number is a factor; otherwise it is not. The divisibility rules can also be used to determine if a number is a factor of another number.

Example 13E

Is 23 a factor of 1955? Is 15 a factor of 1955?

Thinking it through

For the first problem, use a calculator to divide 1955 by 23. The result is 85, so 23 is a factor of 1955.

For the second problem, use a calculator to divide 1955 by 15. The result is 130.33333, so 15 is not a factor of 1955.

The transitive property of factors

The mathematical relationship *is a factor of* possesses the transitive property, as illustrated in Figure 13.3. That is, for example, any factor of 12 must also be a factor of 24 because 12 is a factor of 24.

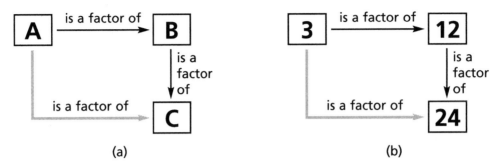

(a)   (b)

FIGURE **13.3** *The transitive property of factors*

What is the *greatest common factor*?

The idea of the *greatest common factor* is similar to the idea of the lowest common multiple. If we list all the factors of two numbers, we see that the two sets of factors have some numbers in common. Because 1 is a factor of all numbers, they must at least have this number in common! The largest of these common factors is called the *greatest common factor* or in some mathematical communities, the *highest common factor*.

Example 13F

Find the greatest common factor of 24 and 30.

Thinking it through

Using 24 and 30, we obtain the following sets of factors:
- The factors of 24 are 1, 2, 3, 4, 6, 8, 12, and 24.
- The factors of 30 are 1, 2, 3, 5, 6, 10, 15, and 30.

The factors in common are 1, 2, 3, and 6. Therefore, the greatest common factor is 6.

This concept is useful in many practical situations. For example, imagine that two classes have 24 and 30 children respectively. We wish to divide the students into a number of groups, with children from each class shared equally among the groups. Clearly, the number of groups must be a factor of both 24 and 30. The largest possible number of groups is therefore 6, as this is the greatest common factor.

Greatest common factors can be illustrated with a rectangular array. The geometric problem is to arrange 30 Xs and 24 Os in a rectangular array with the same combination of Xs and Os in each row. It is possible to achieve this combination with 1 row, 2 rows, 3 rows or 6 rows. So the greatest number of rows possible, 6, is greatest common factor. This result is shown in Figure 13.4, where the 30 Xs and 24 Os are arranged in 6 rows with 5 Xs and 4 Os in each row.

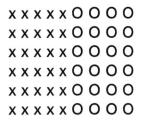

What is a *prime number*?

Any number that has precisely two factors — and no more than two — is called a *prime number*. In practice, we can think of a prime number as a number that cannot be divided exactly by any number apart from 1 and itself. For example, 7 is a prime number because it has precisely two factors: namely, 1 and 7. But 10 is not a prime number because it has four factors: namely, 1, 2, 5, and 10.

A number, such as 10, that has more than two factors is called a *composite number* or, because it can be arranged as a rectangular array with more than one row (see Figure 13.5), a *rectangular number*. A prime number cannot be arranged as a rectangular array, other than with a single row. The first twenty prime numbers are 2, 3, 5, 7, 11, 13, 17, 19, 23, 29, 31, 37, 41, 43, 47, 53, 59, 61, 67, and 71.

```
X X X X X
X X X X X          X X X X X X X
  (a) 10                (b) 7
```

FIGURE 13.5 *(a) 10 is a composite number; (b) 7 is a prime number*

Notice that the number 1 is not a prime number since it has only one factor (itself). Therefore, 1 is the only number that is neither prime nor composite. The exclusion of 1 from the set of prime numbers often puzzles students of mathematics and requires some explanation. By reinforcing the definition of a prime number as having two distinct factors, one and itself, teachers can help students understand the exclusion of 1 as a prime number.

> 1 is the only number that is neither prime nor composite.

Prime factorization

Any composite number has only one combination of prime numbers that, when multiplied together, give the number. For example, the number 24 can be obtained by multiplying together various combinations of numbers, such as: 2 x 12, 2 x 2 x 6, 1 x 2 x 3 x 4, and so on. If, however, we stipulate that only prime numbers can be used in the multiplication, only one combination produces 24: namely, 2 x 2 x 2 x 3. This is called the *prime factorization* of 24. The unique prime factorization of a number is another reason for not including 1 in the set of prime numbers.

> The Greek mathematician Euclid proved, as long ago as 300 BCE, that no largest prime number can exist.

The study of primes is a fascinating branch of number theory. Computers have been employed to search for very large prime numbers. The Greek mathematician Euclid proved, as long ago as 300 BCE, there is no largest prime number! A particularly interesting facet of prime numbers is that no pattern or formula will generate the set of prime numbers.

Number theory and multiples, factors, and primes

Do you feel differently about the numbers 47 and 48? Many people know some differences between these two numbers. To many, 48 seems a friendly number, flexible and amenable. If a group has 48 items, they can be organized in so many ways: 6 sets of 8, 3 sets of 16, 4 sets of 12, and so on. By contrast, 47 is such an awkward number. The difference, of course, is that 47 is prime, but 48 has many factors.

This realization is part of what is sometimes called "having a feel for numbers." Individuals' confidence in working with numbers in everyday situations is improved enormously by having this kind of feel for numbers, by being aware of the significant relationships between them, and by recognizing at a glance which properties they possess and which they do not. The more someone is aware of properties such as multiples, factors, and primes, the more he or she learns to delight in the pattern and fascination of number. Being able to spot at a glance which license plate numbers are multiples of 11 is of no immediate practical use, but it leads to greater confidence when the individual has to respond to numerical situations that do matter.

Check yourself

13.1 Continue the pattern shown earlier in this chapter for multiples of 37 until the pattern breaks down. Then look for a new pattern.

13.2 Multiply each of the following numbers by 9, and check that the digital root in each case is 9:

(a) 47   (b) 172   (c) 9 876 543

13.3 Use the divisibility rules to decide whether the following numbers are multiples of 2, 3, 4, 5, 6, 8, or 9:

(a) 2652   (b) 6570   (c) 2401

13.4 These following license plate numbers are all multiples of 11: 561, 594, 418, 979, and 330. For each, add the two outside digits and subtract the middle one. Do this with a few more three-digit multiples of 11. Can you state a divisibility rule for 11?

13.5 What is the smallest number of people that can be split equally into groups of 8 and of 12? What mathematical concept is used in solving this problem?

13.6 Find all the factors of

(a) 95   (b) 96   (c) 97

Which of these three numbers would be most flexible for breaking up into smaller-sized groups for various activities?

13.7 An assembly room has 48 blue chairs and 80 red chairs. They are to be arranged in rows with the same combination of reds and blues in each row. How many ways can this be done?

13.8 List all the prime numbers between 70 and 100.

13.9 By trying each prime number in turn, find the primes that multiply together to give 4403. (Use a calculator to help you.)

13.10 Start with 1, add 4, add 2, add 4, add 2. Continue this sequence until you pass 60. How many of the terms are prime?

13.11 A famous unproven theorem, called Goldbach's conjecture (after its originator Christian Goldbach, 1690–1764), states that every even number greater than 2 is the sum of two primes. For example, 52 = 5 + 47. Test this conjecture with all the even numbers from 4 to 30.

13.12 Find a number that is a multiple of all the numbers from 1 to 10 inclusive.

➤ Teaching suggestions

1. Encourage students to be fascinated by numbers and number patterns by providing them with opportunities to explore such patterns.
2. Build up students' confidence in numerical situations by exploring the concepts and properties of multiples, factors, and prime numbers.
3. Explore with students some of the divisibility rules for various numbers.
4. Have students use calculators to explore factors, multiples, and primes.
5. Use rectangular arrays to illustrate the concepts of factor, prime number, and composite (rectangular) number.

14

Squares, Cubes, and Number Shapes

Students should learn to explore number sequences, explaining patterns and using simple relationships, and to use some properties of numbers, including squares, cubes, and square roots.

THIS CHAPTER EXPLAINS:

- square numbers;
- cube numbers;
- square roots and cube roots;
- a trial and improvement method for finding square roots and cube roots using a calculator;
- the relationship between sequences of geometric patterns and sets of numbers; and
- triangle numbers.

Why are some numbers called squares?

Connecting number concepts with pictures helps to build up our understanding and confidence, as suggested in the previous chapter in discussing concepts such as factor and multiple. In particular, we saw that a prime number, such as 7, can be represented as a rectangle of dots only in one row, whereas a composite (rectangular) number such as 10 can be shown as a rectangular array with more than one row (see Figure 13.5).

Rectangles that have four equal sides are called *squares*. Numbers, such as 1, 4, 9, 16, and 25, that can be represented by square arrays (Figure 14.1) are called *square numbers*. If we use an array of small squares, called square units, as in Figure 14.1b, rather than dots, as in Figure 14.1a, then the number of squares in the array also corresponds to the total area. For example, the area of the 5 by 5 square grid is 25 square units. Of course, square numbers are also composite (rectangular) numbers, just as squares are rectangles.

(There is one exception: the number 1 is considered a square number, but, as we saw in the previous chapter, it is usually considered to be neither composite nor prime.)

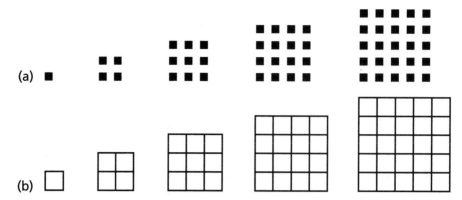

FIGURE 14.1 *Pictures of square numbers, (a) using dots; (b) using a square grid*

> A square number is any number obtained by multiplying a number by itself.

The illustrations in Figure 14.1 help to explain the geometric concept of square numbers. The arithmetic equivalent is that a *square number* is any number obtained by multiplying a number by itself. The number 16 is represented in Figure 14.1 by 4 rows of 4 dots or by 4 rows of 4 squares, corresponding to the multiplication of 4 x 4. Likewise, the representation of 25 as a square corresponds to 5 x 5. A special mathematical notation can be used as a shorthand for writing 5 x 5. It is 5^2, which means 2 fives multiplied together, and it is read as *five squared* or *five to the exponent two* (see the discussion about powers of 10 in Chapter 2).

Square numbers can be obtained using a calculator. For example, to find six squared, just enter 6 x and press the equal sign.

Here is the numerical pattern for the set of square numbers:

$$1 \times 1 = 1^2 = 1$$
$$2 \times 2 = 2^2 = 4$$
$$3 \times 3 = 3^2 = 9$$
$$4 \times 4 = 4^2 = 16$$
$$5 \times 5 = 5^2 = 25$$
$$6 \times 6 = 6^2 = 36$$

What are cube numbers?

Just as some numbers can be represented by square arrays, some, such as 1, 8 and 27, can be represented by arrangements in the shape of a cube. Figure 14.2 shows how the first three cube numbers are constructed from small cubes, called *cubic units*.

The first three cube numbers are made from 1 cubic unit, from 8 cubic units and from 27 cubic units, respectively. The cube of 27 is produced by 3 layers of cubes, with 3 rows of 3 cubes in each layer, and is therefore equal to 3 x 3 x 3. The number of cubic units in the whole construction corresponds to the total volume of the cube. For example, the volume of a 3 by 3 by 3 cube is 27 cubic units. These cubic constructions are difficult to represent in a two-dimensional picture, but readers can build various-sized cubes from cubic units to generate cube numbers for themselves. The same kind of notation is used for cube numbers as square numbers: 3 x 3 x 3 is abbreviated to 3^3 and read as *three cubed* or *three to the power three*. Generating cube numbers with a simple calculator is easy. For example, to obtain six cubed, simply enter 6 x and press the equal sign twice.

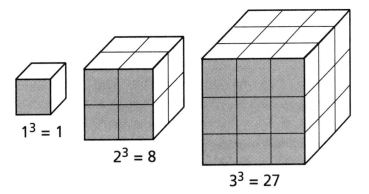

$1^3 = 1$

$2^3 = 8$

$3^3 = 27$

FIGURE 14.2 *Examples of cube numbers*

By analogy with the square numbers above, we can construct the following pattern for the cube numbers:

$$1 \times 1 \times 1 = 1^3 = 1$$
$$2 \times 2 \times 2 = 2^3 = 8$$
$$3 \times 3 \times 3 = 3^3 = 27$$
$$4 \times 4 \times 4 = 4^3 = 64$$
$$5 \times 5 \times 5 = 5^3 = 125$$
$$6 \times 6 \times 6 = 6^3 = 216$$

What are *square roots* and *cube roots*?

A square root or a cube root is the inverse of a square number or a cube number — one of the factors from which these special numbers are constructed.

Example 14A

What is the length of the side of a square that has an area of 729 square units?

Thinking it through

Another way of asking the same question is, which number when multiplied by itself gives 729? Or to put the point yet another way, which number has a square equal to 729?

The answer — which is 27, is called the square root of 729.

We say that 27 is the *positive* square root of 729 because we can also get 729 by multiplying the negative number –27 by itself. However, we are not concerned with negative numbers in this chapter.

The mathematical abbreviation for the (positive) square root of is $\sqrt{729}$. So we could write, for example, $\sqrt{729} = 27$. Finding a square root is the inverse process of finding a square. In other words, one process undoes the effect of the other.

Some examples of square roots are:

$$2^2 = 4, \text{ so } \sqrt{4} = 2$$
$$3^2 = 9, \text{ so } \sqrt{9} = 3$$
$$4^2 = 16, \text{ so } \sqrt{16} = 4$$
$$27^2 = 729, \text{ so } \sqrt{729} = 27$$

The concept of a cube root follows the same logic. In geometric terms, the question is, what is the length of the side of a cube with a total volume of 729 cubic units? Or, in arithmetic terms, what number has a cube equal to 729? The answer, which is 9, is called the cube root of 729.

As with square roots, we can think in terms of an inverse process: finding the cube root is the inverse process of finding the cube. For example, the cube of 14 is 2744, so the cube root of 2744 is 14.

How are square roots and cube roots found?

Finding a square root is simple with a basic calculator. Most have a square root key marked with the square root symbol, √. To find, for example, the square root of 361, we simply enter 361 and press the √ key: and the calculator displays the answer, which is 19.

Trying to find some square roots without using the square root key is, however, instructive. It introduces a mathematical process, sometimes called *trial and improvement* or *trial and error*, which can then be applied to other problems.

Example 14B

Find the side of a square with a total area of 3844 square units.

Thinking it through

Using a calculator, try various numbers, square them, and decide whether you have started too high or too low. Gradually refine your guesses until you get the solution. One approach is:

Try 50	Square it (enter 50 x 50).	Answer: 2500.	Too low.
Try 60	Square it (enter 60 x 60).	Answer: 3600.	Too low.
Try 70	Square it (enter 70 x 70).	Answer: 4900.	Too high.
So the answer lies between 60 and 70.			
Try 65	Square it (enter 65 x 65).	Answer: 4225.	Too high.
Try 63	Square it (enter 63 x 63).	Answer: 3969.	Too high but getting close.
Try 62,	Square it (enter 62 x 62).	Answer: 3844.	Got it.

So the square root of 3844 is 62.

Example 14C

Find the cube root of 85 184.

Thinking it through

Start at 50 and refine your answer.

Try 50,	cube it (enter 50 x 50 x 50).	Answer: 125 000.	Too high.
Try 30,	cube it (enter 30 x 30 x 30).	Answer: 27 000.	Too low.
Try 40,	cube it (enter 40 x 40 x 40).	Answer: 64 000.	Too low.
Try 45,	cube it (enter 45 x 45 x 45).	Answer: 91 125.	Too high.
Try 43,	cube it (enter 43 x 43 x 43).	Answer: 79 507.	Too low
Try 44,	cube it (enter 44 x 44 x 44).	Answer: 85 184.	Got it!

In the two examples above, the numbers were chosen carefully so that the answer is a whole number. This is unlikely to be the case in real situations where a square root or cube root is required. For example, if Hans wants to build a square patio with an area of 200 square meters (m²), the length of each side in meters must be the square root of 200. However, his calculator tells him that $14^2 = 196$ (too low) and $15^2 = 225$ (too high). So the answer lies between 14 and 15. There is no whole number that is the exact square root of 200. But using the trial and improvement method, he can get an answer as close as he wishes, by using decimals. For example, since he finds that $14.1^2 = 198.81$ is too low and $14.2^2 = 201.64$ is too high, the answer must lie between 14.1 and 14.2. (This problem is further pursued in Questions 14.6 and 14.7 in the Check Yourself questions toward the end of the chapter.)

People with little experience in mathematics are often uneasy about this kind of approach, feeling that it is not respectable mathematics. It is, in fact, respectable. Advanced mathematics offers many problems that were once impossible to tackle in practice, but that can now be solved by using numerical methods of this kind, employing a calculator or a computer to do the hard grind of the successive calculations involved.

Do any other geometric shapes describe numbers?

Almost any sequence of geometric shapes or patterns, such as those shown in Figure 14.3, can be used to generate a corresponding set of numbers. Exploring these types of sequences — that is, trying to relate the geometric and numerical patterns — can produce some intriguing mathematics. For example, consider why the first sequence of patterns in Figure 14.3 generates the odd numbers (1, 3, 5, 7, 9, and so on), and why the second sequence generates the multiples of 3 (3, 6, 9, 12, and so on).

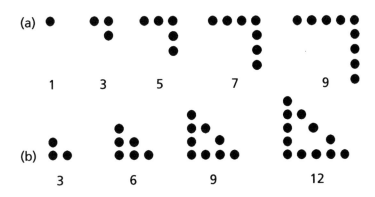

FIGURE 14.3 *Geometric patterns generating sets of numbers*

Some of these patterns turn out to be particularly interesting and are given special names. For example, you may come across the phrase *triangular numbers*. These numbers correspond to the particular pattern of triangles of dots shown in Figure 14.4: 1, 3, 6, 10, 15, and so on. Notice that we get the second triangle by adding 2 dots to the first, the third by adding 3 dots to the second, the fourth by adding 4 dots to the third, and so on.

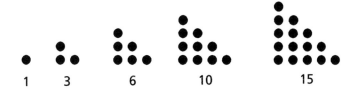

FIGURE 14.4 *Triangular numbers*

The geometric arrangements of dots show that these triangle numbers have the following numerical pattern:

$$1 = 1$$
$$3 = 1 + 2$$
$$6 = 1 + 2 + 3$$
$$10 = 1 + 2 + 3 + 4$$
$$15 = 1 + 2 + 3 + 4 + 5, \text{ and so on}$$

Questions 14.3 and 14.8 in Check Yourself below provide two examples of explaining patterns in number sequences by thinking about the geometric patterns to which they correspond.

Check yourself

14.1 Drawing on the ideas of this and the previous chapter, find at least one interesting thing to say about each of the numbers from 20 to 29.

14.2 Find a triangular number that is also a square number.

14.3 Look at the sequence of square numbers: 1, 4, 9, 16, 25, 36,… Find the differences between successive numbers in this sequence. What do you notice? Can you explain this finding in terms of patterns of dots?

14.4 Choose a number. Square it, and then cube the answer. Now take the original number, cube it, and then square the answer. Are the results the same? Can you find a whole number less than 100 that is a cube number and a square number?

14.5 Use the trial and improvement method to find:

(a) the square root of 3249   (b)   the cube root of 4913

14.6 Use the trial and improvement method for finding the square root of 200 to the nearest hundredth.

14.7 Saro wants to construct a cube with a volume of 500 cm^3. What should be the length of the sides of this cube, to the nearest millimeter?

14.8 List all the triangular numbers less than 100. Find the sums of successive pairs; that is, $1 + 3 = 4$, $3 + 6 = 9$, $6 + 10 = 16$, and so on. What do you notice about the answers? Can you explain this numerical pattern with the geometric patterns for these numbers?

> ## ►Teaching suggestions
>
> 1. Use geometric pictures, such as square arrays of dots and square grids, to explain square numbers. Use cubes constructed from cubic units to explain cube numbers.
> 2. Relate the square of a number with the area of a square grid. With the students, count the number of square units in the grid.

3. Relate the cube of a number with the volume of a cube. With the students, count the number of cubic units used to construct it.

4. Emphasize the idea of inverse processes when discussing squares and square roots; one process undoes the effect of the other.

5. Explicitly teach students the calculator keying sequences for finding squares and cubes.

6. Introduce students to the method of trial and improvement, using a calculator to find square roots (without using the square root key) and cube roots.

7. Encourage students to explore the relationships between sequences of geometric patterns of dots and the corresponding sequences of numbers.

Integers: Positive and Negative

Students should learn to expand their understanding of the number system to negative numbers in context, and to extend methods of computation to include addition and subtraction with negative numbers.

THIS CHAPTER EXPLAINS:

- integers;
- the cardinal and ordinal aspects of number;
- contexts for understanding positive and negative numbers;
- situations in the contexts of temperatures and bank balances that are modeled by the addition and subtraction of positive and negative numbers; and
- how to enter negative numbers on a basic calculator.

What are *integers*?

In mathematics, the word *integer* is related to words such as *integral* (forming a whole) and *integrity* (wholeness). So integers are simply whole numbers. That statement includes both positive and negative whole numbers, as well as zero. The set of integers includes the set of natural numbers described in Chapter 13 *and* their negative counterparts.

Many people have difficulty with the concept of a negative number, mainly because the idea that a number represents a set of things is overemphasized. When teachers want to demonstrate a numerical fact to young children — say, 3 + 4 — the first thing they do is to put out a set of 3 things (counters, blocks, fingers, or the like) and a set of 4 things, and put the two sets together to form a new set. This demonstrates the *cardinal aspect* of number.

No one can visualize, much less demonstrate with objects, a set of three negative things. But this does not mean that negative numbers are some kind of mysterious, abstract mathematical notion. Numbers are not just sets of things. They are also labels used for putting things in order. For instance, the numeral 3 can represent a point on a number line (see Figure 15.1) and the instruction add 4 interpreted as moving 4 steps further along it. In Figure 15.1, the numbers are just labels for putting in order the particular, marked points on the line.

This *ordinal aspect* of number extends our understanding of number quite naturally and simply to include negative numbers.

FIGURE 15.1 *Numbers as points on a line*

Extending the number line (as shown in Figure 15.2) in the other direction, requires using a symbol to designate the points less than zero, which are called *negative numbers*. This extension produces the set of numbers called the *integers*: … –5, –4, –3, –2, –1, 0, +1, +2, +3, +4, +5, …, going on forever in both directions.

Note that although we do not normally write, for example, +4, for positive four but simply 4, we do so in a context in which it is particularly helpful to signal the distinction between the negative and the positive integers.

Students can have fun generating the integers on a calculator. To produce the positive integers, they just enter: 1+1; then they continue to add 1 as many times as they wish. To produce the negative integers, they just enter: – and continue to subtract 1 as many times as desired. (Be warned, however, that various calculators have different ways of displaying negative numbers.)

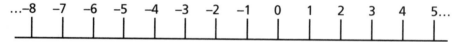

FIGURE 15.2 *Extending the number line*

The number line, either drawn left to right, as in Figures 15.1 and 15.2, or vertically with positive numbers going up and negative numbers going down, is the most straightforward image for associating with positive and negative integers.

Some other settings can also help to make sense of negative numbers. The most familiar is probably the context of temperature. Quite young children can grasp the idea of the temperature falling below zero, associating it with feeling cold and encountering icy roads and they are often familiar with the use of negative numbers to describe winter cold.

One small point about different uses of language should be made here. Mathematicians prefer to refer to the integer –5, as *negative five* rather than *minus five*, saving the word *minus* for a synonym for the operation of subtraction. But weather forecasters tend to say that the temperature is falling to *minus five degrees*. Similarly, they may refer to a positive temperature as *plus five*, rather than *positive five*. These difficulties are not serious, however, and temperature is still one of the best contexts for experiencing positive and negative numbers.

The specification of heights above and below sea level provides another application for positive and negative numbers. And for some people, the context of bank balances is one in which negative numbers make real, if painful, sense. For example, being overdrawn by $5 at the bank can be represented by the negative number –5. Finally, hockey league tables offer another application of positive and negative integers. If two teams have the same number of points, their order in the table is determined by their goal difference, which is the number of goals-for minus the number of goals-against. So, a team with 28 goals-for and 23 goals-against has a goal difference of +5. But a team with 23 goals-for and 28 goals-against has a goal difference of –5. Many students find this context relevant and realistic for experiencing the process of putting in order a set of positive and negative numbers.

How can teachers explain addition of positive and negative integers?

We can make sense of positive and negative integers by using different images to support different operations. With addition, we need contexts and problems that help us to make sense of particular calculations.

For example, using bank balances, interpret an addition statement as follows: the first number represents the starting balance, and the second number represents either a credit (a positive number) or a debit (a negative number).

With this interpretation each of the following examples below can be seen as a mathematical model (see Chapter 3) for a real-life situation.

Example 15A
Simplify $10 + (-2)$.

Thinking it through
Start with $10 and add a debit of $2; the result is a balance of $8. The corresponding mathematical model is $10 + (-2) = 8$.

Example 15B
Simplify $2 + (-7)$.

Thinking it through
Start with a balance of $2 and add a debit of $7; the result is a balance of $5 overdrawn. The corresponding mathematical model is $2 + (-7) = -5$.

Example 15C
Simplify $(-3) + 4$.

Thinking it through
Start with a balance of $3 overdrawn and add a credit of $4, the result is a balance of $1. The corresponding mathematical model is $(-3) + 4 = 1$.

Example 15D
Simplify $(-5) + (-3)$.

Thinking it through
Start with a balance of $5 overdrawn and add a debit of $3 the result is a balance of $8 overdrawn. The corresponding mathematical model is: $(-5) + (-3) = -8$.

We could also interpret these collections of symbols in the context of temperatures, with the first number being a starting temperature and the second either a rise or a fall in temperature. Or we could go to a number line, which, of course, is just like the scale on a thermometer, with the first number being the starting point and the second number a move in either the positive or the negative direction. Question 15.3 of the Check Yourself section invites readers to construct more problems of this kind.

What about subtraction? Why do two minuses make a plus?

The key to making sense of subtraction with positive and negative integers is to eliminate the idea that subtraction means *take away*. This structure applies only to positive numbers; no one can take away a negative number. The calculation 6 – (–3), for example, cannot model a problem about having a set of 6 things and taking away negative 3 things. We make sense of subtracting with negative numbers by drawing on situations that incorporate some of the other structures for subtraction, notably the comparison and the inverse-of-addition structures (see Chapter 6).

The kinds of calculations that we need to give meaning through experience in context include the following examples involving temperatures. First, we think in terms of the comparison structure for subtraction. In this structure, the subtraction *a–b* models a question of the form how much greater is *a* than *b*? Thus, problems that incorporate the comparison structure for subtraction require us to find how much hotter the first temperature is than the second.

Example 15E
Simplify 6 – (–3).

Thinking it through

The problem might be to find how much higher is a temperature of 6 degrees indoors than a temperature of –3 degrees outdoors. Reference to the number line in Figure 15.3(a) makes it clear that the difference between the two temperatures is 9 degrees. The corresponding mathematical model is therefore 6 – (–3) = 9.

Example 15F
Simplify (–3) – (–8)

Thinking it through

When comparing a morning temperature of –3 degrees with the overnight temperature of –8 degrees, we see that the morning temperature is 5 degrees higher than the overnight. The corresponding mathematical operation is subtraction: (–3) – (–8) = 5.

Example 15G
Simplify 6 – 9.

Thinking it through

The idea of comparison makes a lot of sense when we are using subtraction to model a situation in which the first temperature is higher than the second. But in Example 15G, the first temperature is lower than the second. As a result, the answer to the question "how much higher is the first temperature?" is a negative number, which can become a bit confusing.

Perhaps it is easier to relate Examples 15E, 15F, and 15G to problems with the inverse-of-addition structure. In this structure, the subtraction *a–b* models a question of the form, what must be added to *b* to give *a*? In the context of temperatures, we are asking what change takes us from the second temperature to the first. (Note the order.)

So, in Example 15E, the +9 could represent a rise of 9 degrees, which has to be added to a temperature of –3 degrees to produce a temperature of 6 degrees (see Figure 15.3a). In Example 15F, the +5 could represent a rise of 5 degrees, which has to be added to a temperature of –8 degrees to produce a temperature of –3 degrees (see Figure 15.3b). Example 15G then is related to the question, what change in temperature takes us from 9 degrees to 6 degrees? Clearly, this is a fall of 3 degrees; the mathematical model is: $6 - 9 = -3$ (see Figure 15.3c).

Example 15H

Simplify $(-3) - 4$.

Thinking it through

The question is, what change in temperature takes us from 4 degrees to –3 degrees? Clearly, this is a fall of 7 degrees, represented by –7. The corresponding mathematical model is $(-3) - 4 = -7$ (see Figure 15.3d).

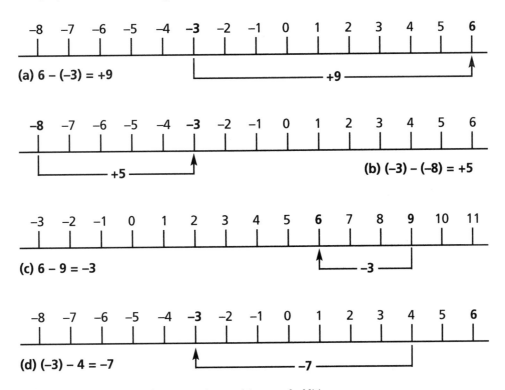

FIGURE 15.3 *Subtractions interpreted as comparison and inverse of addition*

Alternatively, we can pose problems corresponding to those in Examples 15E, 15F, and 15G by stating a starting and a finishing bank balance and then asking what credit or debit has been added. The reader is invited to construct problems of this kind in Question 15.4 of the Check Yourself section.

These illustrations should make it clear that "two minuses make a plus" is a nonsense rule. In a question such as $6 - (-3)$, the first – is a minus sign indicating subtraction, and the second is a negative sign indicating a negative number. If we simply interpret the subtraction as "compare the first number with the second" or "what must be added to the second to give the first?" and put the problems into contexts such as temperatures and bank balances, students will have some chance of understanding what is going on.

How are negative numbers entered on a calculator?

Some calculators have a special key, usually labeled plus or minus sign, that helps the user enter negative numbers. To enter –78, for example, press this key sequence: 78 +/–. To do a calculation such as 184 – (–78), use the following keying sequence: 184 – 78 +/–.

Most calculators also have a memory and a key labeled something like M– that allows a number to be subtracted from whatever is in the memory. This makes it easy to put a number such as –78 into the memory. First, ensure that the memory is clear (often by pressing a key labeled MRC twice), and then press 78 M–. This sequence subtracts 78 from the 0 in the memory to give –78. A key on the calculator enables recall of what is in the memory (it is often the same key as the one that clears the memory — the MRC key). So to do a calculation such as 184 – (–78), you use the MRC key (to clear the memory and then enter) 78 M– (puts –78 in the memory), 184, –, MRC (recalls the –78 from the memory). Try this. It is not nearly as complicated as it looks in print!

However, the context that gives rise to the problem often suggests that the actual calculation makes no use of negative numbers whatsoever. For example, if the problem is to find the difference in height between two points; the first being 184 meters above sea level and the other 78 meters below sea level, the image created in many peoples' minds by the context leads them to simply add 184 and 78.

The conclusion, therefore, is that we rarely need to use calculations with negative numbers to solve real-life problems; but we do need the real-life problems to help to explain the way we manipulate positive and negative numbers when we are doing abstract mathematical calculations!

> We rarely need to use calculations with negative numbers to solve real-life problems; but we do need the real-life problems to help to explain the way we manipulate positive and negative numbers when we are doing abstract mathematical calculations!

Check yourself

15.1 Which of the following are integers?

    (a) 6.8   (b) 472   (c) 0

    (d) –10   (e) –5.5

15.2 Simplify the following:

    (a) $-6 - 4$ (b) $8 - (-4)$ (c) $34 - 56$

15.3 Make up situations about temperature that are modeled by the following additions and give the answers:

    (a) $4 + (-12)$ (b) $(-6) + 10$

15.4 Make up problems about bank balances that are modeled by the following subtractions and give the answers:

    (a) $20 - (-5)$ (b) $(-10) - (-15)$ (c) $(-10) - 20$

15.5 Find how to enter the integer –42 on your calculator in the middle of a calculation. Note how your calculator displays this integer.

15.6 Yesterday Samir was overdrawn at the bank by $187.85. Someone paid a check into his account, and this morning he has $458.64 in credit. Model this situation with a subtraction. Use a calculator to find out the amount of the check that was paid in.

➤ Teaching suggestions

1. Use the number line and the ordinal aspect of number (numbers as labels for putting things in order) to introduce students to the concept of negative integers.

2. Use contexts such as temperatures, multistorey buildings, heights above and below sea level, and bank balances to give meaning to positive and negative numbers.

3. Use problems with temperatures to explain additions with positive and negative integers. Have the first number represent a starting point and the second a rise or fall.

4. To help students experience subtractions with positive and negative integers, use problems that relate to the comparison of two temperatures in order to find how much higher one is than another or the difference in temperature.

5. If necessary, extend this experience to situations with the inverse-of-addition structure, finding the change (up or down) from one temperature to another.

6. Use parallel examples of bank balances, credits, and debits to provide further experience of the structures described in points 3, 4, and 5.

7. Be careful with the language you use about negative numbers. Avoid phrases such as *taking away* a negative number.

8. Make sure that students know how to enter negative numbers on the basic calculators used in their school and that they know how such numbers are displayed.

Fractions

Fractions as representing a part of a whole

Once again we encounter the special difficulty presented by mathematical symbols: that one symbol can represent a number in different kinds of situations in the real world. The mathematical notation used for a fraction can be used in at least four different ways:

- To represent a part of a whole or a unit.
- To represent a part of a set.
- To model a division problem.
- To represent a ratio.

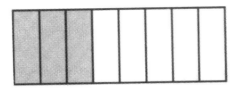

FIGURE **16.1** *The shaded sections are three-eighths of the whole shape*

Consider, for example, the fraction three-eighths, which can be written either as $\frac{3}{8}$ or, often seen in word processing and typesetting, as 3/8. The common interpretation of these symbols is illustrated by the diagrams in Figure 16.1. The most useful fraction examples are chocolate bars (rectangles) and pizzas (circles). A whole, such as a chocolate bar or a pizza, can be subdivided into eight equal sections, called *eighths*, and three of these — *three-eighths* — are then selected.

The concept of fractions can be extended to situations in which a set of items is divided into eight equal subsets and three of these subsets are selected. For example, the set of 40 dots in Figure 16.2a is divided into eight equal subsets (of 5 dots each) in Figure 16.2b. The 15 dots selected in Figure 16.2c can therefore be described as three-eighths of the set.

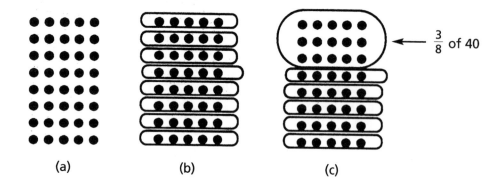

FIGURE 16.2 *Three-eighths of a set of 40*

The fraction $\frac{3}{8}$ can also be used to represent the division of 3 by 8. It might, for example, represent the result of sharing three bars of chocolate among eight people. Notice the marked difference here. In Figure 16.1, one bar of chocolate was being divided; now we are talking about cutting up three bars. The real-world process we have to go through to solve the three-chocolate-bar problem is not immediately obvious.

One way is to set the three side by side, as shown in Figure 16.3, and then to slice through all three bars simultaneously with a knife, cutting each into eight equal pieces. The pieces then nicely form eight equal portions. Figure 16.3 shows that each of the eight people gets the equivalent of three-eighths of a whole bar of chocolate. (Doing this demonstration with pizzas requires placing them one on top of the other, rather than side by side, but otherwise the process is the same, although more gooey.)

When the symbol $\frac{3}{8}$ means divide 3 units by 8, the result of doing the division is three-eighths of a unit. Thus, the symbol $\frac{3}{8}$ represents both an instruction to perform an operation and the result of performing it! We often need the idea that the fraction p/q means p divided by q in order to handle fractions on a calculator. Simply by entering $p \div q$, we obtain the fraction expressed as a decimal.

The symbol $\frac{3}{8}$ represents both an instruction to perform an operation and the result of performing it.

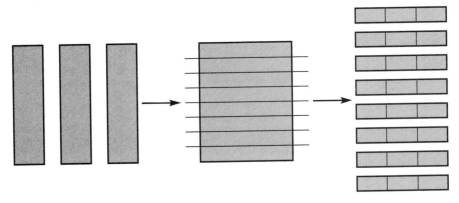

FIGURE 16.3 *Three shared among eight*

As described in Chapter 10, one of the categories of problems modeled by division is comparing two quantities by means of ratio. Because the symbol $\frac{3}{8}$ can mean $3 \div 8$, we can extend the meanings of the symbols to include the ratio of 3 to 8, which is written sometimes as 3:8. For example, when comparing the set of squares with the set of circles in Figure 16.4a, we can say that the ratio of circles to squares is 3 to 8 — in other words, that for every 3 circles there are 8 squares. Arranging the squares and circles as shown in Figure 16.4b shows this to be the case. The reason we also use the fraction notation $\frac{3}{8}$ to represent the ratio 3:8 is that another way of expressing the comparison between the two sets is to say that the number of circles is three-eighths of the number of squares.

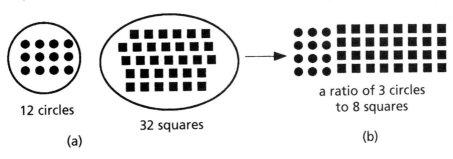

FIGURE 16.4 *A ratio of 3 to 8*

Fraction terminology

Some terminology is associated with learning about fractions. For example, the *numerator* and the *denominator* are, respectively, the top number and the bottom number in the fraction notation. For example, in the fraction $\frac{3}{8}$, the numerator is 3 and the denominator is 8.

> The numerator and the denominator are, respectively, the top number and the bottom number in the fraction notation.

The fraction notation for parts of a unit can also be used where more than one whole unit is to be represented. For example, Figure 16.5, shows eleven-eighths of a pizza, which is written $\frac{11}{8}$. Since eight of the subunits make a whole pizza, this quantity can be written as $1 + \frac{3}{8}$, which is normally abbreviated to $1\frac{3}{8}$ or 1 3/8. This kind of notation is called a *mixed number*.

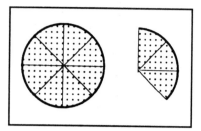

Proper fractions are those that are less than one, and improper fractions are those greater than or equal to one.

FIGURE 16.5 *A fraction greater than 1*

A fraction in which the top number is smaller than the bottom number, such as $\frac{3}{8}$, is sometimes called a *proper fraction*, with a fraction such as $\frac{11}{8}$ being referred to as an *improper fraction*. Thus, proper fractions are those that are less than one, and improper fractions are those greater than or equal to one.

Equivalent fractions

The concept of *equivalence* is one of the key ideas for students to grasp when working with fractions. The concept is that if a fraction represents a part of a unit, then, as listed in Figure 16.6, the fractions three-quarters, six-eighths, and nine-twelfths all represent the same amount of chocolate bar. This kind of *fraction chart* is an important teaching aid for explaining the idea of equivalence.

Sequences of equivalent fractions follow a straightforward pattern. For example, all the following fractions are equivalent:

$$\frac{3}{5}, \frac{6}{10}, \frac{9}{15}, \frac{12}{20}, \frac{15}{25}, \frac{18}{30}, \frac{21}{35}, \frac{24}{40}, \dots, \text{ and so on.}$$

The numbers on the top and bottom are simply the three-times and five-times tables respectively. Given a particular fraction, we can always generate an equivalent fraction by multiplying the top and the bottom by the same number or, vice versa, by dividing by the same number.

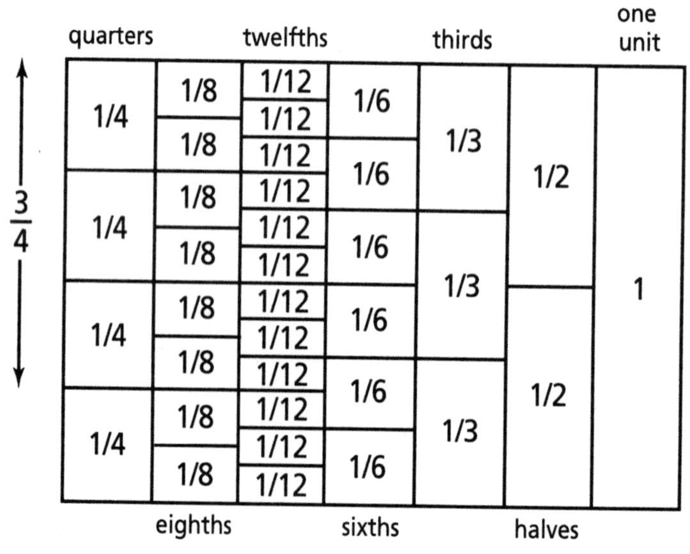

FIGURE 16.6 *A chart showing some equivalent fractions*

For example:

$\frac{4}{7}$ is equivalent to $\frac{36}{63}$ (multiplying top and bottom by 9); and

$\frac{40}{70}$ is equivalent to $\frac{4}{7}$ (dividing top and bottom by 10).

If the two numbers of a ratio are multiplied or divided by the same value, then the ratio stays the same.

If we remember that the fraction notation can also be interpreted as meaning division of the top number by the bottom number, the principle above merely repeats what was said about informal methods of division in Chapter 11: that the answer to a division calculation does not change if both numbers are multiplied or divided by the same value. The same principle applies to ratios: if the two numbers of a ratio are multiplied or divided by the same value, then the ratio stays the same.

Ratios

Using equivalent fractions is an important method for simplifying fractions and ratios. For example, if we are comparing the price of two articles costing \$28 and \$32 by looking at the ratio of the prices, then the ratio 28:32 can be simplified to the ratio of 7:8 (by dividing both numbers by 4). One price is $\frac{7}{8}$ of the other. If we are comparing a journey of 4.2 kilometers with one of 7 kilometers, then we can simplify the ratio of 4.2:7 by first multiplying both numbers by 10 (yielding 42:70) and then dividing both numbers by 14 (yielding 3:5). One journey is $\frac{3}{5}$ of the other.

Comparing Fractions

Notice that when we increase the bottom number of a fraction, we make the fraction smaller, and when we decrease that number, we make the fraction larger. For example, $\frac{1}{2}$ is greater than $\frac{1}{3}$, which is greater than $\frac{1}{4}$, which is greater than $\frac{1}{5}$, and so on. This point is obvious if the symbols are interpreted in concrete terms such as parts of pizzas or chocolate bars.

Comparing two fractions with the same bottom number is easy. For example, $\frac{5}{8}$ of a pizza is clearly more than $\frac{3}{8}$.

Generally, to compare two fractions with different bottom numbers, we need to convert them to equivalent fractions with the same bottom number, which must be a common multiple of the two numbers. This bottom number may be (but does not have to be) the lowest common multiple (see Chapter 13).

Example 16A

Which is greater, $\frac{7}{10}$ of a chocolate bar or $\frac{5}{8}$?

Thinking it through

The lowest common multiple of ten and eight is 40, so convert both fractions to fortieths:

- $\frac{7}{10}$ is equivalent to $\frac{28}{40}$ (multiplying top and bottom by 4); and
- $\frac{5}{8}$ is equivalent to $\frac{25}{40}$ (multiplying top and bottom by 5).

We can then see that the seven-tenths is the better choice (assuming that we like chocolate).

Fraction applications

The most common everyday situations involving calculations with fractions are those that involve calculating a simple fraction of a set or a quantity. For example, a teacher might say, "Three-fifths of my class of 30 are boys." If a sale flyer offers an article priced at $45 at one-third off, the reduced price must be two-thirds of $45. Or someone who encounters fractions in measurements such as three-quarters of a liter or two-fifths of a meter may want to change these to milliliters and centimeters respectively. The process of doing these calculations is straightforward.

Example 16B

Find $\frac{3}{5}$ of 30.

Thinking it through

Divide by the 5 to find one-fifth of 30; then multiply by the 3 to obtain three-fifths:

$\frac{1}{5}$ of 30 = 6, so $\frac{3}{5}$ of 30 = 18.

For other examples in the paragraph above:

$\frac{1}{3}$ of $45 = $15, so $\frac{2}{3}$ of $45 = $30.
$\frac{1}{4}$ of 1000 mL = 250 mL, so $\frac{3}{4}$ of 1000 mL (a liter) = 750 mL.
$\frac{1}{5}$ of 100 cm = 20 cm, so $\frac{2}{5}$ of 100 cm (a meter) = 40 cm.

Anyone who finds division and multiplication applications difficult to calculate alone can use a calculator.

Example 16C

Find three-sevenths of $4500.

Thinking it through

The calculation performed on a calculator is 4500 ÷ 7 x 3. The result is the calculator display of 1928.5714 or, after rounding, $1928.57.

Check yourself

16.1 Give examples in which $\frac{4}{5}$ represents:

(a) a part of a whole or a unit
(b) a part of a set
(c) a division using the idea of sharing
(d) a ratio

16.2 Using the fraction chart in Figure 16.6, state three additional equivalent fractions.

16.3 Assuming you like pizza, which would you prefer: three-fifths of a pizza or five-eighths?

16.4 Put these fractions in order from smallest to largest:

(a) $\frac{3}{4}$
(b) $\frac{1}{6}$
(c) $\frac{1}{3}$
(d) $\frac{2}{3}$
(e) $\frac{5}{12}$

16.5 Pose a problem about prices to which the answer is the price of *A* is three-fifths of the price of *B*.

16.6 Walking to work takes Joan 24 minutes; cycling takes her 9 minutes. Complete the following sentence with an appropriate fraction: "The time it takes to cycle is ☐ of the time it takes to walk."

16.7 Find:

    (a) three-fifths of $100, without using a calculator

    (b) five-eighths of $2500, using a calculator

➤Teaching suggestions

1. Introduce the term *fraction notations* as meaning a number of equal parts of a unit. Make particular use of pizzas (circles) and chocolate bars (rectangles) in the explanation. In this interpretation, the fraction p/q means divide the unit into q equal parts and take p of these parts.

2. When explaining fractions be careful about using *the whole* as a noun; try to use it only as an adjective in such a phrase such as *a whole pizza.*

3. Extend the idea of a fraction, as representing a number of equal parts of a unit to meaning a number of equal parts of a set — for example, two-thirds of a set of 12.

4. Realize that using informal language, such as *top number* and *bottom number*, is quite acceptable when discussing fractions, especially when introducing them or talking with students who are having difficulties.

5. Emphasize strongly the idea of equivalent fractions. Students should make fractions charts, such as Figure 16.6, and find various examples of equivalent fractions.

6. Help students see the pattern in sequences of equivalent fractions. Use this experience to establish the idea that they can change one fraction into an equivalent fraction by multiplying or dividing the top and bottom numbers by the same value.

7. Using examples of sharing pizzas and chocolate bars, establish the idea that p/q can mean p divided by q. For example, three pizzas shared among four people is 3 divided by 4; the result $\frac{3}{4}$ of a pizza each.

8. Introduce students to the use of fractions to compare one quantity with another (that is, finding the ratio), especially in the context of prices. For example, compare two prices of $9 and $12 by stating that one is three-quarters of the other.

9. Explore with students, using concrete illustrations, why making the bottom number of a fraction larger makes the fraction smaller, and making the bottom number smaller makes the fraction larger.

10. Introduce the procedure for finding which is the larger or smaller of two fractions by changing them to equivalent fractions with the same bottom number.

11. Explore with students finding a fraction of a quantity by dividing by the bottom number and then multiplying by the top number. Have them apply this procedure to a range of everyday, practical contexts, using a calculator where necessary.

Calculations with Decimals

Students should learn to understand and use the concept of extending methods of computation to include all four operations with decimals, using a calculator where appropriate.

THIS CHAPTER EXPLAINS:
- the procedures for addition and subtraction with decimal numbers;
- the contexts that may give rise to the need for calculations with decimals;
- multiplication and division of a decimal number by an integer in real-life contexts;
- the results of repeatedly multiplying or dividing decimal numbers by 10;
- how to deal with multiplication of two-decimal numbers;
- some simple examples of division by decimal numbers; and
- how to convert fractions to decimal numbers and vice versa.

Do the procedures for addition and subtraction with decimal numbers differ from those with whole numbers?

The procedures for adding and subtracting decimal numbers are effectively the same as those for adding and subtracting whole numbers. Difficulties arise only if problem solvers forget the principles of place value outlined in Chapter 2. Provided they remember which digits are units, tens, and hundreds or tenths, hundredths, and so on, then the algorithms and informal methods employed for whole numbers (see Chapters 5 and 7) work identically for decimals. The principle that one of these can be exchanged for ten of those guides the whole process.

A useful tip with decimals is to ensure that the two numbers in an addition or a subtraction calculation have the same number of digits after the decimal point. If one has fewer than the other, then fill up the empty places with zeros, acting as placeholders (see Chapter 2). So, for example, 1.45 + 1.8 is written as 1.45 + 1.80; 1.5 – 1.28 is written as 1.50 – 1.28; and 10 – 4.25 would be written as 10.00 – 4.25. The standard algorithms for addition and subtraction then look just the same as when working with whole numbers, but the decimal points in the two numbers are lined up, one above the other, as shown in Figure 17.1.

```
  2.86          1.45          1.50          10.00
+ 4.04         +1.80         - 1.28        -  4.25
 _____        _____        _____         _____
  (a)           (b)           (c)            (d)
```

FIGURE 17.1 *Additions and subtractions with decimals*

Additions and subtractions with decimals

In practice, additions and subtractions with decimals are usually employed to model real-life situations related to money or measurement. Chapter 2 discussed the convention of putting two digits after the decimal point when recording money in dollars. It also suggested that when dealing with measurements of length in centimeters and meters, with a hundred centimeters in a meter, it is a good idea to adopt the same convention — for example, writing 180 cm as 1.80 m, rather than 1.8 m. Similarly, when handling liquid volume and capacity, with 1000 milliliters in a liter, or mass, with 1000 grams in a kilogram, the convention is to write measurements in liters or kilograms with three digits after the point.

If this convention is followed, the decimal numbers arrive for the calculation already written in the required form — that is, each of the two numbers in the addition or subtraction has the same number of digits after the point, with zeros used to fill up empty places.

Example 17A

The four calculations shown in Figure 17.1 might be modeling the following real-life situations:
1. Find the total cost of two articles, priced at $2.86 and $4.04 respectively.
2. Find the total length of wall space taken up by a cupboard that is 1.45 m wide and a bookshelf that is 1.80 m wide.
3. What is the difference in height between a girl who is 1.50 m tall and a boy who is 1.28 m tall?
4. Ming-Li gives the cashier a $10.00 bill for purchases that total $4.25. How much change does she receive?

What about multiplications and divisions involving decimals?

Consider first multiplying a decimal number by a whole number. Once again, a key point is to think about the practical contexts that give rise to the need to do multiplications of this kind. In the context of money, we might need to find the cost of a number of articles at a given price. For example, find the cost of 12 rolls of tape at $1.35 per roll. The model is the multiplication 1.35 x 12. On a calculator, we enter 1.35 x 12, read off the mathematical solution 16.2, and then interpret it as a total cost of $16.20.

Unfortunately, doing this kind of calculation by written or mental methods can lead to all kinds of mixups with the decimal point. So a useful tip is to avoid multiplying decimal numbers. This is easily achieved in the example above by rephrasing the situation as 12 rolls at 135¢ per roll — that is, by writing the cost in cents rather than in dollars. We then multiply 135 by 12 by whatever methods we prefer (see Chapter 9) to get the answer 1620 interpret this as 1620¢, and finally write the answer as $16.20.

Almost all the multiplications involving decimals that elementary school students have to do can be tackled like this. Here's another example: find the length of wall space required to display eight posters each 1.19 m wide. Rather than tackle 1.19 × 8, rewrite the length as 119 cm, calculate 119 × 8, and convert the result (952 cm) back to meters (9.52 m).

The same principle applies to dividing a decimal number by a whole number. The context from which the calculation arises is likely to suggest a way of handling it without the use of decimals. For example, a calculation such as 3.45 ÷ 3 could arise from a problem about sharing $3.45 among 3 people. We can simply rewrite this problem as one of sharing 345¢ between 3 people and deal with it by whatever division process is appropriate (see Chapter 11), concluding that each person gets 115¢. The final step is to put it back into the dollar notation, as $1.15.

What is the rule about moving the decimal point with multiplication and division by 10, 100, and so on? How can it be explained?

On a calculator, enter 10 × 1.2345678, and multiply by 10 eight times. Watch the display carefully. This procedure makes use of the constant facility, which is built into most basic calculators, to multiply repeatedly by 10. The results are shown in Figure 17.2a. It certainly looks as though the decimal point is gradually moving along one place at a time to the right. Now, without clearing the calculator, divide by 10 eight times. This procedure undoes the effect of multiplying by 10 and sends the decimal point back to where it started, one place at a time.

Because of this phenomenon we can think of the effect of multiplying a decimal number by 10 as moving the decimal point one place to the right, and the effect of dividing by 10 as moving the decimal point one place to the left. And since multiplying or dividing by 100 is equivalent to multiplying or dividing by 10 and then by 10 again, this results in the point's moving two places. Similarly multiplying or dividing by 1000 shifts the point three places, and so on for other powers of 10.

(a) Results as displayed on a calculator	(b) Results displayed on the basis of place value
1.2345678	1.2345678
12.345678	12.345678
123.45678	123.45678
1234.5678	1234.5678
12345.678	12345.678
123456.78	123456.78
1234567.8	1234567.8
12345678.	12345678

FIGURE 17.2 *The results of repeatedly multiplying by 10*

To understand this phenomenon, rather than just observe it, realize that it is not the decimal point that is moving but the digits. Look at the results displayed on the basis of place value, in Figure 17.2b. Each time we multiply by 10, all the digits move one place to the left — and the decimal point stays put.

It is not the decimal point that is moving but the digits.

To understand why this happens, trace the progress of one of the digits — for example, the 3. In the original number, it represents 3 hundredths. When we multiply the number by 10, each hundredth becomes a tenth because ten hundredths can be exchanged for a tenth. This is, once again, the principle that ten of these can be exchanged for one of those, as we move right to left. So the 3 hundredths become 3 tenths. In other words, the digit 3 moves from the hundredths position to the tenths position. Next time we multiply by 10, these 3 tenths become three whole units, and the 3 shifts to the units position. Next time we multiply by 10, these 3 units become 3 tens, and so on.

Because the principle that ten of these can be exchanged for one of those as we move from right to left applies to any position, each digit moves one place to the left every time we multiply by 10. And since dividing by 10 is the inverse of multiplying by 10 (one operation undoes the effect of the other), the effect of dividing by 10 is to move each digit one place to the right.

How does this help with the multiplication of two decimal numbers?

Suppose we want to find the area in square meters of a rectangular lawn 3.45 m wide and 4.50 m long. The calculation required is 3.45 x 4.50. For multiplications there is no particular value in carrying around surplus zeros, so we can rewrite the 4.50 as 4.5. Now the calculation we have to complete is: 3.45 x 4.5.

This calculation is fairly difficult, so most people do it on a calculator and read off the answer as 15.525 m². But it may be instructive to look at how to tackle it without a calculator. The solution involves three steps:

1. Get rid of the decimals by multiplying each number by 10 as many times as necessary.
2. Multiply together the two integers that result.
3. Divide the result by 10 as many times in total as you multiplied by 10 in step 1.

So the first step is to get rid of the decimals altogether, using our knowledge of multiplying decimals repeatedly by 10, as follows:

$$3.45 \times 10 = 34.5,$$
$$34.5 \times 10 = 345.0,$$
$$4.5 \times 10 = 45$$

Hence, by multiplying by 10 three times, in total we have changed the multiplication into 345 x 45, a straightforward calculation with integers.

The second step is to multiply 345 by 45, using whatever method is preferred (see Chapter 9), to get the result 15525. Finally, we simply undo the effect of multiplying by 10 three times; we divide by 10 three times, shifting the digits three places to the right and producing the required result, 15.525.

When doing an actual calculation, we don't actually have to think in terms of multiplying and dividing by 10 like this (although few people probably understand what they are doing without an explanation such as the one above). We can simply notice that the total number of times we have to multiply by 10 is determined by the total number of digits after the decimal points in the numbers we are multiplying. For example, 3.45 x 4.5 has two digits after the point in the first number and one in the second, giving a total of three. So we have to multiply by 10 three times in total to produce a multiplication of whole numbers. Then, when we divide our whole-number result by 10 three times, the effect is to shift three digits to positions after the decimal point. The benefit is that the total number of digits after the decimal points in the two numbers being multiplied is the same as the number of digits after the decimal point in the answer.

So our procedure can be rewritten as follows:

1. Count the total number of digits after the decimal points in the numbers being multiplied.
2. Remove the decimal points from the two numbers, and multiply them as though they were integers.
3. Put the decimal point back in the answer, ensuring that the number of digits after the point is the same as the total found in step 1.

For example, to calculate 0.04 x 3.6:

1. Count three digits in total after the decimal points (there are three).
2. Calculate 4 x 36 = 144 (dropping the decimal points altogether).
3. So 0.04 x 3.6 = 0.144 (with three digits after the decimal point).

Figure 17.3 shows how using this principle can let us deduce a whole collection of results from one multiplication result with integers. The examples used are 4 x 36 = 144 (Figure 17.3a) and, to show that the procedure works just the same when there is a zero in the result, 5 x 44 = 220 (Figure 17.3b).

At an appropriate stage in the development of their work with decimals, students can be instructed to use a calculator to compile various tables of this kind and to discuss the patterns that emerge.

x	36	3.6	0.36	0.036
4	144	14.4	1.44	0.144
0.4	14.4	1.44	0.144	0.0144
0.04	1.44	0.144	0.0144	0.00144
0.004	0.144	0.0144	0.00144	0.000144

x	44	4.4	0.44	0.044
5	220	22	2.2	0.22
0.5	22	2.2	0.22	0.022
0.05	2.2	0.22	0.022	0.0022
0.005	0.22	0.022	0.0022	0.00022

Figure 17.3 *Multiplication tables for decimal numbers derived from (a) 4 x 36 = 144 and (b) 5 x 44 = 220*

And what about dividing a decimal by a decimal?

The need to divide a decimal number by a decimal number may occur in a real-life situation with the inverse-of-multiplication division structure (see Chapter 10), perhaps in the context of money or of measurement.

In these cases, we can usually reframe the problem in units that dispense with the need for decimals. For example, to find how many payments of $3.25 we need to make to reach a target of $52 ($52.00), we might first be inclined to model the problem with the division, 52.00 ÷ 3.25. This calculation would be straightforward if we were using a calculator.

Without a calculator, however, problem solvers may get into a muddle with the decimal points. So we rewrite the problem in cents and discard the decimal points altogether. How many payments of 325¢ do we need to reach 5200¢? The mathematical model is now 5200 ÷ 325, which can be solved by whatever method is appropriate.

Similarly, to find how many portions of 0.125 liters we can pour from a 2.500-liter container, we could model the problem with the division 2.500 ÷ 0.125. But it's much less challenging if we change the measurements to milliliters, so that the calculation becomes 2500 ÷ 125 with no decimals involved.

What we are doing here — in changing, for example, 52.00 ÷ 3.25 into 5200 ÷ 325 — is multiplying both numbers by 100. This approach uses the principle established in

Chapter 11: that the result of a division calculation is not changed if both numbers are multiplied by the same thing.

We can use this principle whenever we have to divide by a decimal number. For example, to find 4 ÷ 0.8, simply multiply both numbers by 10 to get 40 ÷ 8; so the answer is 5. To find 2.4 ÷ 0.08, multiply both numbers by 100 to get 240 ÷ 8; so the answer is 30.

One further observation about division by decimals: with decimals, the smaller the number we divide by, the larger the answer. Notice the pattern in the results obtained when, for example, 10 is divided by 2, 0.2, 0.02, 0.002, and so on:

> With decimals, the smaller the number we divide by, the larger the answer.

$$10 ÷ 2 \quad\quad = 5$$
$$10 ÷ 0.2 \quad\quad = 50$$
$$10 ÷ 0.02 \quad\quad = 500$$
$$10 ÷ 0.002 \quad = 5000$$
$$10 ÷ 0.0002 = 50000$$

Each time the divisor gets ten times smaller, the answer gets ten times bigger. This property of division often surprises people, but it is so significant that drawing specific attention to it is worthwhile.

This property is easy enough to make sense of if we think of $A ÷ B$ as meaning, how many Bs are needed to make an A? Clearly, the smaller the B, the greater the number of them that A *can* be divided into.

How can fractions be changed into decimals, and vice versa?

Fractions in which the bottom number is a power of 10, such as tenths, hundredths and thousandths, can be written directly as decimals. Here are some examples to show how this conversion works:

3/10	= 0.3	(0.3 means 3 tenths)
23/10	= 2.3	(the 20 tenths make 2 whole units)
3/100	= 0.03	(0.03 means 3 hundredths)
23/100	= 0.23	(the 20 hundredths make 2 tenths)
123/100	= 1.23	(the 100 hundredths make 1 whole unit)
3/1000	= 0.003	(0.003 means 3 thousandths)
23/1000	= 0.023	(the 20 thousandths make 2 hundredths)

A fraction that we can readily change into an equivalent fraction (see Chapter 16) with a bottom number of 10, 100 or 1000 is also easy to change into a decimal. For example, 1/5 is equivalent to 2/10 (multiplying top and bottom by 2), which is written as a decimal fraction as 0.2. Similarly, 3/25 is equivalent to 12/100 (multiplying top and bottom by 4), which then becomes 0.12.

Here are some further examples, many of which should be memorized:

1/2	is equivalent to	5/10,	which as a decimal is 0.5
4/5	is equivalent to	8/10,	which as a decimal is 0.8
1/4	is equivalent to	25/100,	which as a decimal is 0.25
3/4	is equivalent to	75/100,	which as a decimal is 0.75

1/20	is equivalent to	5/100,	which as a decimal is 0.05
7/20	is equivalent to	35/100,	which as a decimal is 0.35
1/50	is equivalent to	2/100,	which as a decimal is 0.02
3/50	is equivalent to	6/100,	which as a decimal is 0.06
1/25	is equivalent to	4/100,	which as a decimal is 0.04

Otherwise, to change a fraction into an equivalent decimal, recall that one of the meanings of the fraction notation is division (see Chapter 16). So we divide the top number by the bottom number, preferably using a calculator. Sometimes the result obtained is an exact decimal, but often it is a recurring decimal that has been shortened by the calculator (see Chapter 3).

The reverse process is to change a decimal into a fraction. First, we recall that the decimal 0.3 means three-tenths, so it is equivalent to the fraction 3/10. Likewise, 0.07 means seven-hundredths and is equivalent to the fraction 7/100. Then to deal with, say, 0.37 (3 tenths and 7 hundredths), we recognise that the 3 tenths can be exchanged for 30 hundredths, which, together with the 7 hundredths, makes a total of 37 hundredths — the fraction 37/100.

A slight procedural variation is that sometimes the fraction obtained can be changed to an equivalent but simpler fraction by dividing the top and bottom numbers by the same number. Here are a few examples:

0.6	becomes 6/10,	which is equivalent to 3/5	(dividing top and bottom by 2)
0.04	becomes 4/100,	which is equivalent to 1/25	(dividing top and bottom by 4)
0.45	becomes 45/100,	which is equivalent to 9/20	(dividing top and bottom by 5)
0.44	becomes 44/100,	which is equivalent to 11/25	(dividing top and bottom by 25)

Check yourself

17.1 Complete the solution of the problems 1–4 that are modeled by the additions and subtractions in Figure 17.1.

17.2 Remembering that there are 1000 milliliters in a liter and 1000 grams in a kilogram, suggest real-life questions that could be modeled by:

(a) $1.500 - 0.125$, in the context of liquid volume and capacity

(b) $1.120 + 2.500$, in the context of weighing. Answer your questions without using a calculator.

17.3 In the context of money pose a problem that is modeled by 3.99×4. Solve your problem without using a calculator.

17.4 In the context of length pose a problem that might be modeled by $4.40 \div 8$. Solve your problem without using a calculator.

17.5 Given that $4 \times 46 = 184$, find:

(a) 4×4.6 (b) 0.4×46 (c) 0.04×0.046

17.6 Given that $4 \times 45 = 180$, find:

(a) 4×4.5 (b) 0.4×45 (c) 0.04×0.045

17.7 What is the value of 0.01^2? Can you think of a question about area that might be modeled by this calculation?

17.8 Find:

(a) $2 \div 0.5$ (hint: multiply both numbers by 10)

(b) $5.5 \div 0.11$ (hint: multiply both numbers by 100)

17.9 Express these following fractions as equivalent decimals:

(a) 17/100   (b) 3/5   (c) 7/20

(d) 2/3 (use a calculator)   (e) 1/7 (use a calculator)

17.10 Express these following decimals as fractions:

(a) 0.09   (b) 0.79   (c) 0.15

➤Teaching suggestions

1. Try to place calculations with decimals in realistic contexts where the numerals represent money or measurements.

2. Emphasize the importance of having the same number of digits after the decimal point when adding or subtracting money or measurements written in decimal notation. Explain to the students about putting in extra zeros as placeholders where necessary.

3. Show how the principle of one of these can be exchanged for ten of those works when adding or subtracting with decimals in the same way as when working with integers.

4. Remember that realistic multiplication and division problems with decimals involving money or measurements can nearly always be recast into calculations with whole numbers by changing the units (for example, dollars to cents, meters to centimeters). Teach the students how to do this.

5. Base the explanation of multiplying and dividing decimal numbers by 10 (and 100 and 1000) on the principle of place value. Talk about the digits moving, rather than the decimal points moving.

6. Allow students to explore repeated multiplications and divisions by 10 with a calculator, making use of the constant facility.

7. Realize that some students will be able to learn to multiply two decimal numbers without using a calculator. One method is to remove the decimal point and replace it after the multiplication has been done. Explain the procedure in terms of multiplying repeatedly by 10, but teach them the method of counting the digits after the decimal points as well.

8. Show the students how to simplify divisions with decimals by multiplying both numbers by 10, 100, 1000, and so on, as appropriate.

9. Emphasize the principle that the smaller the divisor, the larger the answer. Let students explore this principle with sequences of division on a calculator.

10. Remember that in practice most people do calculations with decimals with a calculator, so be reasonable in the demands put on students for hand-written methods.

11. Have the students explore equivalences between fractions and decimals, using calculators where necessary. Encourage them to learn by heart some of the common equivalences, such as 1/2 = 0.5, 1/4 = 0.25, 3/4 = 0.75, 1/5 = 0.2, 2/5 = 0.4, and so on.

18 Percentages

Students should learn to understand and use, in context, percentages to estimate, to describe, and to compare proportions of a whole; to calculate percentages of quantities; to investigate relationships among fractions, decimals, and percentages; and to use a calculator where appropriate.

This Chapter Explains:

- the meaning of the term percent;
- the use of percentages to express proportions of a quantity or of a set;
- various methods, including the calculator, for evaluating percentages;
- the usefulness of percentages for comparing proportions;
- equivalences among fractions, decimals, and percents;
- the meaning of percents greater than 100; and
- how to calculate a percentage of a given quantity or number, using various methods, including a calculator.

What does *percent* mean?

The skills involved in using percentages are some of the most useful and practical that one can acquire. Percentages are everywhere — in discounts, interest rates, batting averages, prices, sales taxes, population studies, and statistics. However, before getting into the various uses and calculations of percentages, a definition is helpful.

The word *percent* means for each hundred. The Latin root *cent*, meaning a hundred, turns up in many English words, such as *century*, *centurion*, and *centipede*. The concept of a percentage is used primarily to describe a proportion of a quantity or of a set. For example, if a school has 300 students and 180 of them are girls, then the proportion of girls is 60 percent (written as 60%) of the school population. This means that there are 60 girls for every 100 students. If a car trip is 200 km and a total of 140 km of it is on a highway, we can say that 70% (70 percent) of the trip is on a highway, meaning 70 km for each 100 km.

The Latin term *per centum* means per 100.

These examples are similar to the ones used in Chapter 16, when we used fractions to represent a part of a unit or of a set. Indeed, the concept of a percentage is simply a special case of a fraction, with 100 as the bottom number (called a *denominator*). Thus, 60% is an abbreviation for 60/100 and 70% for 70/100.

How is a proportion expressed as a percentage?

The examples above were chosen to make it obvious how to express the proportions involved as so many per hundred. This is not always the case. The following examples demonstrate a number of approaches that can be used to express a proportion as a percentage whenever the numbers can be related to 100. The goal is to find an equivalent proportion for a population of 100 by multiplying or dividing by appropriate numbers.

Example 18A

A school population of 50 includes 30 girls. What percent are girls? What percent are boys?

Thinking it through

Thirty girls out of 50 students is the same proportion as 60 out of 100 (multiply both numbers by 2). Therefore, 60% of the population are girls. Thus, 40% are boys (since the total population must be 100%).

Example 18B

A school population of 250 includes 130 girls. What proportion are girls? What proportion are boys?

Thinking it through

Observe that 130 girls out of 250 students is the same proportion as 260 out of 500 (multiply both numbers by 2). And, 260 girls out of 500 students is the same as 52 per 100 (dividing both numbers by 5). So 52% of the population are girls. Thus, 48% must be boys (52% + 48% = 100%).

Example 18C

A school population of 75 includes 30 girls. What proportion are girls? What proportion are boys?

Thinking it through

Observe that 30 girls out of 75 students is the same proportion as 60 out of 150, which is the same proportion as 120 out of 300 (multiply both numbers by 2). Hence 120 girls out of 300 students is the same as 40 per 100 (dividing both numbers by 3). So 40% of the population are girls, and 60% are boys.

"When I do my math lessons sometimes somebody will point out, 'oh, you could do this or could we take this short cut or could we do this?' There are different ways to do it."

Example 18D

A school population of 140 includes 77 girls. What proportion are girls?

Thinking it through

Observe that 77 girls out of 140 students is the same proportion as 11 out of 20 (dividing by 7), which is the same proportion as 55 per 100 (multiply by 5). Hence, 55% of the population are girls, and 45% are boys.

When the numbers do not relate easily to 100 (as they do in the examples 18A–18D), the procedure is more complicated and is best done with the aid of a calculator.

Example 18E

A school population of 140, includes 73 girls. What percent are girls? What percent are boys?

Thinking it through

Observe that 73 girls out of 140 students means that 73/140 are girls. The equivalent proportion for a population of 100 students is 73/140 of 100. Work this problem out on a calculator: 73 ÷ 140 x 100. Interpret the display (52.14285) by rounding. Just over 52% of the population are girls, so just under 48% are boys.

Most calculators have a percent key (labeled %), that enables this last example to be done easily: 73 ÷ 140%.

Why are percentages used so much?

Percentages are used extensively in media, and in advertising. We are all familiar with claims such as "90% of cats prefer Kittymeat" and "20% of seven-year-olds cannot do subtraction" and with reports such as "a 60% chance of rain on Sunday." The media give us more than enough material to make this topic relevant to everyday life for students. The convention of relating everything to 100 lets us make comparisons in a straightforward manner. It is much easier, to compare 45% with 40% than to compare 4/9 with 2/5. That is why percentages are used so much: they provide us with a standard way of comparing various proportions.

Example 18F

Sarah saves $630 of her annual earnings of $5200. Jose saves $530 of his annual earnings of $4800. How do their saving efforts compare?

Thinking it through

The standard way of comparing these figures is to express the proportions of the savings as percentages. Using a calculator, we find that Sarah saves about 12.12% of her earnings (630 ÷ 5200%), whereas Jose saves about 11.04% of his. (530 ÷ 4800%). Now we can make a direct comparison: Sarah saves about $12.12 and Jose about $11.04 of every $100 of earnings.

How do percents relate to decimals?

The previous chapter explained that a decimal such as 0.37 means 37 hundredths. Since 37 hundredths also means 37 percent, the direct relationship between percents and decimals with two digits after the point is obvious. So, 0.37 and 37% are two ways of expressing the same thing. Here are some other examples: 0.50 is equivalent to 50%, 0.05 is equivalent to 5%, 0.42 is equivalent to 42%. The digits just move two places to the left.

What actually happens is multiplication of the decimal number by 100. This procedure works even if a number has more than two decimal digits. For example, 0.125 = 12.5%, and 1.01 = 101%.

Fractions, Decimals, and Percent Equivalences

We have three ways of expressing proportions of a quantity or of a set:
- using a fraction,
- using a decimal, or
- using a percent.

All three are equivalent.

Students can usefully memorize some of the most common equivalences, such as the following:

fraction	decimal	percent
1/2	0.5	50%
1/4	0.25	25%
3/4	0.75	75%
1/5	0.2	20%
2/5	0.4	40%
3/5	0.6	60%
4/5	0.8	80%
1/10	0.1	10%
3/10	0.3	30%
7/10	0.7	70%
9/10	0.9	90%
1/20	0.05	5%
1/3	0.33 (approx.)	33% (approx.)

Knowledge of these equivalences is useful for estimating percentages. For instance, in Example 18B above, 130 out of 250 students were girls. That is just over half the school population, so without doing the calculation we expect the percentage to be just a bit more than 50% (it is 52%). A proportion of 145 girls out of 450 students is a bit less than a third (150 students), so we expect a percentage of about 33% (it is about 32.22%).

Since we can convert a fraction to a decimal (see Chapter 17) just by dividing the top number (the numerator) by the bottom number (the denominator), we have another direct way of expressing a fraction or a proportion as a percentage.

Example 18G

Of the 37 students who visited the school library yesterday, 23 asked for help in finding material on particular subjects: What proportion sought help?

Thinking it through

The proportion 23 out of 37 corresponds to the fraction 23/37. On a calculator enter: $23 \div 37$ which yields the decimal equivalent 0.6216216. Since the first two decimal places correspond to the percentage, we can read this result as about 62%. If we wish to be more precise, we can include a couple more digits, obtaining 62.16% (see Chapter 12 for a discussion of rounding).

Overall, we can calculate the proportion A out of B as a percentage in four ways: (1) use multiplication and division to change the proportion to an equivalent number out of 100; (2) find $A/B \times 100$, using a calculator if necessary; (3) enter into a calculator: $A \div B\%$;

and (4) use a calculator to find $A \div B$ and read off the decimal answer as a percentage, by shifting all the digits two places to the left.

How can we have 101 percent?

Since 100% represents the whole quantity being considered or the whole population, talking about percentages greater than 100 may seem a bit odd. Coaches, for example, talk about their team having to give 110 percent – meaning, presumably, the players must give everything they have plus a little more.

There are, however, correct uses of percentages greater than 100, not only for expressing a proportion of a whole unit but for comparing two quantities. Just as we use fractions to represent the ratio of two quantities, we can also use percentages in this way.

Example 18H

Greta tutors neighborhood children. She earns $150 in January, $120 in February, and $180 in March. How do her earnings in each of the two later months compare with what she made in January?

Thinking it through

One way of comparing Greta's monthly earnings is to say that the amount she made in February was 80% of what she made in January; 80% is simply an equivalent way of saying 4/5.

The relationship of her March and January earnings is $180/$150. Dividing the top and bottom numbers by 10 yields 18/15 and dividing them by 3 yields 6/5 or 1 1/5, which is the equivalent of 120 percent.

The relationship of her March and February earnings is $180/$120, which is 1 1/2 or 150 percent. Notice the importance of being alert to what is being compared to what.

How do we calculate a percentage of a quantity?

The most common calculation with percentages is to find a percent of a given quantity, particularly in the context of money. Informal methods are available if the percentage can be converted to a simple equivalent fraction. For example, to find 25% of $48, simply change the calculation to 1/4 of $48, which is $12.

When the quantity in question is a multiple of 100, other ways to work out percentages are also available.

Example 18I

What is 37% of $600.

Thinking it through

As 37% of 100 is 37, we can simply multiply $37 by 6 to get an answer of $222.

Many people develop informal methods for building up a percentage, using factors of 100. One of the easiest percentages to find is 10%, and most people intuitively start with it.

Note, however, that the fact that 10% is the same as a tenth makes it a special case; 5% is not a fifth, 7% is not a seventh, and so on. Because we make so much use of 10%, students can get confused about the percent and the fraction. Teachers should make a special point of explaining that this connection works only with 10%.

Example 18J

What is 35% of $80.

Thinking it through

We can use the following reasoning:

If we know that 10% of $80 is $8, then 30% of $80 is $24 (tripling the $8) and 5% of $80 is $4 (halving the $8).

Adding the 30% and 5%, gives 35%, and adding $24 and $4 yields $28.

Intuitive approaches, such as this one to finding percentages, are often neglected in schools. This omission is unfortunate because this kind of manipulation contributes to an increased confidence about handling numbers. Try this method with students to see if they develop a better understanding of percentages.

Example 18K

What is 37% of $946?

Thinking it through

We need to find 37/100 of 946. This problem can be evaluated on a calculator. An appropriate key sequence is 37 ÷ 100 x 946. It gives the result 350.02, so we can conclude that 37% of $946 is $350.02. A more direct calculator method is to reason that 37% is equivalent to 0.37, and then enter 0.37 x 946 or, using the percent key 946 x 37%.

Point out to students that they need to check the reasonableness of this answer — indeed, of any answer, especially one obtained on a calculator. Here they can check for reasonableness of results by estimating the answer: 40% of 1000 is 400.

What about percentage increases and decreases?

One of the most common uses of percentages is to describe the change in a given quantity. We do this by expressing the change as a proportion of the starting value. The following examples illustrate percentage increases and decreases.

Example 18L

In-line skates have a price tag that indicates they were $249.99 and are now $209.99. What is the percentage decrease in the cost of the skates?

Thinking it through

The price reduction is $40 ($249.99–$209.99).

To find the percentage decrease, divide the price difference by the original price ($40/$249.99 = 0.1600) and multiply by 100%. The price has decreased by 16%.

Example 18M

The price tag of a jacket indicates it was $80 and is now reduced by 15%. What is the new price?

Thinking it through

To find the new price, we have to find 15% of $80 ($12) and deduct this amount from the old price, $80 – $12, giving the new price as $68. More directly, we can propose that the new price is the old price (100%) less 15%, so it must be 85% of that old price. Hence, we can just find 85% of $80 by multiplying 80 by 0.85 ($68).

Example 18N

Mario has been making $2500 a month. He receives a 5% raise. How much is his new monthly paycheck?

Thinking it through

If a monthly salary of $2500 is increased by 5%, then to find the new salary we can find 5% of $2500 ($125) and add this amount to the existing salary. Or the problem can be solved more directly. Since the new salary is the existing salary (100%) plus 5%, it must be 105% of the existing salary. So we can get the new salary by finding 105% of the existing salary; which is $2625. We multiply the salary by 1.05 (remembering that 105% = 1.05 as a decimal).

What happens if we add a percentage increase and subtract the same percentage decrease?

If we apply a given percent increase and then apply the same percent decrease, do we get back to where we started? At first thought, many people say yes. They overlook the fact that the first operation changes the base amount for the second one, as illustrated in the following example.

Example 18O

Suppose the price of a share of stock is $20. One month the stock price increases by 10%. The next month the stock price decreases by 10%. What is the final stock price?

Thinking it through

After the 10% increase, the stock price has gone up to $22 ($20 x 0.10 + $20). Next apply the 10% decrease to $22. The amount is a decrease of $2.20 because the percent change applies to the now-existing value of $22. So the stock price becomes $19.80, not the original price of $20.

Check yourself

18.1 A department store is advertising 25% off for some items and one-third off for others. Which reduction is the greater?

18.2 What percentage of students in Grade 6 achieve an A on a mathematics test and what percentage do not achieve that mark if school has

(a) 50 students in the grade and 13 achieve an A?
(b) 300 in the grade and 57 achieve an A?
(c) 80 in the grade and 24 achieve an A?
(d) 130 in the grade and 26 achieve an A?

18.3 A page of an English textbook has 1249 letters, of which 527 are vowels. A page of an Italian textbook has 565 letters, of which 277 are vowels. Use a calculator to determine approximately what percentage of the letters are vowels in each textbook.

18.4 Change

(a) 3/20 into a percent   (b) 65% into a fraction

18.5 Use informal methods to find

(a) 30% of $120   (b) 15% of $450

18.6 The price of a television that costs $275 is increased by 12% one month and decreased by 12% the next. What is the final price? Use a calculator if necessary.

18.7 A shop is advertising a stereo system for $600. The manager tells you that 20% tax must be added to this price. However, she is also offering 10% discount. Which would you prefer the manager to apply first: the tax or the discount?

►Teaching suggestions

1. Explain the meaning of *percent* as *for each hundred*, and show how percentages are used to describe a fraction of a quantity or of a set.
2. Encourage students to find examples of percentages used in newspapers and advertising, and discuss with them what is being claimed.
3. Encourage the use of various methods for expressing a proportion as a percent, using numbers that relate easily to 100.
4. Allow students to use calculators to express more difficult proportions as percents, showing them various ways of doing the calculation.
5. Emphasize the equivalence among fractions, decimals, and percents.
6. Show students how to change a percent into an equivalent decimal and vice versa, by moving the digits two places.
7. Encourage students to memorize common equivalences among fractions, decimals, and percents.
8. Encourage students to use informal methods for finding a percent of a quantity, particularly building up their answers by using percents such as 10% and 5%.
9. Encourage students to use calculators for problems such as finding a percent of a quantity, and explore with them some of the different ways of doing this.
10. Be aware that not all calculators follow the same keying sequence for expressing a proportion as a percent or for calculating percentages of a quantity.
11. Emphasize that the equivalence of 10% and one-tenth is a special case.

19 Data Management

Students should learn to interpret and create frequency tables, including those for grouped discrete data; to collect and represent data appropriately, using graphs and diagrams, including block graphs, pictograms, and line graphs; and to interpret a wider range of graphs and diagrams that represent data, including pie charts.

THIS CHAPTER EXPLAINS:

- the four stages of handling data: collecting, organizing, representing, interpreting;
- the use of tallying and frequency tables for collecting and organizing data;
- the differences among discrete data, grouped discrete data, and continuous data;
- the representation of discrete and grouped discrete data in bar graphs;
- the misleading effect of suppressing zero in a frequency graph; and
- other ways of representing data: set diagrams, pictograms, pie charts, and line graphs.

What do students have to learn about handling statistical data?

Essentially, handling data involves four stages: collecting it, organizing it, representing it, and interpreting it. Students should have experience of all four of these stages. (We adopt the current usage of *data* as a singular noun, meaning a collection of information.)

They should learn how to collect data as part of a purposeful inquiry, setting out to gather answers to specific questions that they raise. Doing so may involve the skills associated with designing simple questionnaires. For example, as part of a geography-focused project on transportation, they may decide to collect data about how students travel to school and seek to make comparisons between, say, students in a rural school and those in a city school.

A useful technique is that of *tallying*, which is based on counting in fives. Data should then be organized in a frequency table. Figure 19.1 shows both these processes for the information collected from a Grade 5 class in a rural school.

(a)		(b) How we travel	Number of pupils

How we travel	Number of pupils
Bus	7
Bike	2
Car	10
Walk	6
Total	25

FIGURE 19.1 *Using (a) tallying and (b) a frequency table*

Various kinds of graphs and diagrams can then be used to represent the data, before the final step of interpreting it. To involve students in the important step of interpretation, three approaches are useful in the classroom: (1) students write about what the graph tells them, particularly in relation to the questions and issues that prompted the collection of the data; (2) students write sentences about what the graph reports, incorporating key words such as *most, least, more than,* and *less than;* and (3) students make up a number of questions that can be answered from the graph and then pose them to each other.

What is discrete data?

The word *discrete* means separate. Discrete data is information about a particular population, such as the children in a class, that sorts the members of the population into distinct subsets.

> Discrete data is information about a particular population that sorts the members of the population into distinct subsets.

The information about traveling to school, shown in Figure 19.1, is a good example of discrete data since it sorts the students automatically into four separate subsets: those who come by bus, by car, by bicycle, or on foot. Other examples of the kind of discrete data that students might collect, organize, display, and interpret include: favorite TV program, chosen from a list of six possible programs; daily newspaper taken at home, including none; and month in which they were born. In each case, the question asked (for example, how did you travel to school today?) identifies a *variable* (for example, the means of transport), and the answer determines a *value* for that variable (for example, bus, car, bike, and on foot). A separate subset is formed for each individual value taken by the variable. The number in each subset is called the *frequency*.

Sometimes the variable is numerical, rather than descriptive. For example, students might be asked how many children are in their family (the possible values of this variable are 1, 2, 3, 4, ...), what size shoes they wear, or how many pets they have. Initially, we should use variables that have no more than a dozen values; otherwise we finish with too many subsets to allow any meaningful interpretation.

We can then display the data in a conventional bar graph. The development of this type of graph has two important stages. The first is reflected in Figure 19.2a, where each square is shaded individually, as though each square represents one child. In interpreting the graph, the students can count the number of squares, as though counting the number of children in each subset, so a vertical axis is unnecessary. (In a still earlier stage, children would write their names on squares of paper that would be arranged in columns, so individual contributions can be identified.)

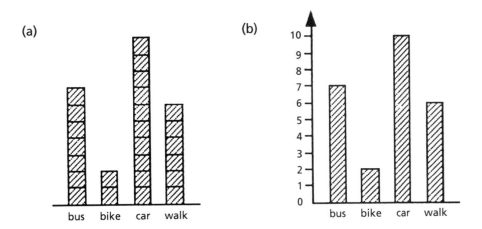

FIGURE 19.2 *Two stages in the use of bar graphs*

Figure 19.2b is based on a more sophisticated idea. Now, the individual contributions are lost and the height of the column, rather than the number of squares in the column, indicates the frequency. We read it by relating the tops of the columns to the scale on the vertical axis, where the numbers label the points on the axis, not the spaces between them. We have progressed from counting to measurement. This step is important because, even though we may still use squared paper to draw these graphs, we now have the option of using different scales, appropriate to the data, on the vertical axis, For example, with a larger population, we might take one unit on the vertical scale to represent 10 people.

Notice that, in Figure 19.2, we have used the convention, common for discrete data, of leaving gaps between the columns. This procedure is appropriate because it conveys pictorially the way in which the variable sorts the population into discrete subsets.

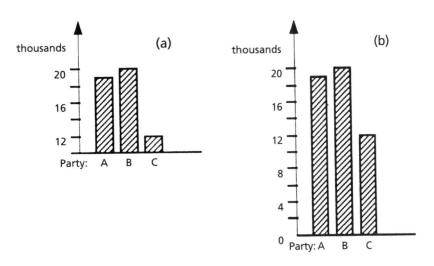

FIGURE 19.3 *Suppression of zero*

In order to present an appropriate picture of the distribution of the data, the columns in a bar graph must be drawn with equal widths. A further important point about bar graphs that represent frequencies is illustrated in Figure 19.3. It was produced prior to a general election to show the numbers of votes gained by three political parties (called A, B, and C) in the previous election. The graph in Figure 19.3a was the version put out by a local Party A candidate to persuade electors that they would be wasting their vote by voting for Party C. It presents a totally false picture of the relative standing of Party C compared to A and B because the frequency axis does not start at zero. Since the purpose of drawing a graph is to provide an instant overview of the relationships within the data, this procedure (called *suppression of zero*) is nearly always inappropriate or misleading and should be avoided. The graph in Figure 19.3b, whose vertical axis properly starts at zero, presents a much more honest picture of the relative share of the vote.

What is meant by *grouped discrete data*?

Discrete data like that in the examples above is the simplest kind of data to handle. Sometimes, however, the variable has too many values for us to sort the population into an appropriate number of subsets. So the data must first be organized into groups.

For example, a group of Grade 5 students were asked how many writing implements (pencils, pens, markers, and so on) they had with them one day at school. The responses were as follows: 1, 2, 2, 3, 4, 4, 5, 5, 5, 6, 6, 8, 8, 8, 9, 9, 10, 10, 11, 13, 14, 14, 14, 15, 15, 18, 19, 25, 26, 32. Clearly, a bar graph cannot represent so many possibilities. The best procedure, therefore, is to group the data — for example, as shown in Figure 19.4. Notice that the range of values in the subsets (0–4, 5–9, 10–14, 15–19, and so on) should be the same in each case; that the groups should not overlap; that they must between them cover all the values of the variable; and that groups with zero frequency (such as 20–24 in Figure 19.4) should not be omitted from the table or from the graph. Of course, the data could have been grouped in other ways, producing either more subsets (for example, 0–1, 2–3, 4–5, and so on: 17 groups), or fewer (for example, 0–9, 10–19, 20–29, 30–39). When working with grouped discrete data like this, we should aim for five to ten groups. More than ten provide too much information to take in; fewer than five mean the loss of much information.

no. of pens etc.	frequency
0–4	6
5–9	10
10–14	7
15–19	4
20–24	0
25–29	2
30–34	1

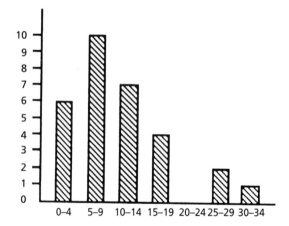

FIGURE 19.4 *Handling grouped discrete data*

What other kind of data is there?

Continuous data is the kind of data produced by a variable that can theoretically take any value on a continuum. For example, if we were collecting data about the waist sizes of a group of adults, the measurements could come anywhere on a tape measure from, say,

50 cm to 120 cm. They are not restricted to particular, distinct points on the scale. For example, the waist measurement of one individual may be about 62.5 cm. If he puts on some weight and the measurement increases to about 64.5 cm, then we know that the waist size could increase continuously from one measurement to the next, on the way taking every possible value in between; it would not suddenly jump from one value to the other. This is a characteristic of a continuous variable.

The contrast with a discrete variable, such as the number of pets a person owns, is clear. If a person has three pets and then gets a fourth, she jumps from three to four, without having to pass through 3.1 pets, 3.2 pets, and so on. Measurements of length, mass, volume, and time intervals are all examples of continuous data.

Yet, we always have to record measurements to the nearest something (see the discussion on rounding in Chapter 12). The effect of such rounding is immediately to change the values of the continuous variable into a set of discrete data. For example, we might measure waist sizes to the nearest centimeter. Now our data on waist measurements is restricted to the following, distinct values: 50 cm, 51 cm, 52 cm, and so on. Thus, in practice, the procedure for handling data produced by recording a series of measurements to the nearest something does not differ from the procedure for handling discrete data with a large number of potential values. Grouping, as explained above, can make it an appropriate activity for elementary school students.

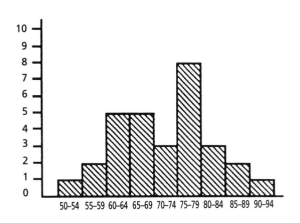

waist measurements to nearest centimetre	frequency
50–54	1
55–59	2
60–64	5
65–69	5
70–74	3
75–79	8
80–84	3
85–89	2
90–94	1

FIGURE 19.5 *A graph derived from a continuous variable*

Students can collect data about, for example, their height (to the nearest centimeter), their mass (to the nearest tenth of a kilogram), the circumference of their heads (to the nearest millimeter), the volume of water they can drink in one sitting (to the nearest tenth of a liter), and the time it takes them to run 100 meters (to the nearest second). Each of these variables is technically continuous, but measurements taken to the nearest something generate a set of discrete data, that can then be grouped appropriately and represented in a graph. The only difference is that the graph should reflect the fact that the data originated from a continuous variable; the convention is to draw the columns with no gaps in between them, as shown in Figure 19.5.

Any further development of handling of continuous data would be beyond the scope of elementary school mathematics.

What are other ways of representing data?

Figure 19.6 shows two more ways of representing the data used in Figure 19.1. The most elementary method is a set diagram, with the actual names of the students written on the various subsets (see Figure 19.6a). In a pictogram, the names are replaced by pictures organized in neat rows and columns (see Figure 19.6b). The pictogram is clearly only a small step from a bar graph, where the pictures are replaced by individual shaded squares. With larger populations, we can use pictograms in which each icon (picture) represents a number of individuals, rather than just one.

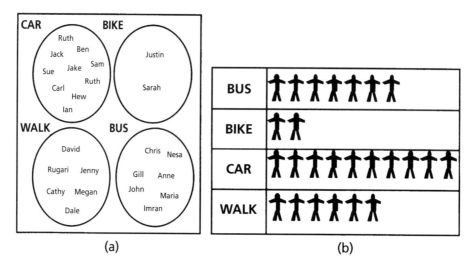

(a)   (b)

FIGURE 19.6 *A set diagram and a pictogram*

A much more sophisticated way of displaying data is the pie chart (Figure 19.7). Here each slice of pie represents the proportion of the population in each subset. The usual practice is to write these proportions as percents (see Chapter 18) within the slice itself, if possible. Pie charts are really appropriate only for discrete data with a small number of subsets — say, six or fewer. They are often used to show what proportion of a budget is spent in various categories.

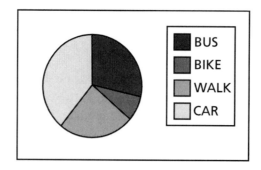

FIGURE 19.7 *A pie chart*

The mathematics for producing a pie chart can be quite complicated for elementary school children unless the data is chosen very carefully. For example, to determine the angle for the slice representing travel by bus, in Figure 19.7, we have to divide 360 degrees by 25 (to determine how many degrees per person in the population) and then multiply by 7. Using a calculator, enter 360 ÷ 25 x 7 (answer 100.8, which is about 101 degrees). This angle then has to be drawn using a protractor.

Fortunately, computers can be used to make pie graphs. If the data in question is entered into a database or on a spreadsheet — many simple examples of these kinds of programs are available for use in elementary schools — there is usually a choice of bar graphs, pie charts, or line graphs (see below) at the press of a button. Thus, elementary school children should certainly learn how to interpret pie charts, but they do not really need to learn how to draw them for themselves.

Another type of graph used sometimes for representing statistical data is the line graph. Figure 19.8. shows the number of new students at an elementary school at the beginning of each school year for a number of years.

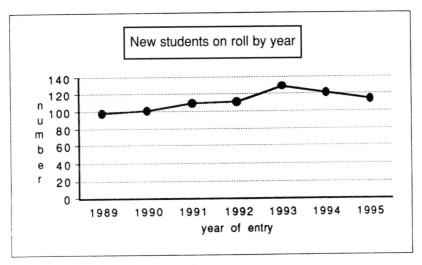

FIGURE 19.8 *A line graph*

A line graph is appropriate for statistical data, particularly when the variable along the horizontal axis is time. The movement of the line, up and down, gives a picture of how the number changes over hours, days, months, years, or decades. Such a graph is useful for showing, for example, the average midday temperature over a series of months, the number of students absent each day in one week, the number of students who have completed their mathematics work by various numbers of minutes past ten o'clock. A line graph is totally inappropriate as a means of presenting discrete data, such as that relating to traveling to school in Figure 19.1, and not really appropriate for all the other examples of statistical data used in this chapter.

Check yourself

19.1 Make up two questions that can be answered from the graphs shown in each of:

(a) Figure 19.2 (b) Figure 19.4 (c) Figure 19.5.

19.2 Which of the following variables are discrete? Which generate discrete data that should be grouped? Which are continuous?

(a) the times it takes various students to count to a thousand
(b) students' heights
(c) the number of living grandparents students have
(d) the amount of money in coins in the possession of various students
(e) each student's favorite kind of music chosen from a list of five possibilities
(f) the mass of the classroom guinea pig recorded each Monday morning for a term.

19.3 Which of the examples in Question 19.2 would be best represented in a pie chart? Which would be best represented in a line graph?

19.4 For part (d) of Question 19.2, the data collected from a group of students ranges from zero to $4.59. How would you choose to group this data in order to represent it in a bar chart?

19.5 In a class of 36 students, 14 come to school by car.
   (a) What angle would be needed in the slice of a pie chart to represent this information?
   (b) What would it be for 14 students out of a class of 33?

➤Teaching suggestions

1. Explore with the students all four stages of handling data: collecting, organizing, representing, interpreting.

2. Realize that motivation is higher when the students collect the data themselves; higher still when it is collected to answer questions they have posed themselves; and even higher when it is about themselves.

3. Teach the skills of handling data and pictorial representation through purposeful inquiries related to topics focusing on other areas of the curriculum, such as geography, history, or science.

4. Teach the technique of tallying, and encourage students to use it when collating data.

5. Have students first handle discrete data with nonnumerical variables (for example, means of travel to school), and then move into discrete data using numerical variables (for example, the number of pets owned). Use examples with no more than ten subsets.

6. Introduce students to set diagrams and pictograms as ways of representing discrete data.

7. Introduce bar graphs first by sticking on or shading individual squares whose number represents frequency. Then use columns whose heights represent frequency.

8. Teach students to interpret pie charts. They are best used with only a small number of subsets.

9. With the students, progress to handling discrete data with so many subsets that the data has to be organized into groups covering a range of values.

10. Have the students deal with continuous variables, such as measurements of length, mass, time, and volume. They should record measurements to the nearest something, thus converting the values of the variable to discrete data, which can then be grouped appropriately.

11. Have the students use database and spreadsheet programs to organize data and to generate graphs (particularly bar graphs and pie charts) for them to interpret.

12. Encourage students to collect examples of graphs and tables of data from the press and advertising — and discuss whether they are helpful or misleading.

13. Introduce line graphs for data related to time.

20 Averages

> Students should learn to understand the mean, the median, and the mode in relevant contexts, and the range as a measure of spread.
>
> **THIS CHAPTER EXPLAINS:**
> - the idea of an average as a representative figure for a set of data;
> - three measures of average: the mean, the median, and the mode;
> - the need for a measure of spread and the idea of range; and
> - the concept of average speed.

Is there more to finding an average than simply adding up some numbers and dividing by how many there are in the set?

The process outlined in this question produces one kind of average figure, called the *mean* (or, to use its full title, the *arithmetic mean*). The purpose of finding an average is to produce a representative figure for a set of numerical data. The mean is one way of doing this, and it is appropriate in many circumstances. But it is not the only way. Sometimes using other kinds of average — in particular, the median and the mode — makes more sense.

> The purpose of finding an average is to produce a representative figure for a set of numerical data.

The important purpose that all three of these measures of average share is offering a suitable way of obtaining one number that can represent a whole set of numbers. Having this *average figure* enables us: (1) to make comparisons among different sets of data by comparing their means, medians, or modes; and (2) to make sense of individual numbers in a set by relating them to these averages.

> An average is a number that can represent a whole set of numbers.

The discussion below uses these different kinds of average to consider the marks out of 100 gained by two groups of students in the same mathematics and English tests. Group A has 14 students, and Group B has 11 students.

Group A: Mathematics 23, 25, 46, 48, 48, 49, 53, 60, 61, 61, 61, 62, 69, 85
Group B: Mathematics 36, 38, 43, 43, 45, 47, 60, 63, 69, 86, 95
Group A: English   45, 48, 49, 52, 53, 53, 53, 53, 54, 56, 57, 58, 59, 62
Group B: English   45, 52, 56, 57, 64, 71, 72, 76, 79, 81, 90

What is the process of finding the mean?

Finding the mean value of a set of numbers involves three steps: (1) find the sum of all the numbers in the set; (2) divide by the number of numbers in the set; and (3) round the answer appropriately, if necessary (see Chapter 12).

For example, to find the mean mathematics score of the Group A students: (1) add all the scores to obtain the sum of 751; (2) divide 751 by 14, using a calculator to get 53.642857; and (3) round this answer to, say, one decimal place, to determine the mean score to be about 53.6.

The logic behind using this amount as a representative figure is that the total marks obtained by the group would have been the same amount as the sum obtained in step (1) if all the students had scored the mean (allowing for the possibility of a small error introduced by rounding). For example, if the 14 students had all scored 53.6, the total of their marks would have been 750.4. In other words, imagine that all the students put all their marks into a pool, which is then shared out equally among all 14 of them. This vision is an application of the concept involved in division structures associated with the word *per* (see Chapter 10): we are finding the marks per student, assuming an equal sharing of all the marks awarded.

A good illustration is finding the mean for the amount of money that a group of people have in their possession. We could do this by having them put all their money on the table and then share it out equally among the members of the group. This process is precisely what is modeled by the mathematical process of finding the mean.

We can now use this process to make comparisons. For example, to compare Group A with Group B in mathematics, we can compare their mean scores. Group A's mean score is about 53.6 (751 ÷ 14), and Group B's mean score is about 56.8 (625 ÷ 11). The difference lends some support to an assertion that, on the whole, Group B has done better on the test than Group A.

We can also use average scores to help make sense of individual scores. For example, Cathy in Group B scored 60 in mathematics and 64 in English. Reacting naively to the raw scores, we might conclude that she did better in English than in mathematics. But comparing her marks with the mean scores for her group leads to a different interpretation: Cathy's mark for mathematics (60) is above the mean (56.8), while the higher mark she obtained for English (64) is actually below the mean for her group (which works out to 67.5). This comparison lends some support to the view that Cathy has done better in mathematics than in English.

What is the *median*?

The *median* is the number that comes in the middle of a set when the numbers in it are arranged in numerical order. Finding this average figure is much easier than calculating the mean. The process of finding the median starts by arranging all the numbers in the set in order from

The median is the number that comes in the middle of a set when the numbers in it are arranged in numerical order.

smallest to largest. Then if the set has an odd number of numbers, the median is the number in the middle. If the set has an even number of numbers, the median is the mean of the two numbers in the middle: that is, halfway between them.

For example, for Group B mathematics, with a set of 11 students, the median is the sixth mark when the marks are arranged in order; hence the median is 47. For Group A mathematics, with a set of 14, the median comes halfway between the seventh and eighth marks (halfway between 53 and 60); hence the median is 56.5.

Interestingly, using the median, rather than the mean, as the measure of average in comparing the two groups leads to a different conclusion: on the whole Group A (median mark of 56.5) has done better than Group B (median mark of 47).

When the set of numbers is small, as in these examples, the median is often a more appropriate representative figure than the mean. The reason is that the median is not affected by one or two extreme values, such as the 86 and 95 in Group B; a couple of scores much higher or lower than the rest, can increase or decrease the value of the mean significantly and produce an average figure that does not represent the group in the most appropriate way. To take an extreme case, imagine that nine students in a group of ten score 1 in a test and the other scores 100. This data produces a mean score of 10.9 but a median of 1. There is surely no argument here that the median represents the performance of the group as a whole most appropriately.

These considerations illustrate the fact that most sets of statistics are open to different interpretations — which is why the phrase "lend some support to" is useful in drawing conclusions from the data in these examples.

Returning to Cathy, who scored 60 for mathematics and 64 for English, we can compare her performance with her group's median scores, of 47 and 71 respectively. These statistics again lend support to the assertion that she has done better in mathematics than in English.

What is the *mode*, and when would you use it?

The *mode* is the number in the set that occurs most frequently. For example, for Group A mathematics, the mode is 61 because this number occurs three times, which is more than any other number in the set. For Group B mathematics, the mode is 43.

> The mode is the number in the set that occurs most frequently.

The mode is actually an ineffective way of determining representative marks for these sets of data. It is useful as a measure of average only when we are dealing with a large set of data and the range of values the data covers is quite small.

An example of a good use of a mode is in discussing an "average" family. In the United Kingdom, the modal number of children in a family is 2, because more families have two children than any other number. In contrast, the mean is 2.4 children. If someone is writing a play featuring an average family, it probably includes two children. Clearly the mode is more use here than the mean, since 2.4 children would be difficult to cast.

Like the mean and the median, the mode enables us to make useful comparisons among different sets when it is an appropriate and meaningful measure of average. For example, when comparing social factors in, say, parts of China, some countries in Africa, and European states, the modal numbers of children per family are significant statistics to consider.

What is meant by *the range as a measure of spread*?

If we compare Group A's marks for mathematics with their marks for English and look just at the mean scores (53.6 and 53.7 respectively), we might conclude that the sets of marks for the two subjects are very similar. Looking at the actual data, it is clear that they are not. The most striking feature is that the mathematics marks are widely spread while the English marks are relatively closely clustered together.

Statisticians have various ways of measuring the degree of *spread* (sometimes called *deviation*) in a set of data. For example, the phrase *standard deviation* is common. These measures of spread have a purpose similar to that of the measures of average: they enable us to compare sets of data and to make sense of individual items of data. For elementary school work, teachers need introduce the range only as a measure of spread. The *range* is the difference between the largest and the smallest values in the set.

When comparing Group A's results in mathematics and English, we can say that although they have about the same mean scores, the range for mathematics is 62 marks (85–23), whereas the range for English is only 17 marks (62–45).

How does the idea of average speed fit in with the concept of an average?

Students' first experience with speed is usually with the movement of a vehicle, measured in kilometers per hour (km/h). (Note that average speed gives us another example of the word, *per*).

The idea of average speed derives from the concept of a mean. Over the course of a journey, a driver's speed changes constantly; sometimes it is even zero. When we talk about the average speed of a journey, it is as though we add up all the kilometers covered during various stages of the journey and then share them equally per hour, using the idea of pooling that is the basis for calculating the mean of a set of numbers. So if a journey covers 400 km in total and takes 8 hours, the average speed is 50 km/h (400 ÷ 8).

The logic here is that if the driver had been able to travel at a constant speed of 50 km/h, then the journey would have taken the same 8 hours. So the average speed (in kilometers per hour) is the total distance traveled (in kilometers) divided by the total time taken (in hours).

We can extend this definition of average speed to apply to trips for which the time is not a whole number of hours. For example, for a trip of 22 km in 24 minutes (0.4 hours), the average speed is 22 ÷ 0.4, which is 55 km/h. The same principle applies, of course, whatever units are used for distance and time. For example, if a toy car takes 5 seconds to run down a ramp of 150 cm, the average speed is 30 cm/s (150 ÷ 5).

Check yourself

20.1 Compare the mean and median scores for Groups A's and B's English results, using the data given above. Which group did better for English on the whole?

20.2 Find the mean score for English for the two groups combined. Is it equal to the mean of the two separate mean scores?

20.3 Find the median scores and the ranges for English and mathematics for the two groups combined.

20.4 John, in Group A, scored 49 for mathematics. How does this score compare to the performance of Group A as a whole?

20.5 Toy car P travels 410 cm in 6 seconds; toy car Q travels 325 cm in 5 seconds. Which has the greater average speed?

20.6 On a car trip of 400 km, Stefan averages a speed of 40 km/h. How long does the trip take? On the way back he averages a speed of 50 km/h. How long does the return trip take? Now (be careful!), what is the average speed for the whole trip, there and back?

➤Teaching suggestions

1. Explain to students the idea of an average being a representative figure for a set of numbers, enabling comparisons between different sets.

2. Explain the idea of the mean, first using the example of pooling money and sharing it out equally. Then extend the idea to other examples.

3. Emphasize that the median is the number in the middle when the numbers are arranged in order. But point out how to work with sets with an even number of numbers.

4. Introduce students to the idea of using the mode as a measure of average when appropriate — for example, when dealing with a large set of numbers with a limited range of possible values.

5. Show students, using examples of sets with approximately the same mean but very different spreads, the importance of looking at the range of values when comparing sets.

6. Encourage students to use and apply these concepts to make comparisons between sets of data and to make sense of individual items of data. Have them use information they have collected themselves in the course of purposeful inquiries.

7. Be aware of useful sources of data for applying these concepts. They include the students themselves (their ages, their heights, distance of home from school, children in their family, and so on), the weather, sports, science experiments (repeating a measurement several times and recording a mean value), and most geography-focused topics (particularly for making comparisons among different areas).

8. Emphasize to students that conclusions drawn from statistics, such as averages, can be uncertain or even misleading.

Probability

What is probability?

Mathematics probability is a measurement that is applied to events. *Probability* measures how strongly we believe that an event will happen. Measurements of this level of belief are described by words ranging from *impossible* to *certain*; we compare our assessment of different events by talking about one being *more likely* or *less likely* than another.

This strength of belief is determined by various kinds of evidence. Sometimes this evidence is simply the accumulation of our experience, in which case our judgment about the likelihood of one event compared to others is fairly subjective. For example, suppose a group of student-teachers writes down some events that might occur during the next 12 months and ranks them from the least likely to the most likely as follows:

1. It will snow in Edmonton during July.
2. The Toronto Blue Jays and the Montreal Expos will oppose each other in the world series in 2000.
3. Steve will get a teaching post.
4. Canada will have a general election.
5. Someone will reach the summit of Mount Everest.

If we suggest that Steve has an interview at school next week for a teaching position for which he is ideally suited, then this extra piece of evidence will have an immediate effect on the student-teachers' strength of belief in event 3, and they will likely change its position in the ranking.

The use of terminology such as *more likely than* and *less likely than*, reflects the fact that probability is based on the ideas of comparison and ordering, which are always the first stages of the development of any aspect of measurement. And they signal that probability requires some kind of measuring scale. For example, we may judge that event 1 above is an almost impossible event, 2 is fairly unlikely and event 5 is almost certain. When we feel that an event is as likely to happen as not to happen, we say that *the chances are even*. To introduce a numerical scale, we can think of awarding marks out of 100 for each event, with 0 marks for one we believe to be impossible, 100 marks for an event we judge to be certain, and 50 marks for even odds. For example, working subjectively, the student-teachers in the group award 1 mark for event 1, 5 marks for event 2, 50 marks for event 4 and 99 marks for event 5. Event 3 starts out at 40 but moves to 75 when the new evidence is obtained.

If we think of these marks out of 100 as percentages and convert them to decimals (see Chapter 18), we have the standard scale used for measuring probability, ranging from 0 (impossible), through 0.5 (even), to 1 (certain). For example, our subjective assessment of the probabilities of events 2 and 5 are 0.05 and 0.99 respectively.

Can probability be measured more objectively?

For a more objective estimate of probability we have three ways of collecting evidence: (1) collect statistical data and use the idea of relative frequency; (2) perform an experiment a large number of times and use the relative frequency of different outcomes; and (3) use theoretical arguments based on symmetry and equally likely outcomes.

Statistical data collection

Statistical data collection methods are used extensively by business firms, such as insurers and marketers, which often assess probabilities by gathering statistical data. To determine an appropriate premium for a life insurance policy for a professor, an insurance company uses the probabilities that she may live to 60, to 70, to 80, and so on. To determine these probabilities, insurers could collect statistical data about university professors living in Toronto and find what proportion of them survive to various ages. If that data shows that out of 250 cases, 216 live to 70, then this evidence suggests that a reasonable estimate for the probability of a university professor's living to this age is 86.4% (216 ÷ 250) or, as a decimal, 0.864.

> Statistical data collection methods are used extensively by business firms, such as insurers and marketers, which often assess probabilities by gathering statistical data.

Since obtaining such data from the entire population is normally impractical, this application of probability is usually based on evidence collected from a sample.

Example 21A

What is the probability that a word chosen at random from a page of text in this book will have four letters in it?

Thinking it through

To answer this question, we can use the last hundred words of the previous chapter as a sample. Since 18 of these words have 4 letters, the relative frequency of four-letter words in the sample is 18%. So an estimate for the probability based on this evidence is 0.18. In general, the larger the sample, the more reliable relative frequency is as an estimate of the probability.

Experimental data collection

The second procedure for obtaining objective estimates for probabilities applies the same idea to an experiment, often the kind of thing that can be experienced in the classroom. The event in question is an outcome of the experiment. For example, the experiment might be to throw three identical dice simultaneously, looking for whether the score on one of them is greater than the sum of the scores on the other two. What is the probability of this outcome?

A useful experience for students is to make a subjective estimate of the probability, based purely on intuition, and then to perform the experiment a large number of times, recording the numbers of successes and failures. For example, they may estimate subjectively that the chances of this outcome would be a bit less than even, so the probability is, say, about 0.40. Then they throw the dice, say 200 times and find that the number of successes is 58. Hence the relative frequency of successes is 29% (58 ÷ 200), so the best estimate for the probability, based on this evidence, is 0.29.

For some experiments, however, we can consider all the possible outcomes theoretically and make estimates for probability using an argument based on symmetry. Experiments with coins and dice lend themselves to this kind of argument. The simplest argument involves tossing one coin. There are only two possible outcomes: heads and tails. Given the symmetry of the coin, there is no reason to assume that either outcome is more or less likely than the other. So we conclude that the probability of a head is 0.5 and the probability of a tail is 0.5.

Notice that the sum of the probabilities of all the possible outcomes must be 1, which represents certainty. We are certain that the coin will come down either heads or tails.

Similarly, throwing a conventional, six-faced die has six possible outcomes, each of which is equally likely on the basis of symmetry. We therefore determine the probability of throwing each number to be one-sixth or about 0.17 (1 ÷ 6 = 0.1666666 on a calculator).

We can also determine the probability of events that are made up of a number of different outcomes. For example, two of the scores on the die faces are multiples of three, so the probability of throwing a multiple of three is two-sixths or about 0.33 (2/6 = 1/3 = 0.3333333 on a calculator).

The general procedure for determining the probability of a particular event by this theoretical approach is: (1) list all the possible equally likely outcomes from the experiment, being guided by symmetry but thinking carefully to ensure that the outcomes listed really are equally likely; (2) perform the experiment over and over again, counting the numbers of times each of these outcomes occur; and (3) divide the second number by the first.

Example 21B

Find the probability that a card drawn from a conventional pack of playing cards will be less than 7.

Thinking it through

The draw has 52 equally likely outcomes: that is, any of the 52 possible cards may be drawn. The event in question (the card is less than 7) could occur in 24 of these. So the probability is 24 ÷ 52, or about 0.46.

It is important to remember that probability is a measure of how strongly we believe an event will happen. If someone says that the probability of a coin's turning up heads is 0.5, he is making a statement about how strongly he believes that it will come up heads. If an argument based on symmetry is valid, theoretical probability does not change from one outcome to the next. Therefore, the statement that the probability of getting a head is 0.5 does not tell us anything about what will *actually* happen next. If a person has just thrown a head, the probability of a head on the next toss is still 0.5. If someone just threw 20 tails in succession, the probability of the next one's being a head is still 0.5 (so long as we can assume that the coin is not bent or weighted in any way that might distort the results).

What the probability does tell us is that in the long run, if the person goes on tossing the coin long enough, the relative frequency of heads (and tails) will gradually get closer to 50%.

This statement does not mean that, with a thousand tosses, we expect exactly 500 of each; in fact, that outcome would be very surprising! But we can expect the proportion of heads to be about 50% and get closer to 50% the more often the coin is tossed.

Students should, therefore, actually do such experiments a large number of times, obtain the relative frequencies of various outcomes for which they have determined the theoretical probability, and observe and discuss the fact that the two are not usually exactly the same. In an experiment with a number of equally likely outcomes, we have no way of predicting the outcome of any given experiment, but we can predict with confidence what will happen in the long run.

What is the theoretically probable outcome of tossing two coins or throwing two dice?

When arguing theoretically about possible outcomes we have to be careful to ensure that they really are all equally likely. For example, one class of students decided that tossing two coins had three possible outcomes: two heads, two tails, and one of each, and they determined the probability to be one-third for each. Then, performing the experiment 1000 times (40 times each for 25 students), they found that two heads turned up 256 times, two tails turned up 234 times and one of each turned up 510 times. So the relative frequencies were 25.6%, 23.4%, and 51%. Obviously, the students were not getting close to the theoretical 33.3%.

The problem was that their three outcomes were not equally likely. Calling the two coins A and B, we can identify four possible outcomes: A and B both heads, A heads and B tails, A tails and B heads, and A and B both tails. So the theoretical probabilities of two heads, two tails, and one of each are 0.25, 0.25 and 0.50 respectively.

Second coin

	Head(H)	Tail(T)
Head(H)	H+H	H+T
Tail(T)	T+H	T+T

First coin

(a) outcomes from tossing two coins

Second die

+	1	2	3	4	5	6
1	2	3	4	5	6	7
2	3	4	5	6	7	8
3	4	5	6	7	8	9
4	5	6	7	8	9	10
5	6	7	8	9	10	11
6	7	8	9	10	11	12

First die

(b) outcomes from throwing two dice

FIGURE 21.1 *Two-way tables for an experiment with two independent events.*

With experiments involving two independent events, such as tossing two coins or throwing two dice, a useful device for listing all the possible outcomes is a two-way table. Figure 21.1a is such a table, showing the four possible outcomes from tossing two coins.

Figure 21.1b similarly gives all 36 possible outcomes of the total sum from throwing both die A and die B. From this table we can discover, for example, that the probability of scoring seven (7 occurs 6 times out of 36: 6/36 = 0.17 approximately) is much higher than scoring eleven (11 occurs 2 times out of 36: 2/36 = 0.06 approximately).

Check yourself:

21.1 What is the most appropriate way to determine the probability that:

(a) a chalkboard eraser will land handle side up when tossed in the air?
(b) a Canadian age 50–59 years has two living parents?
(c) the total score will be an even number when two dice are thrown?

21.2 What is the probability that a word chosen at random in this book will have fewer than six letters in it?

21.3 If Jamie throws a dodecahedron die (one with twelve faces, numbered one through twelve):

(a) What is the probability that she will score a number with two digits?
(b) What is the probability that she will score a number with one digit?

21.4 Look at Figure 21.1b. When two conventional dice (with six faces, numbered one through six) are thrown, what is the probability of:

(a) scoring a multiple of 3?
(b) scoring a multiple of 4?
(c) scoring a number that is a multiple of 3 or 4 (or both)?

21.5 Patrice throws two conventional dice. Write down an outcome that has a probability of 0, and another that has a probability of 1.

➤ Teaching suggestions

1. Introduce probability by getting students to write down events that may occur in the next 12 months and then to rank them from least likely to most likely. Use this opportunity to introduce some of the language of probability, particularly *more likely than* and *less likely than*.

2. Ask the students to describe events that might occur using labels such as *impossible, nearly impossible, not very likely, even, fairly likely, almost certain*, and *certain*.

3. Introduce the idea of measuring probability on a numerical scale by subjectively assigning points out of 100 (percentages) to various events that might occur; work with the students to change the percentages to decimals. Then use these to introduce the probability scale from 0 to 1.

4. Introduce students to the idea of relative frequency, expressed as a percentage and as a decimal, using statistical data they have gathered themselves as part of a purposeful inquiry.

5. Explain to the students how to apply the idea of relative frequency to the outcomes of experiments, interpreting these as estimates of probability.

6. Give students opportunities to compare their intuitive estimates of the probabilities of various outcomes from an experiment with the estimates of probabilities obtained by repeating that experiment a large number of times.

7. By using theoretical arguments based on symmetry, emphasize the importance of identifying equally likely outcomes.

8. Let students compare probabilities determined theoretically with the results of performing experiments a large number of times.

9. Emphasize the idea that probability does not tell anyone anything about what will actually happen next but predicts what will happen in the long run.

10. Although an obvious application of probability is to betting and lotteries, be aware that some parents hold strong views about gambling, so handle this subject in a way that is sensitive to different perspectives on the morality and acceptability of gambling as a pastime.

Algebra

Students should learn to explore number sequences, explaining patterns and using simple relationships; and to interpret, generalize and use simple mappings related to numerical, spatial, or practical situations, expressed initially in words and then in letters as symbols.

THIS CHAPTER EXPLAINS:
- the difference in the meaning of letters used as abbreviations in arithmetic and as used in algebra;
- the idea of a letter representing a variable;
- some other differences between arithmetic thinking and algebraic thinking;
- the order of operators;
- ways of introducing variables to students;
- the important role played by tabulation;
- the ideas of sequential and global generalization;
- independent and dependent variables;
- the meaning of the word mapping in an algebraic context; and
- the usefulness of the trial-and-improvement method for solving equations arising from problems.

Introduction to variables

To explore the concept of variable, two problems are posed using letters as symbols. Write down answers to these problems before each Thinking it through section.

Example 22A

Lise can get 5 francs to the dollar. She has D dollars. She exchanges this money for F francs. What is the relationship between D and F?

Thinking it through

Most people write down $5F = D$ (or $F = 1D$ or $D = F$ or $1D = F$, which are all different ways of saying the same thing). The correct answer is actually $F = 5D$. The table in Figure 22.1a shows various values for D and F. For example, if Lise has 1 dollar ($D = 1$) she can exchange this for 5 francs ($F = 5$); if she has 2 dollars ($D = 2$), she can exchange this for 10 francs ($F = 10$). Similarly, when $D = 3$, $F = 15$, and so on. The table makes it clear that whatever number is chosen for D (1, 2, 3,...) the value of F is 5 times this number (5, 10, 15,...). This is precisely what is meant by the algebraic statement, $F = 5D$.

Even people who are apparently quite well qualified in mathematics often get this equation wrong when this problem is given to them, so it is instructive to analyze the thinking that leads to this misunderstanding. Those who write down $5F = D$ may be thinking that they are writing a statement that says, 5 francs makes a dollar. They are using the F and D as abbreviations for *franc* and *dollar*. This is, of course, how we use letters in arithmetic, when they are actually abbreviations for fixed quantities or measurements. When we write 10 g or 5 m, the g stands for "a gram" and the m stands for "a meter." Letters used in algebra are not abbreviations for measurements. They do not represent a thing or an object. They are variables. The letter D in Example 22A stands for "whatever number of dollars you choose." It does not stand for a dollar but for the number of dollars.

No. of dollars	No. of francs
D	**F**
1	5
2	10
3	15
4	20
5	25

No. of teachers	No. of students
T	**S**
1	20
2	40
3	60
4	80
5	100

(a)   (b)

FIGURE 22.1 *Tabulating values for Examples 22A and 22B*

Example 22B

S is the number of students in a school and T is the number of teachers. The school has 20 times as many students as teachers. Write down an equation using S relating T.

Thinking it through

The relationship between S and T here is not $20S = T$. Those who write this down may think that what they are saying is, 20 students for 1 teacher, using the S to stand for "a student" and T to stand for "a teacher." Again, we see the same misunderstanding. S and T are not abbreviations for a student and a teacher. They stand, respectively, for "the number of students" and "the number of teachers." They are variables. T can be any number, and whatever number is chosen, S is 20 times this number. So the correct algebraic relationship is $S = 20T$. This means the number of students is 20 times the number of teachers or, referring to the tabulation of values in Figure 22.1, the number in column S is 20 times whatever number is in column T.

That so many people get the algebraic statements in these problems wrong is understandable. The choice of D, F, S, T as letters to represent the variables in the problems is actually confusing. Using the first letters of the words *dollar*, *franc*, *student* and *teacher* does rather suggest that they are abbreviations for these things. (Fewer people get these relationships incorrect if other letters such as N and M, are used for the variables.)

This confusion is introduced early in too many algebra lessons. Many people have been subjected to explanations that reinforce the misconception that the letters stand for things. For example, it does not help to explain $2a + 3a = 5a$ by saying 2 apples plus 3 apples makes 5 apples. That statement makes students think of a as an abbreviation for apples. What is actually meant is, whatever number is chosen for a, then a multiplied by 2 plus a multiplied by 3 is the same as a multiplied by 5.

What are some of the other differences between the ways symbols are used in arithmetic and in algebra?

The distinction between the meaning of letters used in algebra (as variables) and in arithmetic (as abbreviations) is one of the most crucial differences between these two branches of mathematics. But teachers should be aware of a number of other significant differences:
  • the use of the equals sign;
  • the need to recognize the mathematical structure of a problem;
  • the distinction between solving a problem and representing it; and
  • the need to recognize what is called the *precedence of operators*.

Doesn't the equals sign always means the same thing?

What the equals sign means in strictly mathematical terms is not necessarily the same thing as the way it is interpreted in practice. When doing arithmetic — that is, manipulating numbers — students mostly think of the equals sign as an instruction to do something with some numbers, to perform an operation. They see $3 + 5 =$ and respond by doing something: that is, adding the 3 and the 5 to get 8. So, given the question, $3 + \square = 5$, many younger students put 8 in the box; they see the equals sign as an instruction to perform an operation on the numbers in the question and respond to the plus sign by adding them up.

Students may also use the equals sign simply as a device for connecting the calculation they have performed with the result of the calculation, as meaning, this is what I did and this is what I got… . Given the problem, you have $28, earn $5 and spend $8, how much do you have now?, many students will quite happily write something like, $28 + 5 = 33 - 8 = 25$. We may object to this way of recording the calculations, arguing that $28 + 5$ does not equal $33 - 8$. But that is not what the student means. What is written down accurately represents the student's thinking about the problem, or the buttons he or she has pressed on a calculator to solve it: like, "I added 28 and 5, and got the answer 33, and then I subtracted 8 and this came to 25."

In algebra, however, the equals sign usually represents equivalence — that what is written on one side is the same as what is written on the other side. Of course, it has this meaning in arithmetic as well; $3 + 5 = 8$ does mean that $3 + 5$ is the same as 8. But students rarely use it to mean this; their experience reinforces the perception of the equals sign as an instruction to perform an operation with some numbers.

In algebraic statements it is the idea of *equivalence* that is strongest in the way the equals sign is used. For example, the equation $p + q = r$ is not actually an instruction to add p and q. In fact, we may not have to do anything at all with the equation. It is simply a statement of equivalence between one variable and a combination of two others.

> In algebraic statments, it is the idea of equivalence that is strongest in the way the equals sign is used.

How is the mathematical structure of a problem recognized in arithmetic and algebra?

In arithmetic, students often succeed through adopting informal, intuitive, context-bound approaches to solving problems. Often they can be successful without being explicitly aware of the underlying mathematical structure. For example, many students are able to solve the problem, how much does it cost for 10 g of chocolate if you can get 2 g per penny? without recognizing the formal structure of the problem as that of division. But even with a calculator, they may then be unable to solve the same problem with more difficult numbers such as, how much does it cost for 750 g of chocolate if you can get 135 g per dollar?

The corresponding algebraic problem is a generalization of all problems with this same structure: how much for A grams of chocolate if you can get B grams per penny? Trying to explain this problem by putting in some simple numbers for A and B and asking what has to be done to these numbers to answer the question is often useless, because the students do not recognize the existence of a division structure here at all. The primitive, intuitive thinking about the arithmetic problem with simple numbers does not make the mathematical structure explicit in a way that supports the algebraic generalization $A \div B$.

It is partly because of this frequent confusion that we have put so much stress on the structures of addition, subtraction, multiplication, and division in Chapters 4, 6, 8 and 10 and that we encourage the frequent use of the question "what is the calculation you enter on a calculator to answer this?" as a device for making the mathematical structure explicit.

What is the distinction between solving a problem and representing it?

The discussion above leads us to a further significant difference between arithmetic and algebra. Given an arithmetic problem to solve that involves more than one operation, the question we ask ourselves is, what sequence of operations is needed to solve this problem? In algebra, the question is, what sequence of operations is needed to represent this problem? For example, consider the following.

Example 22C

A plumber's initial charge is $55 and then the customer pays $45 an hour. How many hours work would yield a bill of $190?

Thinking it through

The arithmetic thinking here might be: $190 - 55 = 135$ and then $135 \div 45 = 3$. Therefore, the number of hours of work is 3. That is the sequence of operations required to solve the problem. The algebraic approach is to let N represent the number of hours (which is, therefore, a variable and can take any value) and then to write $45N + 55 = 190$. This is the sequence of operations that represents the problem. To solve the problem, we have to find the value of N that makes this algebraic equation true.

It is quite possible that the two approaches, as illustrated here, result in the use of inverse operations. To solve the problem using arithmetic methods, we perform subtraction and then division, but to represent the problem algebraically, we think multiplication and then addition. It is this kind of difference in thinking that makes it so difficult for many students to make generalized statements using words or algebraic symbols, even of the simplest kind.

What is meant by *precedence of operators*?

A statement such as 3 + 5 × 2 is potentially ambiguous. If we do the addition first, the answer is 16. But if we do the multiplication first the answer is 13.

Which answer is correct? If we enter this calculation on a basic calculator, the answer is 16. The calculator does the operations in the order they are entered. However, if we use a more advanced, scientific calculator, with the same key sequence, we get the answer 13. These calculators use what is called an *algebraic operating system* (as do many computer applications, such as spreadsheet programs). In other words, they adopt the convention of *giving precedence to the operations of multiplication and division*. So, when we enter 3 + 5 on such a calculator, it waits to determine whether there is a multiplication or a division operation following the 5. If there is one, it is done first. If we actually mean to do the addition first, we would have to use parentheses to indicate this: (3 + 5) × 2, which can also be written as 2(3 + 5), with the multiplication sign omitted but understood.

This convention of precedence of operators is always applied strictly in algebra and is essential for avoiding ambiguity, particularly because of the way symbols are used to represent problems, not just to solve them. So, for example, A + B × C (which is usually written A + BC, with the understanding that BC means B × C) stands for B multiplied by C and then add A; whereas to represent A added to B, and then multiply by C we write (A + B) C. This is usually written C(A + B).

But in arithmetic and therefore in number work in elementary schools, we do not need this convention. The calculations we have to do should always arise from a practical context that naturally determines the order in which the various operations have to be performed, so ambiguity is rare. And since the basic calculators used in elementary schools deal with operations in the order they arrive, there is little point in giving students calculations such as 3 + 5 × 2 and insisting they must do the multiplication first.

As soon as we get into using algebra to express generalizations, however, we need this convention for the order of operators. Students have to learn to recognize it and to use parentheses as necessary to make the order of operations clear.

How can variables be introduced to students?

The central principle in algebra is the use of letters to represent variables, enabling the expression of generalizations. Students should first encounter the use of letters as algebraic symbols for this purpose.

The most effective way of introducing them is through the tabulation of number patterns in columns, with the problem being to express the pattern, first in words and later in symbols. A useful game in this context is What's My Rule? Figure 22.2 shows some examples. In each case the teacher challenges the students first to state the rule being used to find the numbers in column B and then to use this rule to find the number in column B when the number in column A is 100.

For the example in Figure 22.2a, students usually observe first that the rule is for the pattern adding 2. But older elementary school students can usually determine that when the number in A is 100, the number in B is 201, which helps them to recognize that the rule is actually double and add 1.

Later this rule can be expressed algebraically as $B = A \times 2 + 1$, or $B = 2A + 1$. This statement clearly uses the idea of letters as variables and expresses a generalization. The statement means essentially, "the number in column B is the number in column A multiplied by 2, plus 1." Similarly, in Figure 22.2b, the pattern in column B, add 4, is easily determined. What is more difficult to find is its calculation rule: multiply by 4 and subtract 1, although again working out what is in *B* when 100 is in *A* helps to make this rule explicit. This leads to the algebraic statement, $B = A \times 4 - 1$, or $B = 4A - 1$. In this kind of equation, where *A* is chosen and a rule is used to determine *B*, we call *A* an *independent variable* and *B* a *dependent variable*.

A	B
1	3
2	5
3	7
4	9
5	11
6	13
7	15
8	17
9	19
10	21
100	?

(a)

A	B
1	3
2	7
3	11
4	15
5	19
6	23
7	27
8	31
9	35
10	39
100	?

(b)

A	B
1	3
2	8
3	13
4	18
5	23
6	28
7	33
8	38
9	43
10	48
100	?

(c)

A	B
1	99
2	98
3	97
4	96
5	95
6	94
7	93
8	92
9	91
10	90
100	?

(d)

FIGURE 22.2 *What's My Rule?*

The experience of tabulation and finding generalizations to describe the patterns occurs often in mathematical investigations, particularly those involving a sequence of geometric shapes, such as those discussed in Chapter 14 (see, for example, Figures 14.3 and 14.4).

Example 22D

If 6 children can sit around a rectangular table, how many children can sit around various numbers of tables arranged side by side?

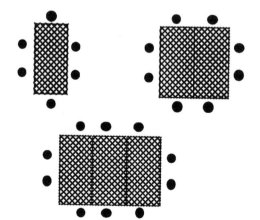

number of tables	number of children
X	Y
1	6
2	8
3	10
4	
5	
6	
7	
8	
9	
10	
100	?

FIGURE 22.3 *An investigation leading to a generalization*

Thinking it through

The number of tables is the independent variable, and the number of children the dependent variable. With 2 tables, we can seat 8 children; with 3 tables, we can seat 10. These results are already tabulated in Figure 22.3. The tabulation can then be completed for other numbers of tables. The answer for 100 tables can be predicted, first in words and then in symbols, with *X* representing the independent variable (the number of tables) and *Y* the dependent variable (the number of children). Completing the table is left as an exercise in Question 22.6 of the Check Yourself section toward the end of the chapter.

What is a mapping?

The examples of tabulation used above all have three components:

1. a set of input numbers (the values of the independent variable),
2. a rule for doing something to these numbers, and
3. a set of output numbers (the values of the dependent variable).

These three components put together constitute what is sometimes called a *mapping*.

Sometimes we are given the input and the rule, and we have to find the output; this process is *substituting into a formula*. Sometimes we are given the input and the output, and the task is to find the rule; this process is *generalizing* (as in the examples of tabulation above). Finally, we can be given the output and the rule and be asked to find the input; this process is *solving an equation*.

What are some methods of solving equations in elementary schools?

Elementary school students should be introduced to solving equations in a manner that reinforces the idea that the letters stand for variables, rather than things or specific numbers. An appropriate approach is to introduce students to the algebraic thinking involved in solving problems through a trial-and-improvement method (see Chapter 14). We can use purely numerical problems, which cannot be solved by simple arithmetic procedures, such as finding square roots and cube roots, as explained in Chapter 14. They can also be practical problems, such as finding areas and perimeters.

Example 22E

A garden is to comprise a patio that is 5 m wide and a square lawn. What should be the length of the side of the lawn if the area of the whole garden is to be 200 m²?

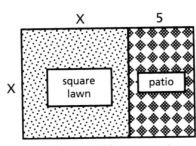

Total area = 200 square metres

side of lawn	area of garden
X	**Y**
20	500
10	150
13	234
11	176
12	204
11.9	201.111
11.8	198.24
11.85	199.6725
etc....	

FIGURE 22.4 *A problem solved by trial and improvement*

Thinking it through

This problem can be approached by trying various inputs for the side of the square and using an appropriate rule to determine the outputs (the corresponding area of the garden). One possible rule is: add 5 to the side of the square and multiply by the side of the square. Expressed in symbols, this rule is $X(X+5)$ so we are actually solving the equation $X(X+5) = 200$.

The first trial is with $X = 20$; it yields 500 (an area of 500 m^2) which is too large. Next we try 10, which gives an area of 150 m^2, which is too small. So we try something in between — say, $X = 13$, which gives an area of 234 m^2, which is too large. We continue this process until we get whatever accuracy we require.

The point about solving equations this way is that the letter involved (X standing for the side of the square) is genuinely perceived as a variable, and our task is to find the value of X that generates the required value for the dependent variable. This concept is much more sophisticated and powerful than the idea that X stands for an unknown number.

Check yourself

22.1 The length of a garden is M meters. Measured in centimeters, it is C centimeters long. What is the relationship between M and C? What criticism could you make of the form of this question?

22.2 If Hari can buy A apples at 30 cents each and B bananas at 42 cents each, what is the meaning of

(a) $A + B$?   (b) $30A$?   (c) $42B$?
(d) $30A + 42B$?

What criticism could you make of the form of this question?

22.3 The first 5 rides in a fair are free. The charge for all the other rides is $3 each. If Wing-y has $12 to spend, how many rides can she have? What are the arithmetic steps used in answering this question? How can the problem be represented algebraically, using N to represent the number of rides?

22.4 What answer do we get if we enter 25 – 5 x 3 on:

(a) a basic calculator?
(b) a scientific calculator that uses an algebraic operating system?

22.5 For each of Figures 22.2c and 22.2d, write down

(a) the sequential generalization
(b) the value of B when A is 100
(c) the global generalization in words

22.6 Complete the tabulation of results in Figure 22.3. Write down:

(a) the number of children if there are 100 tables
(b) the general rule in words

Now repeat this investigation assuming the tables are arranged end to end, rather than side by side.

22.7 Choose a number, double it, add 3, and multiply the answer by our number. The result is 3654. What is our number? Use a calculator and the trial-and-improvement method to answer this question. What equation have you solved?

➤Teaching suggestions

1. Use the What's My Rule? game to introduce students to algebraic thinking through making generalizations, first in words and then in symbols.

2. Tabulate results in an orderly fashion; predict the result for a large number, such as 100; articulate the general rule in symbols.

3. Reinforce algebraic thinking with tabulated results from investigations, having students find patterns in the sequence of numbers obtained.

4. Avoid the fruit-salad approach to explaining algebraic statements. Never refer to $3a + 5b$ as 3 *apples* and 5 *bananas*, or use any words that reinforce the idea that the letters stand for objects or specific numbers.

5. Emphasize the idea that a letter in algebra stands for *whatever number is chosen* — that is, a variable.

6. Reinforce, through language, the idea that the equals sign means is the same as, even in the early stages of recording the results of calculations.

7. Ask students, what is the calculation you would enter on a calculator to solve this problem? to help make explicit the underlying structures of problems (see Chapters 4, 6, 8, and 10).

8. Do not worry about precedence of operators when problem solving. The context giving rise to the calculation will determine the appropriate sequence of operations.

9. Use order of operations when introducing algebraic notation. Explain the different systems used by various calculators and show the need for brackets when some rules are written algebraically.

10. To reinforce the concept of a variable, use trial-and-improvement methods, with a calculator, to solve equations arising from practical or numerical problems.

23

Coordinates..............

Students should learn to use coordinates to specify location and to recognize the number relationships between coordinates in the first quadrant of related points on a line or in a shape.

THIS CHAPTER EXPLAINS:
- how the coordinate system enables us to specify location in a plane;
- axis, x-coordinate and y-coordinate origin;
- the meaning of quadrant in the context of coordinates;
- the difference between the coordinate system for labeling points in a plane and other systems that label spaces;
- some of the ways in which the coordinate system enables us to connect algebraic and geometric relationships;
- how to plot an algebraic relationship as a graph; and
- linear relationships, including those in which one variable is directly proportional to another.

What is meant by *coordinates in the first quadrant*?

The coordinate system is an elegant device for specifying location in two dimensions. Two number lines are drawn at right angles to each other, as shown in Figure 23.1. These are called *axes* (plural of *axis*). Of course, the lines can continue as far as we wish at either end. The point where the two lines meet (called the *origin*) is taken as the zero for both number lines. The horizontal line is called the *x-axis*, and the vertical line the *y-axis*. Then any point in the plane can be specified by two numbers, called its *coordinates*. The x coordinate of a point is the distance moved along the x-axis, and the y coordinate is the distance moved vertically, in order to get from the origin to the point in question. In Figure 23.1, for example, to reach point P, we move 3 units along the x-axis and 4 units vertically, so the x coordinate of P is 3 and the y coordinate is 4. We then state that the coordinates of P are (3,4). The convention is always to give the x coordinate first and the y coordinate second.

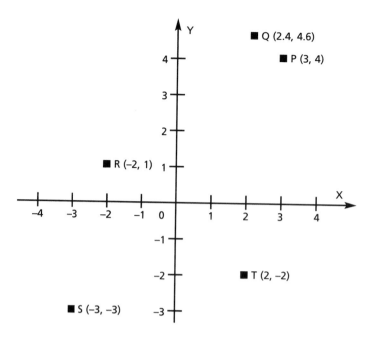

FIGURE 23.1 *The coordinate system*

The axes divide the plane into four sections, called *quadrants*. The first quadrant consists of all the points that have a positive number for each of their two coordinates. The points *P* and *Q* in Figure 23.1 are in the first quadrant. The point *R* (−2,1) is in the second quadrant, *S* (−3, −3) in the third quadrant, and *T* (2, −2) in the fourth quadrant.

> The axes divide the plane into four sections, called quadrants.

The beauty of this system is that we can now refer specifically to any point in the plane. And, of course, we are not limited to integers, as is shown by the point *Q*, which has coordinates (2.4, 4.6).

The coordinate system can be used to describe the movement from one point to another. For example, from *R* to *P* is a movement of 5 units in the positive *x* direction and 3 units in the positive *y* direction; from *T* to *S* is a movement of −5 in the negative *x* direction and −1 in the negative *y* direction.

> An important feature of the coordinate system is that it is the points in the plane, not the spaces between them, that are labeled by the coordinates.

An important feature of the coordinate system is that it is the points in the plane, not the spaces, that are labeled by the coordinates. This convention is similar to the one noted in Chapter 19 with reference to Figure 19.2b, where the numbers on the vertical axis labeled the points on the scale, not the spaces between them.

This convention is important to explain in teaching because students often encounter situations with coordinate systems that are based on labeling the spaces. For example, many board games, computer games, city street maps, and computer spreadsheets label the spaces. A system often employed in these and other similar examples is to use the labels for the columns (A, B, C,...) and the labels for the rows (1, 2, 3,...) to specify individual cells or squares (such as B3). Moving from this kind of labeling of spaces to the labeling of points is a significant step in the development of the idea of the coordinate system used to display algebraic relationships.

How do coordinates help us to understand number relationships and geometry?

The system described above is sometimes called the *Cartesian coordinate system*. It takes its name from René Descartes (1596-1650), a prodigious French mathematician who first made use of the system to connect geometry and algebra. He discovered that by interpreting the inputs and outputs from an algebraic mapping (see Chapter 22) as coordinates and then plotting these as points, we can generate a geometric picture of the relationship. By the reverse process, starting with a geometric picture drawn on a coordinate system, we can generate an algebraic representation of geometric properties. At the elementary school level, we can only touch on these massive mathematical ideas, so a couple of examples will suffice.

First, we can take any simple algebraic relationship of the kind considered in Chapter 22 and explore the corresponding geometric picture. The convention is to use the *x*-axis for the independent variable. For example, the table shown in Figure 22.2a is generated by the algebraic rule, $B = 2A + 1$.

In this case, *A* is the appropriate variable to be represented by the *x*-axis. The pairs of values in the table can be written as coordinates, as follows: (1, 3), (2, 5), (3, 7), and so on. When these are plotted, as shown in Figure 23.2a, they clearly lie on a straight line. These points can then be joined and the line continued indefinitely, as shown in Figure 23.2b.

This straight line is a powerful geometric image of the way in which the two variables, *A* and *B*, are related. An algebraic rule that produces a straight-line graph is called a *linear relationship*. We can use the straight-line graph to read off values of *B* for values of *A* other than those plotted; for example, the arrow in Figure 23.2b shows that when $A = 3.5$, $B = 8$.

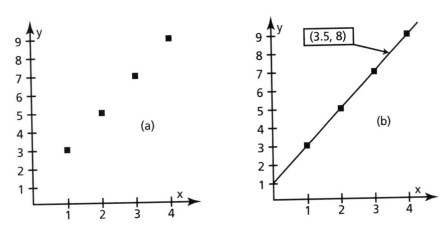

FIGURE 23.2 *The rule B = 2A + 1 represented by coordinates*

Using this process to explore various algebraic rules leads us to recognize a linear relationship as one in which the rule is simply a combination of multiplying or dividing by a fixed number and addition or subtraction. For example, all the following rules are linear relationships:

multiply by 7 and subtract 5 $y = 7x - 5$
divide by 6 and add 4 $y = x/6 + 4$
multiply by 3 and subtract from 100 $y = 100 - 3x$
add 1 and multiply everything by 2 $y = 2(x + 1)$

There are, of course, nonlinear relationships. They reflect other kinds of rules; for example, those involving squaring (multiply the input by itself) and other powers (cubes and so on) that produce sets of coordinates that do not lie on straight lines. These non-linear relationships are beyond the scope of this book.

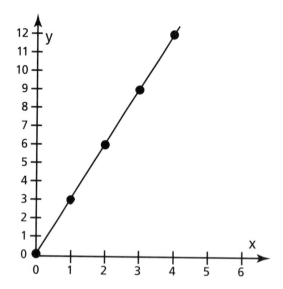

FIGURE 23.3 *The variable* y *is directly proportional to* x

The simplest kind of linear relationship is one in which y is directly proportional to x. This means that y is obtained by multiplying x by a constant factor. Examples of this kind of relationship abound in everyday life. If a liter of juice costs $3.00, x is the number of liters purchased, and y is the total cost in dollars, then the relationship for y is $y = 3x$. This rule generates the coordinates

> The simplest kind of linear relationship is one in which y is directly proportional to x.

(1, 3), (2, 6), (3, 9), and so on, including the possibility that no juice is purchased (0, 0). As shown in Figure 23.3, this rule produces a straight-line graph that, noting again the significance of the (0, 0) possibility, passes through the origin.

Any rule in which y is directly proportional to x, such as $y = 7x$, $y = 0.5x$, $y = 2.75x$, produces a straight-line graph passing through the origin.

An interesting point for discussion relates to situations that involve a discrete variable, one that cannot be broken into pieces. Consider the numbers of bottles of wine someone buys at $9 per bottle. The algebraic rule is a linear relationship: $y = 9x$. But in this case, x is a discrete variable and the points on the line between the whole number values do not have any meaning. We cannot purchase 2.6 bottles of wine.

How are coordinates used to investigate a geometric property?

Using coordinates, we can communicate to someone else a geometric shape that is made up of straight lines. For example, we can ask a class of students to plot the points (1, 2), (3, 2), (3, 6), and (1, 6) and then to join these points producing the rectangle *ABCD* in Figure 23.4. The corners *A*, *B*, *C*, and *D* are called the rectangle's *vertices* (each one is a *vertex*). Similarly, rectangle *PQRS* is produced by plotting (5, 2), (9, 4), (8, 6), and (4, 4).

This exercise raises a question: what rules or numerical patterns determine the coordinates of the four vertices of a rectangle? Notice that the movement from *P* to *S* (−1 in the *x* direction, 2 in the *y* direction) is the same as that from *Q* to *R*; *S* to *R* and *P* to *Q* are also identical. A particularly interesting rule relates the coordinates of opposite vertices. (We leave the reader to discover it; see Question 23.4 in the Check Yourself section below.)

In this way, we can analyze geometric properties, such as the characteristics of a rectangle, by means of algebraic relationships. The potential for exploring the connection between algebraic and geometric relationships makes the coordinate system a fundamental part of mathematics at every level.

> The potential for exploring the connection between algebraic and geometric relationships makes the coordinate system a fundamental part of mathematics at every level.

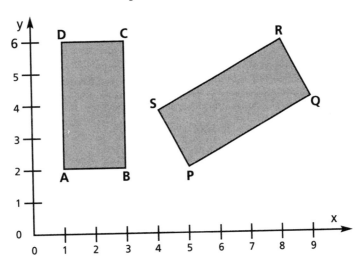

FIGURE 23.4 *Using coordinates to draw rectangles*

Check yourself

23.1 In chess, a knight's move is two steps horizontally (left or right) and one step vertically (up or down), or two steps vertically and one step horizontally. Starting at (3,3), which points can a knight reach in one move? Plot them on graph paper and join.

23.2 On graph paper, plot some of the points corresponding to each of panels b, c, and d in Figure 22.2. Are the algebraic rules here linear relationships?

23.3 Give an example of a variable that is directly proportional to each of the following independent variables:

(a) the number of cartons of eggs purchased, with six eggs in each carton
(b) the number of dollars exchanged at a bank for some foreign currency
(c) the bottom number in a set of equivalent fractions

23.4 Plot the three points (1, 2), (0, 3), and (3, 6) on graph paper. Join them and find the fourth point needed to complete a rectangle. Using this example and the two rectangles in Figure 23.4, state the rule for connecting the coordinates of opposite vertices of a rectangle. Use this rule to determine the fourth vertex of a rectangle if the first three vertices are (4, 4), (5, 8), and (13, 6). Check your answer by plotting the points and joining them.

23.5 Plot the following points and join them in order to form a rectangle: A $(0, 0)$, B $(4, 0)$, C $(4, 3)$, and D $(0, 3)$. Now keep A and B fixed but change C and D by adding 1 to each of their x-coordinates. What happens to the shape? Repeat this procedure and produce another shape. Repeat this procedure a third time. The shapes you are making are all examples of parallelograms. What relationships can you suggest for connecting the coordinates of the four vertices of a parallelogram? Use these relationships to find the fourth vertex if the first three are $(1, 1)$, $(4, 2)$, and $(4,4)$.

➤ Teaching suggestions

1. Explain carefully to students the use of coordinates to specify the location of points in a plane, rather than spaces as in street maps.
2. Give students experience of activities in which they use the coordinate system to describe movements from one point to another.
3. In looking at coordinates with elementary school students, work in other quadrants. The principles are the same in the other quadrants, and exploring them can provide some useful experience of interpreting and applying negative numbers.
4. Have students interpret, as sets of coordinates, tables of values obtained by exploring algebraic relationships (as in Chapter 22). Plot these coordinates and discuss the results.
5. Investigate with the students whether or not particular relationships produce straight-line graphs when plotted as coordinates.
6. When a real-life relationship produces a straight-line graph, discuss with the students whether or not the points between those plotted have meaning.
7. Show students how relationships in which one variable is directly proportional to another can be shown as a straight-line graph passing through the origin.
8. Give students opportunities to analyze simple properties of geometric shapes, such as rectangles and parallelograms, by looking for patterns and rules in the coordinates of their vertices.

Measurement

Students should learn to choose appropriate standard units of length, mass, capacity, and time; to make sensible estimates with them in everyday situations; and to convert one metric unit to another.

THIS CHAPTER EXPLAINS:
- the role of comparison and ordering as a foundation for measurement;
- the principle of transitivity in the context of measurement;
- conservation of length, mass, and liquid volume;
- nonstandard and standard units;
- the idea that all measurement is approximate;
- the difference between a ratio scale and an interval scale;
- the distinction between mass and weight;
- the distinction between volume and capacity;
- two aspects of the concept of time: time interval and recorded time;
- SI and other metric units of length, mass, volume, and time, including the use of prefixes; and
- the importance of estimation and the use of reference items.

What principles are central to teaching measurement to elementary school students?

Several principles are central to learning about measurement. They include: comparison and ordering; transitivity; conservation; nonstandard and standard units; approximation; a context for developing number concepts; and the meaning of zero.

Comparison and ordering

First, the foundation of all aspects of measurement is *direct comparison*: putting two and then more than two objects (or events) in order according to the attribute in question. The language of comparison, discussed in relation to subtraction in Chapter 6, is of central importance here. Two objects are placed side by side, and students determine which is the longer, which is the shorter. Two items are placed in the pans of a balance, and students determine which is the heavier, which is the lighter. Water is poured from one container to another to determine which holds more, which holds less. Two students perform a specified task, starting simultaneously, and observe which takes a longer time, which takes a shorter time.

Notice that this stage involves no units, only direct comparison that leads to putting two or more objects or events in order. (Recall that the first stage of learning about probability in Chapter 21 employed this same procedure: simply comparing two or more events and deciding which was more likely or less likely than which.)

Transitivity

An important mathematical principle here is that of *transitivity*. Chapter 13 demonstrated this mathematical property applied to the relationships "is a multiple of" (illustrated in Figure 13.1) and "is a factor of" (illustrated in Figure 13.3). Figure 24.1 illustrates the principle of transitivity more generally, but does it always hold true? If we know that A is related to B (as indicated by an arrow) and B is related to C, is it a logical consequence that A is related to C?. With some kinds of relationships, such as "is a factor of", it does follow logically, and we can draw the arrow connecting A to C. In other cases, however, the same consequence does not follow. For example, the relationship "is a mirror image of" can be applied to a set of shapes; if shape A is a mirror image of shape B, and B is a mirror image of shape C, then it is not true that A must automatically be a mirror image of C. So this relationship is not transitive.

We can now see that whenever we compare two objects or events using a measuring attribute such as their lengths, their masses, their capacities, or their duration, then we are making use of a transitive relationship. The arrows used in Figure 24.1 could represent any one of the measuring relationships used to compare two objects or events, such as: "is longer than," "is lighter than," "holds more than," or "takes less time than." In each case, because A is related to B and B is related to C, then it follows logically that A is related to C.

This principle of transitivity is fundamental to ordering a set of more than two objects or events. Once we know A is greater than B and B is greater than C, for example, it is this principle that allows us not to have to check A against C. Grasping this principle is a significant step in the development of students' understanding of measurement. The teacher should explain however, that although transitivity is frequent, it does not exist in all kinds of relationships.

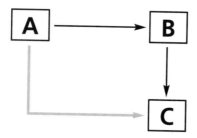

FIGURE 24.1 *The transitive property*

Conservation

The principle of conservation is another fundamental idea in learning about measurement of length, mass, and liquid volume. Students meet this principle first in the context of conservation of number. They have to learn, for example, that if they rearrange a set of counters in different ways, they do not alter the number of counters. Similarly, if two objects are the same length, each remains that length when one is moved to a new position. This is the principle of *conservation of length.*

Students experience *conservation of mass* when they balance two lumps of Plasticine, rearrange each lump in some way (such as breaking one up into small pieces and molding the other into some shape or other), and then check that they still balance. *Conservation of liquid* volume is more difficult for many children to grasp. When they empty the water from one container into another that is differently shaped, as shown in Figure 24.2, they tend to focus their attention on the heights of the liquid in the containers and thus have trouble with the idea that the volume of water has not been changed by the transformation. One way to convince them is to pour the water back into the original container. (This experiment is often easier to carry out with sand, rice, or some other material that flows freely but does not spill easily and thus lose volume.)

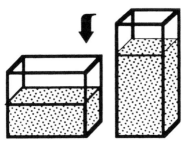

FIGURE 24.2 *Conservation of liquid volume*

Nonstandard and standard units

Fundamental to the idea of measuring is the use of a *unit*, which is a quantity in which other quantities can be expressed. Grams, meters, liters, and hours are a few of the measurement units common in everyday life. Notice that these examples are all standard units: each is officially and carefully defined so that a meter in Vancouver is the same length as a meter in Los Angeles, in Paris, or in Melbourne.

Using nonstandard units to introduce the idea of measuring in units is a well-established tradition in teaching elementary school mathematics. For example, students can measure the length of items of furniture in hand spans, the mass of a book in erasers, and the capacity of a container in drinking cups. Many adults use nonstandard units of length in everyday life, especially when making measurements for practical jobs around the house and garden.

The value of this approach is that students get experience in measuring in units by using familiar, nonthreatening objects and words first, rather than going directly into mysterious things called milliliters and grams.

A nonstandard unit is often a size more appropriate than a standard unit for early measuring experiences. For example, most of the things around the classroom that students may want to measure have a mass of several hundred grams. For practical purposes, the gram is a very small mass to begin with, and the kilogram is far too large. Erasers and glue sticks are much more appropriate sizes of units for measuring mass in the early stages.

Eventually, of course, students must learn about standard units. The experience of working with nonstandard units often makes this need explicit; for example, when two students measure the length of the hall in paces, they are likely to get different answers.

Approximation

The next major principle of measurement is that nearly all measurements are approximate. When we measure length, mass, time, or capacity, all we can ever achieve is a measurement to the nearest something. How close we come depends on the level of accuracy of our measuring device.

The principle of measuring to the nearest something and the associated language (see Chapter 12 for a discussion on rounding) should be introduced to elementary school students from the earliest stages. Even when they measure in nonstandard units, they will encounter this idea when determining that the length of the table is nearly 9 hand spans, about 9 hand spans or between 8 and 9 hand spans.

Development of number concepts

Throughout this book, we stress the central importance of measurement experiences as a context for developing number concepts. We use measurement problems and situations to reinforce ideas such as place value (Chapter 2), the various structures for the four operations (Chapters 4, 6, 8, and 10) and calculations with decimals (Chapter 17).

Ratio scales and interval scales

Measurements such as length can be compared in the form of *ratio scales*. For example, if a student is 90 cm tall and an adult is 180 cm tall, we can say that the adult is twice as tall as the student. Similarly, we can compare masses, capacities and time intervals by ratio.

Measurements such as recorded time are different. It makes no sense to compare, say, 6 o'clock with 2 o'clock by saying that one is three times the other. This is an example of what is called an *interval scale*, on which comparisons can be made only by reference to the difference (the *interval*) between two measurements. We can, for example, say that 6 o'clock is four hours later than 2 o'clock. Of course, we can compare the measurements on a ratio scale by referring to difference (for example, the adult is 90 cm taller than the student), but the point about an interval scale is that we cannot use its measurements for comparisons by ratio; we can use them only for difference.

Temperature measured in degrees centigrade (or Fahrenheit) is another example of an interval scale. Asserting that 15 degrees is three times as hot as 5 degrees is meaningless; the two temperatures should be compared by their difference.

An interesting point here is that what really distinguishes a ratio scale from an interval scale is that zero means "nothing" in a ratio scale but is significant in an interval scale. When the recorded time is zero hours, time has not disappeared. When the temperature is zero degrees, there is still a temperature outside, and we can feel it. But a length of zero meters is no length; a mass of zero grams is nothing; a bottle holding zero milliliters of wine is empty; a time of zero seconds is no time at all.

Some complexities

Teaching measurement to elementary school students offers an opportunity to guide them to understanding several points that confuse many adults but are not really difficult if we use the correct vocabulary and approach.

Measuring mass and weight

We face a real problem about the language used to describe what we are measuring when, for example, we put a book in one pan of a balance and equalize it with, say, two hundred grams (200 g) in the other. Many people say that what we have found out is that the book weighs 200 g or that its weight is 200 g. Such statements are technically incorrect. What we have discovered is that the book weighs the same as a mass of 200 g or that the mass of the book is 200 g. *Mass* and *weight* are not interchangeable words in scientifically correct language, although they are often used as synonyms in everyday speech.

The units we use for weighing, such as grams and kilograms, are actually units for measuring the mass of an object, not its weight. The *mass* is a measurement of the quantity of matter in an object. This is not the same thing as the amount of space it takes up; that is the *volume* of the object. A small chunk of lead may have the same mass as our book but take up much less space because the molecules making up the piece of lead are packed together much more tightly than those in the book. The reason that problems with the concept of mass are common is that we cannot experience it directly. We cannot see the mass of the book, feel it, or perceive it in any way. When we hold a book, we experience its *weight*, which is the force exerted on it by the pull of gravity. We can feel the weight because we have to exert force to hold the book up. Of course, a weight and mass are directly related: the greater the mass, the greater the weight, and therefore the heavier the object feels when it is held. However, the big difference between mass and weight is that whereas an object's mass is invariant (it does not change unless the object is changed in some way), the weight changes depending on how far the object is from the center of the earth (or whatever is exerting the gravitational pull on the object).

> The mass is a measurement of the quantity of matter in an object.

We are all familiar with the idea that astronauts' weight changes in space and on the moon because the gravitational pull being exerted on them there is less than it is on the earth's surface. In some circumstances (for example when they are in orbit) this pull is effectively canceled out and they experience "weightlessness". An astronaut can then place a book on the palm of his or her hand and it weighs nothing. On the moon's surface, the force gravity exerts on the book and the astronauts — that is, their weight — is about one-sixth of what it is on the earth's surface. However, their masses remain unchanged. The book is still 200 g, as it was on earth, even though its weight has been changing constantly. (So a good way of "losing weight" is to go to the moon, but doing so does not affect waist size. What dieters really want to do is to lose mass!)

> A good way of "losing weight" is to go to the moon, but doing so does not affect waist size. What dieters really want to do is to lose mass!

An important point to note is that balance scales actually measure mass. We put the book in one pan, balance it with a mass of 200 g in the other pan, and because the book "weighs" the same as a mass of 200 g, we conclude that it also has a mass of 200 g. We would get the same result using the balance scales on the moon. However, the pointers on spring-type weighing devices, such as many kitchen scales and bathroom scales, respond directly to weight. They would give a different reading if we took them to the moon. But, of course, they are calibrated for use on the earth's surface, so when Doug stands on the bathroom scales and the pointer indicates 78 kg, he can rely on that reading as a measurement of his mass. On the moon, the pointer would indicate 13 kg; this amount is not his mass.

Because weight is a force, it should be measured in the units of force. The standard unit of force in the metric system is the newton, appropriately named after Sir Isaac Newton (1642–1727), the mathematical and scientific genius who first articulated this distinction between mass and weight. A *newton* is defined as the force required to increase the speed of a mass of one kilogram by one metre per second every second. A newton is actually about the weight of a small apple, and a mass of a kilogram has a weight of nearly 10 newtons. But elementary school students don't have to know any of this. Teachers may come across spring-type weighing devices with a scale graduated in newtons, but these are not appropriate for use in elementary schools.

One way to introduce the word *mass* to elementary school students is to use "masses" (rather than "weights") to refer to the plastic or metal objects used for weighing objects in a balance. We can say we have a box of ten-gram masses and a box of hundred-gram masses. Then when we have balanced an object against some masses, we can say, as a step toward using the correct language, that the mass of the object is so many grams or that it weighs the same as a mass of so many grams.

Measuring volume and capacity

The *volume* of an object is the amount of three-dimensional space that it occupies. By historical accident, liquid volume and solid volume are conventionally measured in different units although the concepts are exactly the same. Liquid volume is measured in liters (L) and milliliters (mL), whereas solid volume is measured in units such as cubic meters (m^3) and cubic centimeters (cm^3). In the metric system, the units for liquid and solid volume are related in a simple way: one milliliter is the same volume as one cubic centimeter; or one liter is the same volume as one thousand cubic centimeters (see Figure 24.3).

> The volume of an object is the amount of three-dimensional space that it occupies.

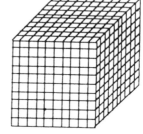

A one-liter box   One thousand cubic centimeters

FIGURE 24.3 *A liter is the same volume as a thousand cubic centimeters*

> The capacity of a container is the maximum volume of liquid it can hold.

Only containers have capacity. The *capacity* of a container is the maximum volume of liquid it can hold. Hence capacity is measured in the same units as liquid volume. For example, if a water glass holds 250 mL when filled to the brim, its capacity is 250 mL.

Measuring time

Students have to learn to handle two quite different aspects of time. The first is the idea of a time *interval*, which is the length of time occupied by an activity or the time that passes from one instant to another. Time intervals are measured in units such as seconds, minutes, hours, days, weeks, years, decades, centuries, and millennia. The second aspect is the idea of recorded time, the time at which an event occurs. We use various conventions for reading the time of day, such as o'clocks, a.m. and p.m., the 24-hour system, together with various ways of recording the date, including reference to the day of the week, the day of the month, and the year. For example, we say that the meeting starts at 1530 on Monday, 7 October 1999, using the concept of recorded time, and that it is expected to last for 90 minutes, using the concept of time interval.

Time is one aspect of measurement that is not often expressed in decimal units. The relationships between the units used (60 seconds in a minute, 60 minutes in an hour, 24 hours in a day, and so on) are challenging for elementary school students. They find it difficult, for example, to use a subtraction algorithm for finding the intervals from one time to another. Teachers should, therefore, use an informal process of adding-on in working with pupils on problems of this kind.

Example 24A

Find the length of time of a journey that starts at 10:45 a.m. and finishes at 1:30 p.m.

Thinking it out

From the moment the journey begins, the interval is 15 minutes to 11 o'clock, then 2 hours to 1 o'clock, and then a further 30 minutes, making a total of 2 hours and 45 minutes.

Learning about time is also complicated by the fact that the hands on a conventional dial clock go round twice in a day. Because the 12-hour clockface is widely associated with a circle, avoid using that shape to represent a day — in, for example, a pie chart of "how I spend a day" or a circular diagram showing the events of a day. For this last illustration, try a diagram like the one shown in Figure 24.4. Students can add pictures or verbal descriptions of what they are doing at various times of day.

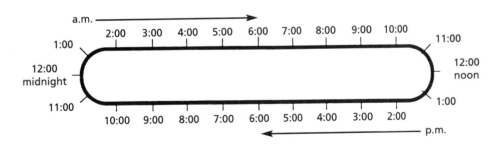

FIGURE 24.4 *A picture of a day*

Additional complications in students' dealing with time relate to the variety of watches and clocks they use and to the range of ways of saying the same time. Students have to be able to read a conventional dial clock as well as a digital display in both 12-hour and 24-hour versions. They also have to learn that the following phrases represent the same time of day: twenty to four in the afternoon, 3:40 p.m., and 15:40 (also written sometimes as 1540 or 15.40). Incidentally, using, for example, *fifteen hundred* to refer to the time 1500 in the 24-hour system is an unhelpful abuse of mathematical language. It reinforces the misunderstanding, mentioned in Chapter 2, of thinking that *00* is an abbreviation for *hundred*. The statement that "the time is fifteen hours" is correct and more helpful.

A couple of further small points relate to noon and midnight. First, note that a.m. and p.m. are abbreviations for *ante meridian* and *post meridian*, which mean *before noon* and *after noon* respectively. Thus, 12 noon is neither a.m. nor p.m. It is just 12 noon. Similarly, 12 o'clock midnight is neither a.m. nor p.m. In the 24-hour system, midnight is the moment when the recorded time of day starts again, so it is not 2400, but 0000 or zero hours.

What metric units and prefixes do elementary school teachers need to know?

The internationally accepted system of metric units is called *SI (Système International)*. This system specifies one base unit for each aspect of measurement. For length, the SI unit is the meter; for mass, it is the kilogram (not the gram); for time, it is the second. Solid volume is measured in cubic meters. The same base unit can be applied to liquid volume; the more common international usage is the liter as the standard unit for capacity and liquid volume.

Other units can be obtained by attaching various prefixes to these base units. The preference is for those related to a thousand: for elementary school use, these are *kilo* (k), which means a thousand, and *milli* (m), which means a thousandth. So this book uses, for example, kilograms (kg) and grams (g), where 1 kg = 1000 g, and liters (L) and milliliters (mL), where 1 liter = 1000 mL. (NB: the symbol l, previously used for liter, can be confused in print with the numeral 1.) Similarly we can have kilometers (km) and meters (m), with 1 km = 1000 m, and meters and millimeters (mm), with 1 m = 1000 mm. These uses of the prefixes kilo and milli are the only ones likely to be needed in the elementary school.

For practical purposes, teachers need other prefixes, especially *centi* (c), which means a hundredth. This gives us the really useful unit of length, the centimeter (cm), where 1 m = 100 cm. Some teachers also find it helpful — for example, in explaining place value and decimal measures of length (see Chapter 2) — to use the prefix *deci* (d), which means a tenth, as in decimeter (dm), where 1 m = 10 dm. Some wine bottles are labeled 0.75 L, 7.5 dL (deciliter) or 750 mL (milliliters).

Gaining experience in metric measurement

Teachers should give students a variety of opportunities to practice real-life estimation of lengths, heights, widths and distances, liquid volume and capacity, and mass. On a trip to a local supermarket, for example, encourage them to notice which items are sold by mass (although the store will likely call it weight) and which by volume. Have them estimate the mass or volume of various items and then check their estimates against the package labels. This exercise helps significantly to build up confidence in handling less familiar units.

One way of becoming a better estimator is to learn the sizes of some specific reference items. Students should be encouraged to do this for length, mass, and capacity and then to relate other estimates to these.

Here are some references:
- The mass of an individual package of crackers is 30 g.
- The mass of a standard-size can of condensed soup is about 300 g (including the can).

- A standard pop can has a capacity of about 350 mL.
- A standard large can of fruit juice holds about 1.5 L. A tetrapack holds 250 mL.
- A wine bottle holds 750 mL.
- A standard carton of milk or juice holds 1 L (1000 mL); an individual-portion carton holds 250 mL.
- A liter of water has a mass of a kilogram (1000 g).
- A child's finger is about 1 cm wide.
- Student rulers are 30 cm long.
- A sheet of standard letterhead or computer paper is about 21.5 cm by 28 cm.
- The distance from my nose to my outstretched finger-tip is about 1 m (100 cm).
- The classroom door is about 200 cm or 2 m high.

Imperial measures

Many adults still find metric units less familiar than the Imperial units they grew up with. They use quick mathematical conversions.

For those who wish to relate miles to kilometers, the most common equivalence used is that 5 miles is about 8 kilometers. A simple method for doing this conversion is to read off the corresponding speeds on the speedometer of a car; those in most models are calibrated in both miles per hour and kilometers per hour, showing clearly that 30 miles is about 50 km, 50 miles is about 80 km, and 70 miles is about 110 km.

This conversion has an intriguing connection with a sequence of numbers called the Fibonacci sequence, named after Leonardo Fibonacci (c. 1170–c. 1250), an Italian mathematician. The sequence runs 1, 1, 2, 3, 5, 8, 13, 21, 34, 55, 89, etc. Each number is the sum of the two previous numbers. So, for example, the next number after 89 is 144 (55 + 89). Purely coincidentally, it happens that one of these numbers in miles is approximately the same as the next one in kilometers. For example, 2 miles is about 3 km, 3 miles is about 5 km, 5 miles is about 8 km, 8 miles is about 13 km, and so on. This works remarkably well to the nearest whole number for quite some way! (See Question 24.4 in Check Yourself below.)

Check yourself

24.1 Are the following relationships transitive:

    (a) "is earlier than" applied to times of the day?
    (b) "is half of" applied to lengths?

24.2 Measure the length of a sheet of standard typing or computer paper to the nearest millimeter. Give the answer

    (a) in millimeters   (b) in centimeters   (c) in decimeters
    (d) in meters

24.3 On earth the mass of a liter of water is 1 kg (1000 g). What is it on the moon?

24.4 Given that 1 mile is 1.6093 km, use a calculator to find how far the Fibonacci sequence rule for changing miles to kilometers is correct to the nearest whole number.

➤ Teaching suggestions

1. Help students develop their understanding of and skills in measurement through practical, purposeful activities.

2. Introduce new aspects of measurement through direct comparison and ordering.

3. Introduce the idea of measuring via nonstandard units that are familiar and appropriately sized. Use these experiences to establish the need for a standard unit.

4. Refer to the things used for weighing objects on a balance as *masses* and use the phrasing *weighs the same as a mass of so many grams.* Then encourage students to say, the mass is so many grams. But acknowledge that most people incorrectly say, the weight is so many grams.

5. With older students in elementary school, discuss the relationship between gravity and weight and the idea that space travel does not change mass.

6. Do some work on solid volume, measured in cubic centimeters.

7. Explore the measurements of liquid volume and capacity, in liters and milliliters. The scope for practical experience with water or sand and various containers makes it an important component of elementary school mathematics.

8. Make collections and displays of packages, discussing which items are sold by mass or by volume and the units used.

9. Explore with students various methods for finding the length of time from one recorded time to the next. Teach an informal adding-on approach.

10. Do not represent a day with a circle, because of the association with a 12-hour clockface.

11. Help students learn to choose and use appropriate measuring devices. Discuss the idea of accuracy. Make explicit the notion that measurement is always to the nearest something.

12. Ensure that students have practical experience working with metric units, especially the meter, centimeter, millimeter, liter, milliliter, kilogram, and gram. Also refer to the kilometer and decimeter.

13. Make considerable use of estimation as a class activity, encouraging students to learn the measurements of specific reference items.

Angles

Students should learn to understand and use, in context, right angles, fractions of a turn, and degrees in measuring rotation, and to use the associated language.

THIS CHAPTER EXPLAINS:
- the dynamic and static views of angles;
- comparison and ordering of angles;
- the use of turns and fractions of a turn for measuring an angle;
- degrees;
- acute, right, obtuse, straight, and reflex angles; and
- the sum of the angles in a triangle, a quadrilateral, and so on.

What is an angle?

An angle is a measurement. We can think of an angle in two ways. The first is the dynamic view: the angle between two intersecting lines is a measurement of the size of the rotation involved when we point along one line and then turn to point along the other.

This way of introducing the concept of an angle to students is particularly useful, because it lends itself to practical experience. The students can point themselves in one direction and then turn through various angles to point in other directions. And with angles formed by lines drawn on paper, students can run a physical pointer, such as a pencil or a finger, along one line and then rotate about the intersection (called the *vertex*) to point along the other line.

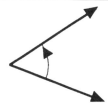

counterclockwise rotation

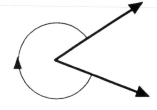

clockwise rotation

FIGURE 25.1 *Angle as a measure of rotation*

Note that turning from one direction to another always involves two angles: one when we rotate clockwise and another when we rotate counterclockwise, as shown in Figure 25.1.

The second way of thinking about an angle is the static view. Here we focus on the shape formed by the two lines: how pointed is it? Notice that in this view an angle is still a measurement — of the difference in direction between the two lines. For example, the angle in Figure 25.2a is greater than that marked in the one in Figure 25.2b; the two lines in panel b are pointing in nearly the same direction, whereas the two in panel a differ much more in direction.

Thinking of an angle as the difference in direction between two lines helps to link the static view of an angle with the dynamic one of rotation. The obvious way to measure the difference in two directions is to turn from one to the other and to measure the amount of turn.

FIGURE 25.2 *Angle as a measure of the difference in direction*

Like any aspect of measurement, the concept of an angle enables us to make comparisons and to order (see Chapter 24). We can do this dynamically, by physically doing the rotations involved (for example, with a pencil) and judging which is the greater rotation and which is the smaller. We can also experience the comparison by cutting out one angle and placing it over another to determine which is the more pointed (the smaller angle). Figure 25.3 shows a set of angles ordered from smallest to largest.

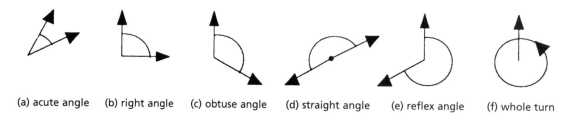

(a) acute angle   (b) right angle   (c) obtuse angle   (d) straight angle   (e) reflex angle   (f) whole turn

FIGURE 25.3 *A set of angles in order from smallest (a) to largest (f)*

We can use the dynamic view to measure angles in turns and fractions of a turn. The process is equivalent to making measurements of length, mass, and capacity in nonstandard units. For example, students can point north and turn all the way around until they are pointing north again. Figure 25.3f shows such a whole turn, pointing in one direction and rotating back to the same direction. If, however, students point north and then turn to point south, they have moved through an angle that can be called a half-turn. Similarly, rotating clockwise from north to east is a quarter-turn.

Figure 25.3b shows a quarter-turn from a horizontal position to a vertical position. This quarter-turn is called a *right angle*. Figure 25.3d illustrates why a half-turn, formed by two lines pointing in opposite directions, is called a *straight angle*.

Degrees

The next stage in teaching about angles is to introduce a standard unit for measuring them. This unit is called a *degree*. The notation is a symbol — ° — and 360° degrees is equal to a complete turn. Hence a right angle (quarter-turn)is 90°, and a straight angle (half-turn) is 180°. There is evidence that the Babylonians used this system of measuring angles with a base of 360 degrees as long ago as 2000 BCE. It may be related to the Babylonian year's being 360 days long.

What are acute, obtuse, and reflex angles?

Angles are classified, in order of size, as acute, right, obtuse, straight, and reflex. Figure 25.3 illustrates that an *acute angle* (panel a) is an angle less than a right angle (that is, less than 90°). An *obtuse angle* (panel c) is an angle between a right angle and a straight angle (that is, more than 90° but less than 180°). A *reflex angle* (panel e) is an angle greater than a straight angle but less than a whole turn (that is, more than 180° but less than 360°).

Properties of angles

The sum of the angles in a triangle is always 180°. One way to demonstrate this fact is to draw a triangle on paper, mark the angles, tear off the three corners and fit them together, as shown in Figure 25.4, to discover that together they form a straight angle (or two right angles) of 180°. The same thing can be done with the four angles of a quadrilateral (a shape with four straight sides) to discover that they fit together to make a whole turn (or four right angles) of 360°.

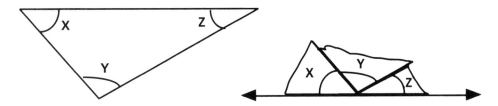

FIGURE 25.4 *The three angles of a triangle fitted together to make a straight angle*

The experiments just described use the static view of angle. It is also possible to illustrate the same principle using the dynamic view, by taking a pointer (say, an arrow or a pencil) for a walk round a triangle. As shown in Figure 25.5, step 1 is to place the arrow along one side of the triangle, for example, on *AC*. Step 2 is to slide the pointer along the line segment until it reaches *A* and then rotate it through the angle. For step 3, we slide up *AB* to *B* and rotate through that angle. Finally, in step 4, we slide down to *C* and rotate through that angle. The pointer has now rotated through all three angles (their sum) and is facing in the direction opposite to which it started. Hence the three angles together make a half-turn (or two right angles).

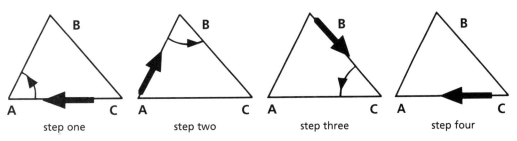

FIGURE 25.5 *The three angles of a triangle together make a half-turn*

Clearly this procedure works for any triangle, not just the one shown here.

The same procedure can be applied to a four-sided figure, such as the quadrilateral shown in Figure 25.6. Now we find that the pointer does a complete rotation, finishing up pointing in the same direction as it started. So we conclude that the sum of the four angles in a four-sided figure is a full turn.

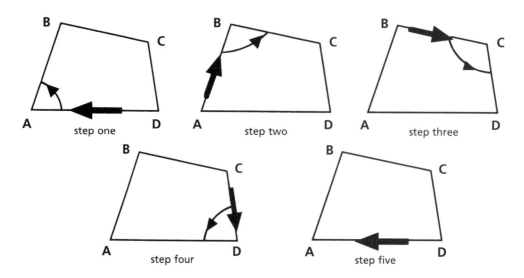

FIGURE 25.6 *The four angles of a quadrilateral together make a whole turn.*

The delight of this activity is that it can easily be extended to five-sided figures, six-sided figures, seven-sided figures, and so on. The results can then be tabulated, using the approach given in Chapter 22, in order to formulate a sequential generalization and a global generalization. This exercise is left for the reader in Question 25.2 in the Check Yourself section.

Check yourself

25.1 Put the following angles in order and classify them as acute, right, obtuse, straight or reflex:

(a) 89°   (b) one-eighth of a turn
(c) 150°   (d) 90°
(e) three-quarters of a turn   (f) 200°
(g) two right angles   (h) 95°

25.2 Use the idea of taking a pointer around a shape, rotating through each of the angles in turn, to find the sum of the angles in:

(a) a five-sided figure   (b) a six-sided figure
(c) a seven-sided figure

Give the answers in right angles; tabulate them; and formulate both the sequential and the global generalizations. What is the sum of the angles in a figure with 100 sides?

➤ Teaching suggestions

1. Emphasize the dynamic view of an angle, giving the students plenty of practical experience of rotating objects, themselves, and pointers (such as fingers and pencils).

2. When teaching angles include the important stages of developing a measurement concept: comparison, ordering, and the use of nonstandard units (turns and fractions of turns).

3. Have students compare and order angles by cutting some out and placing them on top of each other.

4. Emphasize the idea of rotation from zero when explaining to students how to use a protractor.

5. Use a transparent protractor on an overhead projector to demonstrate to students how to use this device for measuring angles.

6. When explaining about angles, draw some diagrams in which one of the lines is not horizontal.

7. Have the students cut out pictures from magazines, mark angles on them, and display them in sets as acute, right, obtuse, straight, and reflex.

8. Explore with students by using both the static and the dynamic methods for discovering the sum of the angles in a triangle, a quadrilateral, and so on.

9. Use dynamic geometric software to encourage students to explore various relationships in geometry and angles.

26

Transformations.... and Symmetry

> Students should learn to understand and use, in context, the congruence of simple shapes; to recognize reflective and rotational symmetries; and to transform two-dimensional shapes by translation, reflection, and rotation.
>
> **THIS CHAPTER EXPLAINS:**
> - the fundamental ideas of transformation and equivalence;
> - translation, reflection and rotation, as types of congruence; and
> - reflective and rotational symmetry for two-dimensional shapes.

What is congruence?

Congruence is a concept used to describe shapes whose lengths of lines and measures of angles remain the same under a translation, a rotation, and a reflection.

Two fundamental questions in mathematics are, how are things the same? and how are they different? The first question directs our attention to what is called an *equivalence*, the second to a *transformation*. For example, in Chapter 16, we saw that we can transform a fraction, such as 2/3 into 4/6, by multiplying the top and bottom numbers by 2. The two fractions are, in a sense, different. They use different top and bottom numbers, and two pieces of a pizza cut into three is not exactly the same as four pieces of pizza cut into six. But the two ways of cutting up do result in the same amount of pizza. So, in an important sense, the two fractions are the same.

> Congruence is a concept used to describe shapes whose lengths of lines and measures of angles remain the same under a translation, a rotation, and a reflection.

Chapter 24 applied a similar line of reasoning in discussing the conservation of liquid volume. In the example shown in Figure 24.2, the water in the container is transformed in some ways when it is poured into another container. It is a different shape, it has a different height, and so on. But the volume of the water stays the same. If a teacher draws a large diagram on the chalkboard and asks the class to copy it on paper, the students will do so, even though none of them have a piece of paper large enough to produce a diagram as big as the teacher's. Their diagrams differ in size, but in many other respects, they are the same as the one on the board.

Much of what we have to understand in mathematics comes down to recognizing how things can differ yet be the same: the equivalences that exist within various transformations, and which transformations preserve which equivalences. This way of thinking is central to developing an understanding of shape and space.

> Much of what we have to understand in mathematics comes down to recognizing how things can differ yet be the same: the equivalences that exist within various transformations, and which transformations preserve which equivalences.

An example of congruency

In a mathematics lesson, students were asked to draw on graph paper as many different shapes as possible made up of five square units. Figure 26.1 shows four of the shapes that one student drew. Her teacher says that they are all the same shape. Silvie insists they are all different. Who is correct? The answer is that they are both correct. The shapes are all the same in some senses and all different in others.

First, consider how they are the same. All four shapes are made up of five square units. Each shape has six sides: one that is four units long, one that is three units long, one that is two units long, and three that are one unit long. When the angles are measured inside the shaded portion of Figure 26.1, each shape has five 90° angles and one 270° angle. And the sides and the angles are arranged in the same way in each of the shapes to make what we might recognize as a letter L. Surely they are identical, the same in every respect?

> A practical way to show congruency is to cut out one shape. It will fit exactly over another that is congruent.

They certainly are *congruent*. A practical way to show congruency is to cut out one shape; it will fit exactly over another that is congruent.

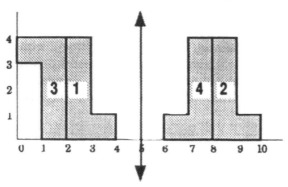

FIGURE 26.1 *The same but different*

The pages in this book are congruent: one page fits exactly over the next. The computer disks being used while writing this book were all congruent.

What is a translation?

How are the shapes in Figure 26.1 different? For example, how is shape 2 different from shape 1? Silvie's argument was that they are in different positions on the paper: Shape 1 is here and Shape 2 is over there, so they are not the same shape. "Surely," she said, "every time I draw the shape in a different position, I have drawn a different shape."

The shapes are indeed different if we take position into account. In order to do this, we need a system of coordinates, as outlined in Chapter 23. The transformation applied to shape 1 to produce shape 2 is called a *translation*. We saw in Chapter 23 that we can use the coordinate system to describe movement. The translation here can be specified by saying, for example, that to get from shape 1 to shape 2, we move 6 units in the horizontal direction (on the *x*-axis) and 0 units in the vertical direction (on the *y*-axis). Any such movement is a translation.

What is a rotation?

If we decide that, for the time being, we do not count translations as producing shapes that are different, what about shape 3? Does it differ from shape 1? Silvie's idea is that shape 1 is an L-shape the right way up, but shape 3 is upside down, so they are different. And they are different if we take orientation on the page into account.

In order to do this, we need the concept of direction, and, as we saw in Chapter 25, to describe a difference in direction we need the concept of angle. To transform shape 1 into shape 3, we can apply a rotation. To specify a rotation, we have to indicate the point about which the turn occurs and the angle through which the shape is rotated. If shape 1 is rotated through an angle of 180° (either clockwise or counterclockwise), about the middle of its left-hand side — the point with coordinates (2,2) — then it is transformed into shape 3. Imagine copying shape 1 on to tracing paper, placing a pin in the point (2,2), and turning the tracing paper through 180°. The shape would land directly on top of Shape 3. Any movement of our shape in which it turns through some angle about a given center is a *rotation*.

What is a reflection?

If we decide that, for the time being, we do not count rotations or translations as producing shapes that are different, what about shape 4? Does it differ from shape 1? Silvie's idea is that the two are mirror images of each other. We can see the point by coloring the shapes, say red, before cutting them out. Shapes 1, 2, and 3 can all be placed on top of each other and match exactly with the red faces uppermost. But Shape 4 only matches if we turn it over so that the red face is down.

The transformation that has been applied to shape 1 to produce shape 4 is a reflection. To specify a reflection, all we have to do is identify the mirror line. In the case of shapes 1 and 4, the mirror line is the vertical line that passes through 5 on the *x*-axis, shown as a double-headed arrow in Figure 26.1. Each point in shape 1 is matched by a corresponding point in shape 4 on the other side of the mirror line and is the same distance from that line. For example, the corner of the letter L with the reflex angle in shape 1 is 2 units to the left of the mirror line, and the corresponding point in shape 4 is 2 units to the right of the mirror line. Any movement of our shape like this, obtained by producing a mirror image in any given mirror line, is a *reflection*.

Reflective symmetry

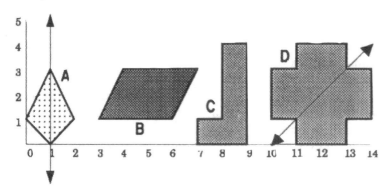

FIGURE 26.2 *Are these shapes symmetrical?*

Sometimes when we reflect a shape in a particular mirror line it matches itself exactly, in the sense that the mirror image coincides precisely with the original shape. Shape A in Figure 26.2 is an example of this phenomenon. The mirror line, which is shown as a double-headed arrow, divides the shape into two identical halves that are mirror images of each other. If we cut the shape out, we can fold it along the mirror line and match the two halves exactly.

Another approach is to color the shape, cut it out, and turn it over. Turned face down, the shape still fits exactly into the hole left in the paper. The shape is said to have *reflective symmetry* (sometimes called *line symmetry*), and the mirror line is called a *line of symmetry*.

Shape D in Figure 26.2 also has reflective symmetry. It can be divided into two matching, mirror-image halves along four possible lines of symmetry. The diagram shows only one of these lines of symmetry. Finding the others is left for Question 26.2 in the Check Yourself section toward the end of the chapter).

Notice that if we color shape D, cut it out, and turn it face down, it fits exactly into the hole left in the paper. But shape C does not have reflective symmetry. If we color it, cut it out, and turn it face down, we cannot fit it into the hole left in the paper.

Rotational symmetry

Shape B is perhaps a surprise. It does not have reflective symmetry. (Anyone who thinks that one of the diagonals is a line of symmetry should copy the shape on to paper and try the coloring, cutting out, and turning face down procedure or try folding it in half along the diagonal.) It does, however, have a kind of symmetry. To see this point, we can use tracing paper. Trace the shape and then rotate it around the center point through a half-turn. The shape matches the original shape exactly. A shape that can be turned onto itself like this is said to have *rotational symmetry*. The point about which we rotate it is called the *center of rotational symmetry*. If we color Shape B and cut it out, there are two ways in which we can rotate it into the hole left in the paper without turning it face down. Therefore, we say that the shape has rotational symmetry of order 2. Shape D also has rotational symmetry (see Question 26.2 in Check yourself below). Shapes A and C do not have rotational symmetry.

The ideas of reflective and rotational symmetry are fundamental to attractive designs and patterns and are employed effectively in a number of cultural traditions. Students can learn first of all to recognize these kinds of symmetry in the world around them and gradually learn to analyze them and employ them in creating designs of their own.

Check yourself

26.1 Describe the congruences that transform shape 2 in Figure 26.1 into:

(a) shape 1   (b) shape 4   (c) shape 3

26.2 In shape D in Figure 26.2, where are the three unmarked lines of symmetry? What is the order of rotational symmetry of this shape?

26.3 Is it possible to draw a two-dimensional shape with exactly two lines of symmetry that are not at right angles to each other?

26.4 Is it possible to draw a shape with exactly two lines of symmetry that does not have rotational symmetry?

➤ Teaching suggestions

1. Explore geometrical designs from various cultural traditions to provide a rich experience of transformations and symmetry.
2. Use some of the numerous computer programs available to provide elementary school students with opportunities to explore transformations and symmetry.
3. Be aware that the most important emphasis for students' learning about shape and space in elementary school is the opportunity for practical experience of coloring in shapes, cutting them out, folding them, turning them over, rotating them, looking at them in mirrors, fitting them together, making patterns, matching them, sorting them, classifying them, and so on. The teacher's approach here should be much less structured than in other aspects of the mathematics curriculum.
4. To promote useful discussion in work with shapes, frequently use the two questions about transformation and equivalence:

    (a) how are they the same?   (b) how are they different?

5. Use the tracing-paper approach to explore the ideas of rotation and rotational symmetry.
6. Use the coloring, cutting out, and turning face down approach to explore the ideas of reflection and reflective symmetry.
7. Have the students make a display of magazine cutouts that illustrate different aspects of symmetry.

27
Classifying Shapes

Students should learn to recognize geometrical features and properties and to use these to classify shapes.

THIS CHAPTER EXPLAINS:
- the importance of classification as a process for making sense of the shapes in the world around us;
- polygons, including the meaning of regular polygon;
- acute-angled, right-angled, and obtuse-angled triangles;
- equilateral, isosceles, and scalene triangles;
- parallelograms, rectangles, squares, rhombuses, and the relationships between them;
- tessellations;
- polyhedra, including the meaning of regular polyhedron;
- prisms and pyramids; and
- reflective symmetry applied to three-dimensional shapes.

The language of geometry

We need the special language of geometry in order to classify shapes into categories. Classification is an important intellectual process that helps us to make sense of our experiences. By coding information into categories, we condense it and gain some control over it. Classification is at the heart of mathematics. The intellectual process involved is another example of the "same but different" principle discussed in Chapter 26. We form categories in mathematics by recognizing attributes shared by various elements (such as numbers or shapes) and then form these elements into a set.

> Classification is at the heart of mathematics.

Although the elements in the set differ, they have something the same about them. When a set is particularly interesting or significant, we give it a name.

Because it is important that we can determine definitely whether or not a particular element is in the set, the next stage of the process is often to formulate a precise definition.

For example, in Chapter 13, we noted the attribute shared by the numbers 2, 3, 5, 7, 11, 13, 17,...: that they have no factors apart from 1 and themselves. This led to putting them into a set and giving them a name, *prime numbers*. Because of some uncertainty about whether or not the number 1 is prime, we turned to a definition: namely, that a prime number is one that has precisely two factors.

In Chapter 13, we also suggested that awareness of various ways of classifying numbers contributes to a greater confidence with numbers. The same is true of shapes. We may recognize that certain shapes have an attribute in common (such as having three sides), form them into a category, give the set a name (here, the set of triangles), and then, if necessary, make the classification more explicit with a precise definition. This process of classifying and naming leads to a greater confidence in handling shapes and a better awareness of the shapes that make up the world around us.

To participate in this important process of classification of shapes, we need mathematical ideas related to the significant properties used to put shapes into various categories. These include, for example, whether the edges of the shape are straight, the number of sides and angles, whether various angles are equal or right-angled, and whether sides are equal in length or parallel. We also need to know the various terms used to name the sets, supported where necessary by a definition.

What are the main classes of two-dimensional shapes?

A two-dimensional, closed shape made up entirely of straight edges is called a polygon.

The first classification of two-dimensional shapes separates those that have only straight edges from those, such as circles, semi-circles, and ellipses, that have curved edges. A two-dimensional, closed shape made up entirely of straight edges is called a *polygon*.

Polygons can be further classified according to the number of sides: *triangles* with three sides, *quadrilaterals* with four, *pentagons* with five, *hexagons* with six, *heptagons* with seven, *octagons* with eight, and so on.

We can also categorize polygons into those that are regular and those that are not. A *regular polygon* is one in which all the sides are the same length and all the angles are the same size. For example, a regular octagon has eight equal sides and eight angles of which each is equal to 135°. To calculate the angles in a regular polygon, use the rule $(180 (N - 2))$ degrees deduced in Question 25.2 (Chapter 25) to determine the total of the angles in the polygon (for example, for an octagon, the sum is $180 (8 - 2) = 1080°$) and then divide the result by the number of angles (for the octagon, $1080° \div 8 = 135$ degrees).

When people talk about shapes, they often misuse the word *regular*. In fact, it is not synonymous with *symmetric* or even *geometric*. For example, the rectangular shape of the cover of this book is not a regular shape because two of the sides are longer than the other two.

A fascinating way of forming the regular polygons uses the fact that the number of lines of symmetry increases as the number of sides increases. For example, a regular triangle has three lines of symmetry, a regular quadrilateral (a square) has four, and so on. To investigate this relationship, tape two mirrors so they can open out like the covers of a book. Draw a straight line on a sheet of paper and place the two mirrors across the line, opened at 120°, so that they reflect the line. With care, they can be arranged so that a viewer sees a regular triangle in them. Then slowly close the two mirrors. As they move, the image successively forms each of the regular polygons.

Categories of triangles

Triangles can be categorized in two basic ways: by their angles and by their sides. Figure 27.1 shows examples of triangles categorized in these ways.

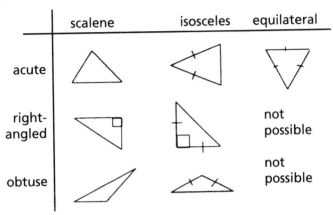

FIGURE 27.1 *Categories of triangles*

First we can categorize triangles as being acute-angled, right-angled, or obtuse-angled. (See Chapter 25 for the classification of angles.) An *acute-angled triangle* is one in which all three angles are acute (less than 90°). A *right-angled triangle* is one in which one of the angles is a right angle (90°). No triangle can have two right angles since the sum of the three angles has to be 180°; the third angle would have to be zero. An *obtuse-angled triangle* is one with an obtuse angle (greater than 90° and less than 180°). Again, a triangle can have only one such angle because the sum of the three angles must equal 180°. This condition also makes it impossible to have any triangle that contains a reflex angle.

Second, we can categorize triangles as being equilateral, isosceles, or scalene. An *equilateral (equal-sided) triangle* is one in which all three sides are equal. Because of the nature of triangles, the only possibility for an equilateral triangle is one in which the three angles are also equal (to 60°). So an equilateral triangle must be a regular triangle. This equality is true only of triangles. For example, an equilateral octagon (one with eight equal sides) need not have equal angles. Imagine joining eight equal strips of card with paper-fasteners or tape and manipulating the structure into many different shapes, all of which are equilateral octagons but only one of which is a regular octagon.

> We can categorize triangles as being equilateral, isosceles, or scalene.

An *isosceles triangle* is one with two sides equal. In Figure 27.1 the equal sides have a small marker. An isosceles triangle has a line of symmetry passing through the middle of the angle formed by the two equal sides. We can discover practically that a triangle with two equal sides always has two equal angles. If it is cut out and folded in half along the line of symmetry, the two angles opposite the equal sides match each other.

Finally, a *scalene triangle* has no sides equal.

Using these categorizations, we can determine eight different kinds of triangle, as shown in Figure 27.1.

Categories of quadrilaterals

The most important set of quadrilaterals is the set of *parallelograms* — those with two pairs of opposite sides parallel. Figure 27.2 shows some examples of parallelograms. Two lines drawn in a two-dimensional plane are said to be *parallel* if, theoretically, they would never meet if continued indefinitely. This relationship exists between the opposite sides in each of the shapes drawn in Figure 27.2. Chapter 26 showed that not all parallelograms have reflective symmetry. In Figure 27.2, only the parallelograms A, B, and C have reflective symmetry. But they all have rotational symmetry of at least order two: the opposite angles match onto each other, and the opposite sides match onto each other, when the shape is rotated through a half-turn. In other words, the opposite angles of a parallelogram are always equal and the opposite sides are always equal.

Parallelograms can thus be classified in two main ways: by their angles and by their sides.

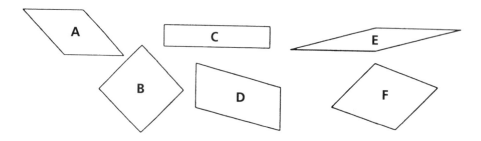

FIGURE 27.2 *Examples of parallelograms*

The most significant aspect of the angles of a parallelogram is whether or not they are right angles. If they are (see shapes B and C shown in Figure 27.2), the shape is called a *rectangle.* In a parallelogram opposite angles are equal, and the four angles add up to four right angles. Thus, in a rectangle, all the angles must be right angles.

From a practical perspective, the rectangle is probably the most important four-sided shape simply because so much of western society is based on it. It is almost impossible to look anywhere and not see rectangles. In the rural areas of some African countries, the environment is based on the circle: people sit on circular stools in circular houses in circular villages. Interestingly, children who grow up in such an environment are often more confident than North American or European children in handling the mathematics of circles and rectangles.

Rhombus

A *rhombus* is a parallelogram in which all four sides are equal (see shapes A and B in Figure 27.2). A *square* (shape B) is, therefore, a rhombus that is also a rectangle (or a rectangle that is also a rhombus). It is also a quadrilateral with all four sides equal and all four angles equal (to 90°), so *square* is another name for a regular quadrilateral.

Teachers should be aware of an important point about language here. A square is a special kind of rectangle, and a rectangle is a special kind of parallelogram. Likewise, a square is a special kind of rhombus, and a rhombus is a special kind of parallelogram. Sometimes people speak of about "squares or rectangles" as though they were different things, neglecting the fact that squares are a subset of rectangles. If we need to distinguish between rectangles that are squares and those that are not, we can refer to *square rectangles* (such as B in Figure 27.2) and *oblong rectangles* (such as C).

What is a tessellation?

Another way to classify two-dimensional shapes is to distinguish between those that tessellate and those that do not. A shape is said to *tessellate* if it can be used to make a tiling pattern — a tessellation — which means that the shape can be used over and over again to cover a flat surface, the shapes fitting together without any gaps.

In practical terms, we are asking whether the shape can be used as a tile to cover the kitchen floor (without worrying about what happens when we reach the edges). The most common shapes used for tiling are squares and other rectangles, which fit together neatly without any gaps, as shown in Figure 27.3a. Figure 27.3b demonstrates an often-overlooked fact: all triangles tessellate. With the three angles of the triangle called *a*, *b*, and *c*, it is instructive to identify the six angles that come together at a point where six triangles meet in the tessellation, as shown. Because *a*, *b*, and *c* add up to 180°, a straight angle, they fit together at this point, neatly lying along straight lines. By repeating this arrangement in all directions, we can make it clear that triangles can be used to form a tessellation.

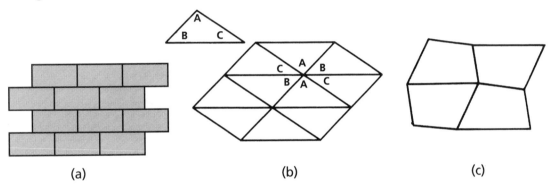

(a) (b) (c)

FIGURE 27.3 *Tessellations*

Any quadrilateral also tessellates (see Figure 27.3c). Because the four angles sum to 360°, we can arrange four quadrilaterals to meet at a point with the four different angles fitting together without any gaps. This pattern can then be continued indefinitely in all directions.

Interestingly, apart from the equilateral triangle and the square, the only other regular polygon that tessellates is the regular hexagon, as seen in the familiar honeycomb pattern.

Three-dimensional shapes

The first classification of three-dimensional shapes is to separate those that have curved surfaces, such as a *sphere* (a perfectly round ball), a *hemisphere* (a sphere cut in half), a *cylinder* (like a soup can) and a *cone* (see the nearest road-repair crew). A shape that is made up entirely of flat surfaces (also called *plane surfaces*) is a *polyhedron*. (plural: polyhedra). To describe a polyhedron we need to refer to the flat surfaces, which are called *faces* (not *sides*); the lines where two faces meet, called *edges*, and the points where edges meet, which are called *vertices* (plural of *vertex*).

With polyhedra as with polygons, the word *regular* is used to identify those in which all the faces are the same shape, all the edges are the same length, and all the angles between edges are equal.

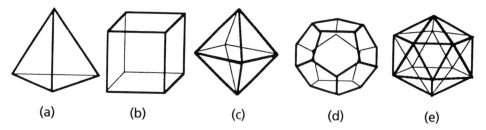

(a)   (b)   (c)   (d)   (e)

FIGURE 27.4 *The regular polyhedra*

Whereas the number of different kinds of regular polygons is infinite, there are only five kinds of regular polyhedra. Figure 27.4 shows them all: the *regular tetrahedron* (four faces, each of which is an equilateral triangle); the *regular hexahedron*, which is usually called a *cube* (six faces, each of which is a square); the *regular octahedron* (eight faces, each of which is an equilateral triangle); the *regular dodecahedron* (twelve faces, each of which is a regular pentagon); and the *regular icosahedron* (twenty faces, each of which is an equilateral triangle).

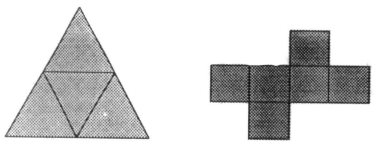

FIGURE 27.5 *Nets for a regular tetrahedron and a cube*

These and other solid shapes can be constructed by drawing a two-dimensional net, such as those shown for the regular tetrahedron and cube in Figure 27.5, cutting the shape out, folding, and gluing it together. (The cutout should incorporate some flaps in appropriate positions for gluing. The outlines in the figure do not include such flaps.) Constructing solid shapes is an excellent mathematical activity for elementary school students, in which a whole range of spatial concepts and practical skills come together.

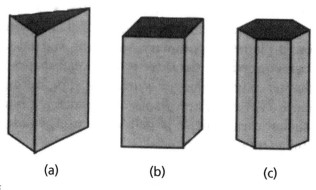

(a)   (b)   (c)

FIGURE 27.6 *Some prisms*

Figure 27.6 illustrates a *triangular prism* (panel a), a *rectangular prism* (panel b), and a *hexagonal prism* (panel c). We can think of prisms as being made from cheese: a shape is a prism if we can slice the cheese along its length so that each slice is identical. Note that all these shapes are called *prisms*, although the word is often used colloquially to refer just to the triangular prism. Note also that another name for a *rectangular prism* is a *cuboid*; it is a three-dimensional shape in which all the faces are rectangles.

Another category of three-dimensional shapes is the set called pyramids, illustrated in Figure 27.7. A *pyramid* is made up of a polygon forming the base and then a series of faces rising from each of its edges to some point above, called the *apex*. The result is a series of faces meeting at the apex. Note that a triangular-based pyramid (see Figure 27.7a) is actually a tetrahedron, and that a square-based pyramid (see Figure 27.7b) is the kind we associate with ancient Egypt.

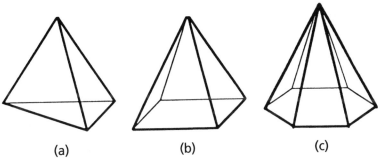

(a)   (b)   (c)

FIGURE 27.7 *Pyramids*

Reflective symmetry

Like some two-dimensional shapes, some three-dimensional shapes have reflective symmetry. Chapter 26 described how some two-dimensional shapes have reflective symmetry, with a line of symmetry dividing the shape into two matching halves, one a mirror image of the other. The same applies to three-dimensional shapes, except that it is now a *plane of symmetry* that divides the shape into the two halves. Think of taking a broad, flat knife and slicing right through the shape, producing two halves that are mirror images of each other, as illustrated with a cone in Figure 27.8. The cone, of course, has an infinite number of planes of symmetry, since any vertical slice through the apex of the cone can be used.

All the three-dimensional shapes illustrated in the figures in this chapter have reflective symmetry. For example, the regular tetrahedron in Figure 27.4 has three planes of symmetry. Students can experience this idea by slicing various fruits in half or by using solid shapes made out of modelling clay.

FIGURE 27.8 *A plane of symmetry*

Check yourself

27.1 Why is it impossible to have an equilateral right-angled triangle or an equilateral obtuse-angled triangle? (See Figure 27.1.)

27.2 What are the sizes of the three angles in a right-angled isosceles triangle?

27.3 What is another name for:

(a) a rectangular rhombus?
(b) a regular quadrilateral?
(c) a triangle with rotational symmetry?
(d) a rectangular prism?
(e) a triangular-based pyramid?

27.4 Which of the following shapes tessellate?

(a) a parallelogram   (b) a regular pentagon   (c) a regular octagon.

27.5 How many planes of symmetry can you identify for a cube?

➤Teaching suggestions

1. Help students develop geometric concepts, such as those discussed in this chapter, by experiencing classification that uses various attributes of shapes. They should first work informally, looking for exemplars and nonexemplars and discussing the relationships between shapes in terms of sameness and difference.

2. Remember that the role of the definition is not to enable students to formulate a concept initially but to sharpen it once it has been formed informally and to deal with doubtful cases.

3. Give students opportunities to explore the properties of various shapes, including various kinds of triangles and quadrilaterals and regular and irregular shapes. Have them fold, trace, and match, looking for reflective and rotational symmetries. Draw out their implications.

4. Remember when talking about quadrilaterals that a square is a special rectangle and that a rectangle is a special parallelogram.

5. Investigate with the students which shapes tessellate and which do not, discovering, for example, that all triangles and all quadrilaterals do. Have them use a plastic or cardboard shape as a template, drawing round it in successive positions.

6. Have the students construct three-dimensional shapes from nets. This excellent, practical activity draws on a wide range of geometric concepts and practical skills.

28

Perimeter and Area

Students should learn to find the perimeters of simple shapes and the circumferences of circles, as well as areas and volumes.

THIS CHAPTER EXPLAINS:
- the concepts of area and perimeter;
- the ideas of varying the area for a fixed perimeter and varying the perimeter for a fixed area;
- a similar idea with volume and surface area; and
- the ratio of a circle's circumference to its diameter.

How can a teacher explain the ideas of perimeter and area so that students don't get them confused?

Area can be defined as the measurement of the amount of two-dimensional space inside a given boundary. The *perimeter* of an object is the length of that boundary — the distance around the object. Think of a field: the area is the size of the field and the perimeter is the amount of fencing around the edges.

Fields and fences provide a clear visual image for students that can be used to explain the concept of area and perimeter. They can draw pictures of various fields on graph paper, such as the one shown in Figure 28.1. They can then count the number of units of fencing around the edges to determine the perimeter; it is 18 units

> Area can be defined as the measurement of the amount of two-dimensional space inside a given boundary. The perimeter of an object is the length of that boundary or distance around the object.

in the figure. Be sure that they count the units of fencing, not the squares around the edge, being especially careful going around corners not to miss any units of fencing. To determine the area, they can fill the field with "sheep" (using small cubes to represent the animals). The number of sheep they can get into the field is a measure of the area. That area is, of course, the same as the number of square units inside the boundary: in this case, 16 square units.

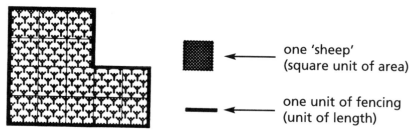

FIGURE 28.1 *Fields and fences*

What is the relationship between perimeter and area?

In general, the perimeter and the area of a two-dimensional shape have no particular relationship. This absence, which is a surprise for many people, provides us with an interesting counterexample of the principle of conservation (see Chapter 24). When we rearrange the fencing around a field into a different shape without changing the overall perimeter, the area is not conserved. In other words, any given perimeter can surround a range of possible areas.

This lack of relationship makes an interesting investigation for students. Again, it is best couched in terms of fields and fences. The first challenge is to find as many different fields as possible that can be enclosed within a given amount of fencing. Figure 28.2 shows a collection of shapes drawn on graph paper, all of which represent fields made by rearranging 12 units of fencing, yielding various areas. An important discovery is that the largest area is obtained with a square field. This is the best use of the farmer's fencing material. (If we were not restricted to the grid lines on graph paper, a circle would provide the largest area. Imagine the fencing to be totally flexible and push it out as far as possible in all directions in order to enclose the maximum area.)

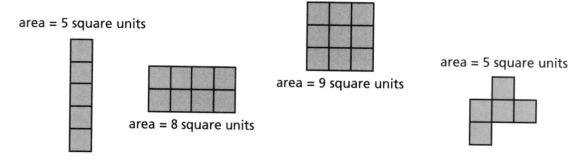

area = 5 square units

area = 8 square units

area = 9 square units

area = 5 square units

FIGURE 28.2 *All these shapes have a perimeter of 12 units*

The second challenge is the reverse problem: to keep the area fixed and find the different perimeters. In other words, what amounts of fencing are required to enclose differently shaped fields all with same area? Figure 28.3 shows a collection of fields that all have same area: 16 square units. Once again, the square is the superior solution, requiring the minimum amount of fencing for the given area.

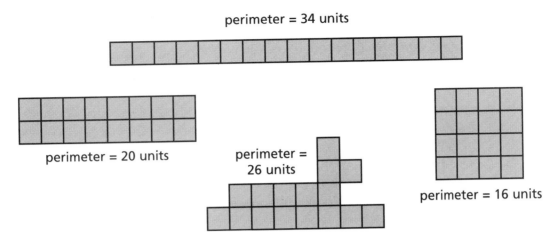

perimeter = 34 units

perimeter = 20 units

perimeter = 26 units

perimeter = 16 units

FIGURE 28.3 *All these shapes have an area of 16 square units*

If we cannot actually make a square using only the grid lines on the graph paper (for example, the problem involves a fixed perimeter of 14 units or a fixed area of 48 square units), we still find that the shape that is closest to a square gives the best solution. In other words the general result, getting away from graph paper, is that a circle provides the minimum perimeter for a given area, and a square provides the minimum quadrilateral solution. In some societies, land has been priced by counting the number of paces around the boundary — that is, by the perimeter. A shrewd operator in such an arrangement could buy square pieces of land and sell them off in long thin strips.

The volume and surface area of solid shapes offer an interesting parallel. Figure 28.4 illustrates two cuboids (see Chapter 27), each with a volume of 12 cubic units. They are made by arranging 12 unit cubes in different ways. In cuboid a, the total surface area (that is, the total number of square units on the six faces of the cuboid) is 32 square units, and in cuboid b it is 40 square units. Thus, covering cuboid a with paper would require 32 square units of paper, but covering cuboid b would require 40 square units.

The fact that rearranging the volume changes the surface area explains why we sometimes need less wrapping paper if we arrange the contents of our parcel in a different way. The closer we get to a cube (or more generally to a sphere), the smaller the surface area.

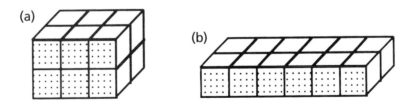

FIGURE 28.4 *Two cuboids with the same volume, 12 cubic units*

Circles

A *circle* is a shape consisting of all the points at a given distance from a given point. That given point is called the *center*. The distance from the center to any point on the circle is called the *radius*. The distance from one point through the center to the opposite point on the circle is called the *diameter*. Clearly, the length of the diameter is twice the length of the radius. The perimeter of a circle is also called the *circumference* (see Figure 28.5).

One of the most amazing facts in all mathematics relates to circles. If we measure the circumference of a circle and divide it by the length of the diameter, we always get the same answer.

For a practical classroom experience, students can use many differently sized circular objects, such as jar lids and pots. To measure the diameter, place the object on a piece of paper, draw the object, and measure the largest distance between the sides of the circle.
To measure the circumference, wrap tape carefully around the object, mark where a complete circuit begins and ends, unwind the tape, and measure the distance between the marks.

If we measure the circumference of a circle and divide it by the length of the diameter we always get the same answer.

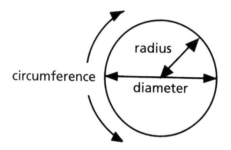

FIGURE 28.5 *Terms used with circles*

Allowing for experimental error, which can be considerable with such crude approaches to measuring the diameter and the circumference, students should find that the circumference divided by the diameter gives an answer of between 3 and 3.3. (Any results that are way out should be checked and measured again, if necessary). This result — that the circumference is always a bit more than three times the diameter — was known in ancient civilizations and used in construction.

If we can measure more accurately, we can determine that the ratio of the circumference to the diameter of a circle is about 3.14. This ratio is so important it is given a special symbol, the Greek letter π (pi). The value of π can be found theoretically to any number of decimal places. It begins like this: 3.14159265358979323384626433... and goes on forever without ever recurring (see Chapter 3). For practical purposes, rounding this value to two decimal places — as 3.14 — is sufficient.

Once we have this value, we can find the circumference of a circle, given the diameter. We multiply the diameter by π, using a calculator if necessary. And we can find the diameter of a circle, given the circumference, by dividing the circumference by π.

A common misunderstanding is that pi is equal to 22/7 or three and one-seventh. Three and one-seventh is an approximation for the value of π in the form of a fraction. As a decimal, three and one-seventh is equal to 3.142857.... Thus, 22/7 is correct only to two decimal places and therefore no better an approximation than 3.14. In the days of calculators, 3.14 is bound to be a more useful approximation for π than 22/7.

Check yourself

28.1 What are the dimensions of the field that gives the maximum area for 25 units of fencing? For calculation, use only rectangles drawn on the grid lines of graph paper.

28.2 What are the dimensions of the field that gives the minimum length of fencing for an area of 48 square units? For calculations, use only rectangles drawn on the grid lines of graph paper.

28.3 How can cubes of the following volumes be arranged in the shape of a cuboid to produce the minimum surface area?

(a) 27-unit cubes?   (b) 48-unit cubes?

28.4 How much ribbon is needed to go once round a cake with a 25-cm diameter?

28.5 Roughly what is the diameter of a circular running track that is 400 m in circumference?

▶Teaching suggestions

1. Use the illustration of fields and fences to explain area and perimeter, and pose problems about area and perimeter in these terms.
2. Let students investigate the way in which a fixed perimeter can produce a range of different areas, and vice versa.
3. Introduce students to solid volume by arranging and rearranging various numbers of unit cubes in the shape of cuboids. Use numbers with plenty of factors, such as 12 and 24. Older elementary students can investigate the way the surface area changes.
4. Give students practical experience of measuring the diameters and circumferences of circular objects, leading to the discovery that the ratio is always about three, or three and a bit.
5. Introduce older students to π, using, for practical purposes, the value 3.14 as an approximation for this ratio.

Answers to Check Yourself Questions

The answers provided are, of course, only examples of possible valid responses, especially when the question asks for the invention of a sentence, a question, or a problem.

Chapter 2: Place value

2.1: CLXXXVIII, CCLXVII, CCC, DCXIII, DCC (188, 267, 300, 613, 700)

2.2: Four thousand one hundred (4099 + 1 = 4100)

2.3: (a) $516 = (5 \times 10^2) + (1 \times 10^1) + 6$; (b) $3060 = (3 \times 10^3) + (6 \times 10^1)$; (c) $2305004 = (2 \times 10^6) + (3 \times 10^5) + (5 \times 10^3) + 4$

2.4: 6 dollar coins, 2 dimes, 4 pennies

2.5: 3.2 is 3 flats and 2 longs; 3.05 is 3 flats and 5 small cubes; 3.15 is 3 flats, one long, and 5 small cubes; 3.10 is 3 flats and 1 long. In order, they are: 3.05, 3.10, 3.15, 3.2.

2.6: 3.405 m and 2.500 m (or 2.5 m or 2.50 m)

2.7: (a) $0.25; (b) 0.25 m; (c) $0.07; (d) 0.045 kg; (e) 0.050 liters; (f) 0.005 m

Chapter 3: Mathematical modeling

3.1: Mathematical model is 4.95 + 5.90 + 9.95; mathematical solution, using a calculator, is 20.8; interpretation is that the total cost is $20.80.

3.2: Mathematical model is 27.90 ÷ 3; mathematical solution (calculator answer) is 9.3. This is an exact but slightly inappropriate answer, because of the convention of 2 figures after the decimal point for money; interpretation is that each person pays $9.30. (However, a tip should be added to this value.)

3.3: Mathematical model is 39.70 ÷ 3; mathematical solution (calculator answer) is 13.233333. This answer has been truncated; interpretation is that each person owes $13.23 and a little bit. However, realistically two people pay $13.23, but one has to pay $13.24 (each amount plus tip).

3.4: Mathematical model is 50 ÷ 0.89; mathematical solution (calculator answer) is 56.1797. This is an exact but inappropriate answer; interpretation is that Luc can buy 56 bars of chocolate.

3.5: Mathematical model is 500 ÷ 35; mathematical solution (calculator answer) is 14.285714. This answer has been truncated; interpretation is that Maria will take 15 months to reach her target.

Chapter 4: Addition structures

4.1: "I buy two articles costing $5.95 and $6.99. What is the total cost?"

4.2: "My salary was $19 750 and then I had a raise of $450. What is my new salary?"

4.3: "If the recipe requires 250 mL of water and 125 mL of milk, what is the total volume of liquid?"

4.4: "The class's morning consists of 15 minutes registration, 25 minutes assembly, 55 minutes mathematics, 20 minutes break, 65 minutes English. What is the total time used this morning?"

Chapter 5: Addition calculations

5.1: Put out 2 dollar coins and 8 pennies; then 1 dollar coin, 5 dimes, and 6 pennies; then 9 dimes and 7 pennies. There are 21 pennies; exchange 20 of these for 2 dimes, leaving 1 penny; there are now 16 dimes; exchange 10 of these for 1 dollar, leaving 6 dimes; there are then 4 dollars; the total is 4 dollars, 6 dimes, and 1 penny, i.e., 461.

5.2: 500 + 200 makes 700; 30 + 90 makes 120, that's 820 in total so far; 8 + 4 makes 12, add this to the 820 and get 832.

5.3: (a) 98 is 2 less than 100; 423 + 100 is 523, take off 2, answer 521. (b) Take 3 off 314 and add it to 297, so the sum becomes 300 + 311; answer is 611. (c) Take 8 off the 309 and add it to the 492, making 301 + 500; answer is 801.

Chapter 6: Subtraction structures

6.1: 51 years; 2050−1999; example of the inverse-of-addition structure

6.2: 78 pages; 256−178; example of the inverse-of-addition structure

6.3: 27 years; 52 − 25; example of the comparison structure

6.4: 185 points; 750 − 565; example of the inverse-of-addition structure

6.5: "Chocolate milk is \$3.95 and white milk is \$2.99. How much cheaper is the white milk?"

6.6: "The temperature in London is 25°, in Yellowknife it is −6°. What is the temperature difference between the two cities?"

6.7: "There are 250 students in a school. Of these, 159 have school lunches. How many do not have school lunches?"

6.8: "I want to buy a computer costing \$1489, but I have only \$1350. How much more do I need?"

Chapter 7: Subtraction calculations

7.1: Put out 6 dollar coins, 2 dimes, and 3 pennies; take away 1 penny, leaving 2 pennies; not enough dimes, so exchange 1 dollar for 10 dimes, giving 12 dimes; take away 7 of these, leaving 5 dimes; now take away 4 dollars; the result is 1 dollar, 5 dimes, and 2 pennies, i.e., 152.

7.2: Put out 2 thousands and 6 units; not enough units to take away 8, no tens to exchange and no hundreds, so exchange 1 thousand for 10 hundreds, leaving 1 thousand; now exchange 1 hundred for 10 tens, leaving 9 hundreds; then exchange 1 ten for 10 units, leaving 9 tens and giving 16 units; can now take away 8 units, 3 tens, and 4 hundreds; the result is 1 thousand, 5 hundreds, 6 tens, and 8 units, i.e., 1568.

7.3: Add 42 to both numbers to give 763 − 500; answer, 263.

7.4: (a) 998 − 458 is 540, so 1000 − 458 is 542. (b) 819 − 519 is 300, so 819 − 523 is 4 less than this, i.e., 296. (c) 606 − 206 is 400, so 605 − 206 is 399.

Chapter 8: Multiplication structures

8.1: "I bought 29 boxes of eggs with 12 eggs in each box..." (29 groups of 12); "There are 12 classes in the school with 29 children in each class..." (12 groups of 29).

8.2: "I bought 12 uniform shirts for a team at \$25 per shirt. What was the total cost of the shirts?"

8.3: The box can be seen as 4 rows of 6 yogurts or 6 rows of 4 yogurts.

8.4: "If the length of the wing in the model is 16 cm, how long is the length of the wing on the actual airplane?" (16 x 25 = 400 cm).

8.5: 4827 x 1.02 = 4923.54 The new monthly salary is $4923.54.

Chapter 9: Multiplication calculations

9.1: The four areas are 40 x 30, 40 x 7, 2 x 30, and 2 x 7, giving a total of 1200 + 280 + 60 + 14 = 1554.

9.2: 4 x 90 = 360, 40 x 9 = 360, 40 x 90 = 3600, 4 x 900 = 3600, 400 x 9 = 3600, 40 x 900 = 36000, 400 x 90 = 36000, 400 x 900 = 360000

9.3: The six areas are 300 x 10, 300 x 7, 40 x 10, 40 x 7, 5 x 10, and 5 x 7, giving a total of 3000 + 2100 + 400 + 280 + 50 + 35 = 5865.

9.4: (a) 248 x 25 = 124 x 50 = 62 x 100 = 6200; (b) Think of the 16 as 10 + 5 + 1; now 72 x 10 is 720; so 72 x 5 is 360; and 72 x 1 is 72. Therefore 72 x 16 = 720 + 360 + 72 = 1152.

Chapter 10: Division structures

10.1: Scale factor is 20 (300 ÷ 15); example of the ratio structure.

10.2: Price is $0.50 per kg (7.00 ÷ 14); example of the inverse-of-multiplication structure.

10.3: I can afford 8 CDs (100 ÷ 12.50); example of the inverse-of-multiplication structure, using the idea of repeated subtraction.

10.4: I need 25 months (300 ÷ 12); example of the inverse-of-multiplication structure, using the idea of repeated addition.

10.5: "A package of four chocolate bars costs $2.40; how much per bar?"

10.6: "A teacher earns $3200 a month, a bank manager earns $4800. How many times greater is the bank manager's salary?" (4800 ÷ 3200 = 1.5); the bank manager's salary is 1.5 times that of the teacher.

Chapter 11: Division calculations

11.1: In 288 ÷ 6, 288 is the dividend, 6 is the divisor (288 ÷ 6 = 48).

11.2: From 126 take away 10 sevens (70), leaving 56, then 5 sevens (35), leaving 21, which is 3 sevens; answer is therefore 10 + 5 + 3, i.e., 18.

11.3: From 851 take away 20 twenty-threes (460), leaving 391; then 10 more (230), leaving 161; then 5 more (115), leaving 46; which is 2 twenty-threes; answer is therefore 20 + 10 + 5 + 2, i.e., 37.

11.4: From 529 take away 50 eights (400), then 10 more (80), then 5 more (40), then 1 more (8), leaving a remainder of 1; answer is 66 remainder 1.

11.5: 154 ÷ 22 is the same as (88 + 66) ÷ 22 which equals (88 ÷ 22) + (66 ÷ 22); hence the answer is 4 + 3, i.e., 7.

11.6: (a) Multiply both numbers by 2 to give 770 ÷ 110; divide both by 10 to give 77 ÷ 11; answer is therefore 7. (b) 420 ÷ 21 would be 20, so 419 ÷ 21 is 19 remainder 20.

Chapter 12: Remainders and rounding

12.1: The mathematical model is 124 x 5.95 (or 5.95 x 124); the mathematical solution is 737.8; interpretation: the total cost of the order will be $737.80; to the nearest ten dollars, the total cost of the order will be about $740; to three significant figures, the total cost of the order will be about $738.

12.2: The mathematical model is $365 \div 7$; the solution is 52 remainder 1. The answer to Jackie's problem is: there are 52 weeks in a year, plus one extra day; the remainder represent the one extra day. The calculator solution is 52.142857; this answer has been truncated. The figures after the point represent a bit of a week.

12.3: (a) $327 \div 40 = 8.175$ (calculator), or 8 remainder 7. So 9 buses are needed. We round up (otherwise we would have to leave 7 children behind); (b) $500 \div 65 = 7.6923076$ (calculator), or 7 remainder 45. So we can buy 7 donuts. We round down (and have 45 cents change for something else).

12.4: Calculator result is 131.88888; the average height is 132 cm to the nearest cm.

12.5: (a) 3; (b) 3.2; (c) 3.16

12.6: There are 205 books per shop; that's 3485 books altogether, so remainder is 15 books.

Chapter 13: Multiples, factors, and primes

13.1: $3 \times 37 = 111$, $6 \times 37 = 222$, $9 \times 37 = 333$, $12 \times 37 = 444$, $15 \times 37 = 555$, $18 \times 37 = 666$, $21 \times 37 = 777$, $24 \times 37 = 888$, $27 \times 37 = 999$ (pattern breaks down when four-digit answer are achieved)

13.2: (a) $47 \times 9 = 423$; sum of digits = 9; (b) $172 \times 9 = 1548$; sum of digits = 18; sum of these digits = 9; (c) $9876543 \times 9 = 88888887$; sum of digits = 63; sum of these digits = 9

13.3: (a) 2652 is a multiple of 2 (ends in even digit), 3 (sum of digits is multiple of 3), 4 (last two digits multiple of 4), and 6 (multiple of 2 and 3); (b) 6570 is a multiple of 2 (ends in even digit), 3 (sum of digits is multiple of 3), 5 (ends in 0), 6 (multiple of 2 and 3), and 9 (digital root is 9); (c) 2401 is a multiple of none of these (it is actually $7 \times 7 \times 7 \times 7$)

13.4: A three-digit number is a multiple of 11 if the sum of the two outside digits subtract the middle digit is either 0 (e.g., 561, 594, 330) or 11 (418, 979).

13.5: 24 (the lowest common multiple of 8 and 12)

13.6: (a) Factors of 95 are 1, 5, 19, and 95; (b) Factors of 96 are 1, 2, 3, 4, 6, 8, 12, 16, 24, 32, 48, and 96; (c) Factors of 97 are 1 and 97 (it is prime); clearly 96 is the most flexible

13.7: Factors of 48 are 1, 2, 3, 4, 6, 8, 12, 16, 24, and 48; factors of 80 are 1, 2, 4, 5, 8, 10, 16, 20, 40, and 80; common factors are 1, 2, 4, 8, and 16; could have 16 rows of 3 blue and 5 red, or 8 rows of 6 blue and 10 red, or 4 rows of 12 blue and 20 red, or 2 rows of 24 blue and 40 red, or 1 row of 48 blue and 80 red!

13.8: 71, 73, 79, 83, 89, and 97 (N.B. not 91, because this is 9×13)

13.9: $4403 = 7 \times 17 \times 37$

13.10: 1, 5, 7, 11, 13, 17, 19, 23, 25, 29, 31, 35, 37, 41, 43, 47, 49, 53, 55, 59, and 61; they are all prime except 25, 35, 49, and 55.

13.11: $4 = 2 + 2$, $6 = 3 + 3$, $8 = 3 + 5$, $10 = 3 + 7$, $12 = 5 + 7$, $14 = 7 + 7$, $16 = 3 + 13$, $18 = 5 + 13$, $20 = 7 + 13$, $22 = 11 + 11$, $24 = 7 + 17$, $26 = 3 + 23$, $28 = 5 + 23$, $30 = 13 + 17$

13.12: The smallest answer is 2520.

Chapter 14: Squares, cubes, and number shapes

14.1: Some possible answers: 20 is a factor of 100; 21 is a triangle number; 22 is a multiple of 2 and 11; 23 is a prime number; 24 has eight factors; 25 is a square number; 26 is a multiple of 2 and 13; 27 is a cube number; 28 is a triangle number; 29 is a prime number.

14.2: 36 is both a triangle number and a square number.

14.3: The differences between successive square numbers are 3, 5, 7, 9, 11..., the odd numbers; these are the numbers of dots added to each square in Figure 14.1a in order to make the next one in the sequence.

14.4: The answers should be the same. Whole numbers less than 100 which are both cubes and squares are 1 and 64.

14.5: (a) 57; (b) 17

14.6: 14.14 m

14.7: The cube root of 500 is between 7.93 and 7.94; so the length of the side of the cube should be about 7.9 cm (79 mm).

14.8: The answers are the square numbers: 4, 9, 16, 25, 36, and so on; two successive triangles of dots in Figure 14.4 can be fitted together to make a square number.

Chapter 15: Integers: positive and negative

15.1: 472, 0, and –10 are integers.

15.2: (a) –10; (b) 12; (c) –22

15.3: (a) The temperature one winter's day is 4°; that night it falls by 12 degrees; what is the night-time temperature? (Answer: –8); (b) The temperature one winter's night is –6°; when it rises by 10 degrees the next day. What is the temperature? (Answer: 4)

15.4: (a) If I am overdrawn by $5, how much must be paid into my account to make the balance $20? (Answer $25); (b) If I am overdrawn by $15, how much must be paid into my account so that I am only overdrawn by $10? (Answer $5); (c) If I have $20 in my bank balance, what debit would produce a balance of $10 overdrawn? (–$30)

15.5: My basic calculator displays –42 with the negative sign at one end of the display and the 42 at the other.

15.6: The mathematical model is 458.64 – (–187.85); the cheque paid in was $646.49.

Chapter 16: Fractions

16.1: (a) A bar of chocolate is cut into 5 equal pieces and I have 4 of them. (b) 4/5 of a class of 30 children is 24 children. (c) Share 4 pizzas equally between 5 people. (d) If I earn $400 a week and you earn $500 a week, my earnings are 4/5 of yours.

16.2: (a) 1/4 = 2/8 = 3/12; (b) 1/2 = 2/4 = 3/6 = 4/8 = 6/12; (c) 3/4 = 6/8 = 9/12; (d) 4/4 = 8/8 = 12/12 = 6/6 = 3/3 = 2/2 = 1; (e) 2/12 = 1/6; (f) 4/12 = 2/6 = 1/3; (g) 8/12 = 4/6 = 2/3; (h) 10/12 = 5/6

16.3: 3/5 is 24/40; 5/8 is 25/40; 5/8 is larger.

16.4: Convert all fractions to twelfths: 1/6 (2/12), 1/3 (4/12), 5/12, 2/3 (8/12), 3/4 (9/12).

16.5: Compare by ratio the prices of two coffee pots, pot A costing $15, pot B costing $25.

16.6: 9/24 or 3/8 (three-eighths)

16.7: (a) 1/5 of $100 is $20, so 3/5 is $60; (b) $1562.50 (2500 ÷ 8 x 5)

Chapter 17: Calculations with decimals

17.1: (a) Mathematical solution is 6.90, total cost is $6.90. (b) Mathematical solution is 3.25, total length is 3.25 m. (c) Mathematical solution is 0.22, difference in height is 0.22 m or 22 cm. (d) Mathematical solution is 5.75, change is $5.75.

17.2: (a) I have a 1.500-liter bottle of water and pour out one glass of 0.125 liters (125 mL); how much is left? Answer: 1.375 liters; (b) Find the total mass (weight) of a bag of potatoes of 2.500 kg and a bag of onions of 1.120 kg. Answer: 3.620 kg.

17.3: How much for four paperbacks on sale costing $3.99 each? Answer: $15.96 (399 x 4 = 1596, so 3.99 x 4 = 15.96).

17.4: Divide a 4.40-m length of wood into 8 equal parts; each part is 0.55 m (55 cm) long. (Change the calculation to 440 cm divided by 8.)

17.5: (a) 18.4; (b) 18.4; (c) 0.00184

17.6: (a) 18 (or 18.0); (b) 18 (or 18.0); (c) 0.0018

17.7: 0.0001. Find the area in square meters of a square of side 0.01 m (1 cm).

17.8: (a) $2 \div 0.5 = 20 \div 5 = 4$; (b) $5.5 \div 0.11 = 550 \div 11 = 50$

17.9: (a) 0.17; (b) 0.6; (c) 0.35; (d) 0.6666666 (approximately); (e) 0.1428571 (approximately)

17.10: (a) 9/100; (b) 79/100; (c) 15/100 = 3/20

Chapter 18: Percentages

18.1: Since one-third is about 33%, this is the greater reduction.

18.2: (a) 13 out of 50 is the same proportion as 26 out of 100. So 26% achieve an A and 74% do not. (b) 57 out of 300 is the same proportion as 19 out of 100. So 19% achieve an A and 81% do not. (c) 24 out of 80 is the same proportion as 3 out of 10, or 30 out of 100. So 30% achieve an A and 70% do not. (d) 26 out of 130 is the same proportion as 2 out of 10, or 20 out of 100. So 20% achieve an A and 80% do not.

18.3: English, about 42%; Italian, about 49%

18.4: (a) 3/20 = 15/100 = 15%; (b) 65% = 65/100 = 13/20

18.5: (a) 10% of $120 is $12, so 30% is three times this value or $36.
(b) 10% of $450 is $45; so 5% is $22.50. Therefore, 15% is $45 + $22.50 = $67.50.

18.6: $271.04 (one way of doing this is 275 x 1.12 x 0.88)

18.7: It makes no difference! In one case the calculation could be 600 x 1.20 x 0.90; in the other it could be 600 x 0.90 x 1.20. The results are the same, $648.

Chapter 19: Handling data

19.1: (a) Which way of traveling to school is used by most children? How many fewer children walk than come by car? (b) How many children have fewer than five writing implements? Which group has no children in it? (c) How many have waist measurements in the range 60 to 64 cm, to the nearest centimeter? How many have waist measurements to the nearest centimeter which are greater than 89 cm?

19.2: (a) Continuous; (b) continuous but should be grouped; (c) discrete; (d) discrete, but should be grouped; (e) discrete; (f) continuous

19.3: Examples (c) and (e), having a small number of possibilities, are best displayed on a pie chart. Example (f) is best displayed on a line graph, with the horizontal axis representing time.

19.4: Fifty-cent intervals will produce 10 groups: $0.00–$0.49, $0.50–$0.99, $1.00–$1.49, and so on.

19.5: (a) 14/36 x 360 = 140 degrees; (b) 14/33 x 360 is about 153 degrees (calculator answer: 152.72726)

Chapter 20: Averages

20.1: Group A English, mean = 53.7, median = 53; Group B English, mean = 67.5, median = 71. Both averages support the view that Group B did better.

20.2: The mean for English for the two groups combined is 59.8 (1494 ÷ 25). This is less than the mean of the two separate means (the mean of 53.7 and 67.5 is 60.6). Because there are more students in Group A, their mean has a greater "weighting" in the combined mean.

20.3: With 25 in the set, the median is the 13th value when arranged in order. For English, the median is 56; for mathematics, the median is 53. The range for English is 45 (90 – 45) and the range for mathematics is 72 (95 – 23).

20.4: For mathematics, John's mark (49) is less than the mean (53.6) and less than the median (56.5), but well above the bottom of the range.

20.5: P (about 68 cm per sec) had a greater average speed than Q (65 cm per sec).

20.6: The journey there takes 10 hours and the journey back takes 8 hours. Total journey is 800 miles in 18 hours, so overall average speed is about 44.4 mph (800 ÷ 18).

Chapter 21: Probability

21.1: (a) By experiment: finding the relative frequency of successful outcomes in a large number of trials; (b) By collecting data from a large sample of people aged 50 – 59 years in Canada; (c) Using an argument based on symmetry, considering all the possible, equally likely outcomes

21.2: As 59% in Chapter 20 have less than 6 letters; estimate of probability is 0.59.

21.3: (a) 3/12 = 0.25; (b) 9/12 = 0.75

21.4: (a) 12/36 = 0.33 approximately; (b) 9/36 = 0.25; (c) 20/36 = 0.56 approximately

21.5: Examples: probability of scoring 1 is 0; probability of scoring less than 13 is 1.

Chapter 22: Algebra

22.1: $C = 100M$. Using C and M is misleading, since they look like abbreviations for "a centimeter" and "a meter," instead of variables (e.g., the number of centimeters).

22.2: (a) The total number of pieces of fruit bought (b) The cost of the apples in cents (c) The cost of the bananas (d) The total cost of the fruit. Using A and B is misleading, since they look like abbreviations for "an apple" and "a banana"; so $10A + 12B$ looks like "10 apples and 12 bananas."

22.3: Wing-y has 9 rides. Arithmetic steps: 12 divided by 3, add 5. Algebraic representation: $3(N - 5) = 12$

22.4: (a) 60; (b) 10

22.5: For Figure 22.2c: (a) add 5; (b) 498; (c) multiply by 5, subtract 2; (d) $B = 5A - 2$. Other answers include $B = 3 + 5(A - 1)$. For Figure 22.2d: (a) subtract 1; (b) 0; (c) subtract from 100; (d) $B = 100 - A$.

22.6: Side by side: (a) 204; (b) multiply by 2, add 4 or $Y = 2X + 4$. End to end: (a) 402; (b) multiply by 4, add 2 or $Y = 4X + 2$

22.7: My number is 42; the equation is $X(2X + 3) = 3654$.

Chapter 23: Coordinates

23.1: The points are (1, 2), (1, 4), (2, 5), (4, 5), (5, 4), (5, 2), (4, 1), and (2, 1). Joined up in this order they form an octagon.

23.2: They are all linear relationships, producing straight-line graphs.

23.3: (a) The total number of eggs; (b) The equivalent number of francs; (c) The top number in the fractions in the set

23.4: The fourth vertex is (4, 5). The sum of the x-coordinates of two opposite vertices is the same as the sum of the x-coordinates for the other two opposite vertices. The same is true of the y-coordinates. The fourth vertex to go with (4, 4), (5, 8), and (13, 6) is therefore (12, 2), because 4 + 13 = 5 + 12, and 4 + 6 = 8 + 2.

23.5: A sequence of parallelograms is produced. The rules are exactly the same as those given for rectangles. The fourth vertex is (1, 3); if you join the points in a different order it could also be (1, –1) or (7, 5).

Chapter 24: Measurement

24.1: (a) Yes; if A is earlier than B and B is earlier than C, then A must be earlier than C. (b) No; for example, 20 cm is half of 40 cm and 40 cm is half of 80 cm, but 20 cm is not half of 80 cm.

24.2: (a) 279 mm; (b) 27.9 cm; (c) 2.79 dm; (d) 0.279 m

24.3: It will still be 1 kg. It will weigh less, but the mass does not change.

24.4: It works as far as 55 miles, which is 89 km to the nearest km (88.5115). The next value, 89 miles, is 143 km to the nearest km (143.2277), rather than the Fibonacci number, 144.

Chapter 25: Angle

25.1: one-eighth of a turn (acute), 89° (acute), 90° (right), 95° (obtuse), 150° (obtuse), two right angles (straight), 200° (reflex), three-quarters of a turn (reflex)

25.2: (a) 540°; (b) 720°; (c) 900°. The sequential rule is "add two 180°." For a figure with N sides the global rule for the sum of the angles is $180(N-2)$. When $N = 100$, the sum of the angles is 17640°.

Chapter 26: Transformations and symmetry

26.1: (a) Translation, –6 units in x-direction, 0 units in y-direction; (b) Reflection in vertical line passing through (8, 0); (c) Rotation through half-turn about (5, 2), clockwise or counterclockwise

26.2: (a) A diagonal line passing through (11, 3) and (13, 1); (b) A vertical line passing through (12, 2); (c) A horizontal line passing through (12, 2). Order of rotational symmetry is four.

26.3: No

26.4: No

Chapter 27: Classifying shapes

27.1: Because all the angles in an equilateral triangle must be 60 degrees.

27.2: 90, 45, and 45 degrees

27.3: (a) Square; (b) square; (c) equilateral triangle; (d) cuboid; (e) tetrahedron

27.4: The parallelogram tessellates, as do all quadrilaterals.

27.5: Nine

Chapter 28: Perimeter and area

28.1: The maximum area is given by the square field, 5 units by 5 units, i.e., 25 square units.

28.2: The minimum length of fencing is 28 units, for a field which is 6 units by 8 units.

28.3: (a) As a cube with side 3 units; total surface area = 54 square units; (b) As a cuboid, 4 units by 4 units by 3 units; total surface area = 80 square units (16 + 16 + 12 + 12 + 12 + 12).

28.4: About 78.5 cm (25 x 3.14); 80 cm to be on the safe side.

28.5: About 127 m (400 ÷ 3.14)

Index

A

acute angle, 176, 177, 189
acute-angled triangle, 189
addition, 21-23, 25-29
    aggregation, 21-23
    algorithm, 26
    augmentation, 22, 23
    calculations, 25-29
    carrying, 26-27
    of decimals, 113-114
    exchange principle, 25, 26-27
    explaining, 25
    front-end approach, 26, 28
    informal methods, 28
    language, 22, 26
    with manipulatives, 29
    mental, 26, 28
    of negative numbers, 22
    real-world applications, 22-23
    repeated, 45, 59
    self-checks and answers, 23, 28, 201-202
    structures, 21-23
    teaching suggestions, 23, 29
    understanding, 25
    using coins, 26
aggregation, 21-23
    repeated, 45, 46, 48
algebra, 149-157
    equals sign, meaning of, 151
    equivalence, 151
    generalizations, 154, 155
    letters, meaning of, 150-151, 156
    mapping, 155
    precedence of operators, 153
    representing problems, 152, 156
    scientific calculators, 153, 156
    self-check and answers, 156-157, 207
    solving problems, 152, 155-156
    structure of a problem, 152
    symbols, differences in, 151-153
    tabulation, 149-150, 154-156
    teaching suggestions, 157
    trial and improvement, 155-157
    variables, 149-151, 153-156
    what's my rule?, 153-154
algebraic operating system, 153
algorithm(s)
    addition, 26
    defined, 15
    long multiplication, 16, 51
    short division, 65-67
    subtraction, 40, 42
angles, 175-179
    comparisons, 176
    degrees, 177

    difference in direction, 176
    generalizations, 178
    ordering, 176
    parallelograms, 190
    quadrilaterals, 178
    rotation, 175-178
    self-check and answers, 178, 208
    teaching suggestions, 179
    triangles, 177
    turns, 176, 177
    types, 176, 177
    vertex and vertices, 175
answers to self-checks, 201-208
ante meridian, 172
anxieties, 2-5
apex, 193
approximation, 168
area
    conservation of, 196
    explaining, 195-196
    fields and fences, 195-196
    of a rectangle, 48, 52-53
    self-check and answers, 198-199, 208
    surface, 197, 199
    teaching suggestions, 199
arithmetic mean, 137
arrays
    rectangular, 47-49, 52, 83
    square, 89, 90
augmentation, 22, 23
average(s), 137-141
    calculating, 75, 78
    comparisons, 137-141
    deviation, 140
    mean, 75, 78, 137, 138, 140
    median, 138, 140
    mode, 139
    per, 138, 140
    purpose, 137
    range as a measure of spread, 140
    real-world applications, 138-140
    self-check and answers, 140-141, 206–207
    speed, 140, 141
    spread, 140
    teaching suggestions, 141
    types, 137-139
axes, 159

B

Babylonian number system, 10
Ball, 1, 6
bar graphs, 130-133, 136
base-ten blocks
    for addition, 29
    for division, 59